DEFINING MOMENTS

a memoir

DONALD GREEN

PRAISE FOR DEFINING MOMENTS

"Among the great people I have met over the years Don Green stands tall. His story, written with honesty, humility, and his sense of humor, is a great read. It teaches through example that it is possible to reach success without losing self."

— Congresswoman Lynn Woolsey (Ret.)

"Don Green's story reads like a novel. I am reminded of Hermann Hesse's Siddhartha, who fully engages and therefore fully experiences life's challenges and joys."

— Jane Rogan Dwight

"To have universal accessibility, a memoir must include a spiritual component. *Defining Moments* has that dimension. Donald Green's book is not simply the success story of the "Father of Telecom Valley"; it also shows us something of the soul of the man, from the challenges of a wartime childhood to facing the process of aging with dignity. And along the way the author presents an in-depth view of how family, music, and common-sense spirituality can play a part in all our lives."

— Brother Tolbert "Toby" McCarroll
Author: Thinking With The Heart

"Although I know Don Green, I didn't know about the hardships he endured as a young boy during the war. *Defining Moments* is interesting, entertaining, and well written."

— Greg Steele

"One would expect Don Green to write an engrossing tale about his remarkable Telecom life; but to tell it as a page-turner, that's a pleasant surprise. Perhaps growing up in wartime England could have made him a first-class novelist!"

— Corrick Brown, Conductor Emeritus,
Santa Rosa Symphony

"I've had the privilege of working with Don for the past forty years. We traveled together throughout the United States, South America, Europe, the Far East, and Australia. The adventures were countless, the fun endless—and that comes through in his engaging book."

— Chet Stephens, former vice president of DTS

"Don is a hero and a visionary in so many ways, and has given so much to our local community. The story of his life and career, from a modest English upbringing to a key player in the digital revolution, is gripping and inspiring . . . Read his tale—you won't be disappointed."

— Robert Worth, Music Director, Sonoma Bach;
Professor Emeritus, Sonoma State University

"'Inspired by the insanity of it all . . .' That's Don Green reporting with a keen mind and a light heart on his extraordinary life. In these deceptively breezy memoir pages he reflects on the twists and turns of fate—not to mention, perseverance—that have shaped him. Between history and happenstance, good instincts and received wisdom, he both found his way and made his way. It's a whale of a tale well told. Green sweeps us along from 'I was three years old and a goat,' through 'I learned that we'd used more dynamite than was necessary,' to a seminal phone call: 'It sounded like you said $6.8 billion. That's Billion with a capital B?' to, later in life, 'Now I had a problem: one dog, one rope, and one very steep cliff.' You see what I mean? It's a great story, and one rollicking, great read."

— Amanda McTigue

DEDICATION

To my wife Maureen and all the other members of
the Green family. And to the many people who worked
closely with me in the various enterprises I founded.

ACKNOWLEDGEMENTS

My heartfelt thanks to the members of the memoir team, without whom this book would not have been possible. I'm especially grateful to editor-in-chief Steve Boga, editor Kimberly Feare, communications editor Alexandra Espinosa Cunningham, consultant Julie Floyd, and printing coordinator Derek Landen (Lithocraft II).

A special thank you to my son David Green for his beautiful bird photographs, which are used throughout the book as a tribute to my passion for birds.

CONTENTS

PART I   BRITAIN

PART II   CANADA

PART III   CALIFORNIA

FOREWORD

As Don Green's personal assistant, I was to accompany him to a thirty-year DTS (Digital Telephone Systems) reunion. Don was DTS founder and, from 1969 to 1986, its CEO.

As I drove his Bentley to Tiburon, I had no idea how memorable it would be.

"You can drop me off in front and park down the street," Don told me.

Don, 83, had contracted Parkinson's disease and was unsteady on his feet; I was more than a little worried about leaving him alone. At the same time I sensed that this situation was different. I could feel his confidence. He was excited and yet seemed to possess an inner calm.

I hurriedly parked the car and ran to catch up. As we entered the spacious home of one of Don's past employees, Don was greeted warmly by those who recognized him. Most did, but not everyone; I overheard a conversation between two women.

"Who is that?"

"I'm not really sure."

"Do you think it's John?"

"No, I don't think so."

We came to a large patio adjacent to a pool, all set in a backyard lushly landscaped with plants of every variety. Don, beaming, blended into the crowd, joyfully accepting handshakes and slaps on the back. Worried that he might be knocked down, I guided him toward a cushioned patio chair.

A man in his sixties walked up to Don and offered a big smile and an eager handshake. "Is this really who I think it is? Donald Green? Is that you?!"

Flashing a smile, Don shook his hand. "I think so," he said dryly.

"Oh boss! It is so good to see you!"

All eyes were now on Don. Everyone at the party wanted to speak with him, and most did. A middle-aged man approached, waited politely for Don to finish his conversation, then launched into a story loud enough for all to hear:

"I just want you all to know how important and influential Donald Green has been. I was working on construction when Don gave me my first real job. A friend asked me if I wanted to work for a great company that was going places. I agreed to come to DTS for an interview. Immediately I could tell this company was unique. People wore bell bottoms, went to work happy, believed they were making a difference. I am very glad my friend told me about DTS, and I believe it shaped my future. Because of the chance that Don gave me, I was able to accept other opportunities in my life that have brought me much success." The man raised his glass. "Here's to Don Green, the best boss I ever had." Others raised their glasses and drank; Don beamed.

For the next couple of hours, I watched people happily joking, laughing, and reminiscing about the good 'ol times. Don sat with his former assistant, Lynn Woolsey, later a California Congresswoman, and they happily chatted about the past. They reminded me of two celebrities, surrounded by fans who had become good friends.

Snatches of conversation reached my ears:

A man said, "One time we had a party and the snow-cone machine stopped working. Don tore that machine apart trying to fix it. He was just like everybody else, and he really cared."

An elderly woman said, "How many companies have you worked for that have a thirty-year reunion? It just doesn't happen. We had such a good time, such a great community of people."

When it was time to go, everyone wanted to help Don to the car. Five men carried him down the stairs. It was like watching soldiers hoisting their wounded commander.

As Don got into the car, one man, tears in his eyes, said to me, "Please take good care of my boss."

As we drove away, exchanging waves and shouts to the dozens left behind on the sidewalk, I glanced at Don and noted that he had tears in his eyes. So did I.

— Julie Floyd

On a Sunday morning, November 8, 2015, Julie Floyd was killed when she lost control of her car. Julie, a member of the writing team, was working on this memoir until she left for three months to study yoga in Thailand. She was a beautiful person inside and out and loved by all. She will be missed.

Julie Floyd

Proceeds from this book are being donated to the Santa Rosa Youth Orchestras.

DEFINING MOMENTS

PART I

BRITAIN
(1931-1954)

CHAPTER ONE
Leaving Home

Before boarding the train, I took one last look at my mother's sad face. Instinctively I reached down and patted the box attached at my waist that held my gas mask. It was September 2, 1939, and I was eight years old.

I'd overheard grownups talking. Britain was about to declare war on Germany . . . 800,000 children evacuated to the countryside . . . the government urging country families to take in city children. Now I was one of those children.

I'd also heard that host families wanted strong, healthy children who could do farm work. Being healthy, I would live and work on Mr. and Mrs. Johnson's farm, in a place called Wigan, some forty miles from my hometown of Liverpool.

As I sat looking out the window of the train, I tried to imagine what the future held for me and my family. The chocolate bar my father had given me sat uneaten in my pocket. I reached for the bar and held it for a moment, trying to quiet my racing thoughts.

When would I see my parents and brother again? Or see home? My head hurt from thinking, but I had no more answers than when I started. I lay my head against the window, closed my eyes, and pictured myself back in my room . . . having tea with Mum . . . reading my Biggles book . . .

I must have dozed, for I was jolted in my seat by someone shouting, "Wigan next stop!" It all came back to me then—where I was going: away from everything I'd known. Uncertainty and homesickness welled up inside me and threatened to spill down my cheeks. "Be brave," I told myself. My father's strong image came to mind, lending me courage.

When the train stopped, I grabbed my suitcase, descended the stairs, and stepped timidly onto the platform. Mr. Johnson was there to greet me, which he did with no great ceremony. He was a thin wiry man with a sallow complexion. His wife was his physical opposite, plump and rosy-cheeked. Though not outwardly affectionate, she had a nice smile and seemed friendly.

Soon after I arrived, Mr. Johnson took me on a tour of the farm. His northern accent was heavy and his teeth were few, and I had to concentrate to understand him. People from northern England, I learned, speak with lots of thees and thous, sprinkled with their own slang. I heard Mr. Johnson say something to his son, Nate, that sounded like this: "Shut up, thee, before I swelp your head off."

Mr. Johnson led me toward the barn. As we got close, a feral kitten darted out from inside. With lightning speed Mr. Johnson reached down, grabbed the kitten by the neck, and smashed its tiny skull against the wall; it fell limp to the ground.

I stood motionless, trying to make sense of what seemed a senseless act of brutality. For the past weeks I'd often pictured life on a farm, but it had never included kitten killing.

Our next stop was the edge of a large wheat field surrounded by hedgerows. We stood there for some minutes watching the noisy combine cutting the wheat. As it worked toward us, the noise growing louder, deafening, I wondered what we were waiting for. I soon found out.

As the cranking machine got closer, I saw them . . . rabbits! Dozens of them, dashing frantically ahead of the machine, heading for the hedgerows. Mr. Johnson gestured to his dog. "Fetch, boy!" he commanded, and the dog raced off. He returned with a rabbit clenched between his teeth. "Good dog."

Mr. Johnson took the rabbit from the dog's mouth, then startled me with his swift and powerful blow to the back of the rabbit's neck. I stood there, mouth agape, stunned and nauseated.

Mr. Johnson looked down at me and said, "Now it's thou's turn. If thou is going to live on a farm, thou must know about death." I gulped and nodded. The dog brought another rabbit. Mr. Johnson took the rabbit and handed it to me. Imitating Mr. Johnson as best I could, I hit the animal on the back of its neck and threw it where its unfortunate kin lay. That wasn't so bad, I thought.

But then, to my wide-eyed horror, the merely stunned rabbit got up and dashed into the hedgerow. The dog threw me a look that I took to be disgust.

* * *

I had a tiny bedroom with an icy floor. At 6:30 every morning, Mrs. Johnson roused me from my sleep by shouting my name. After splashing water on my face, I made my way to the kitchen, where it was light and warm, the air permeated with the aroma of hot porridge. I downed a large bowl of it, then dressed and headed outside to do my morning chores.

The early-morning air was stinging cold. My job was to open some gates and bring in twenty cows for milking. Nate had taught me how to hook up the cows to the milking machine.

The machines pumping in unison created a hypnotic sound that sent my mind wandering. I saw myself starring in a Western, one I'd seen three weeks earlier at the cinema. There I was, astride my faithful steed, wearing a black cowboy hat, chaps, and swinging a large lasso above my head. My men and I were herding hundreds of cows to better grazing pasture . . .

I was lassoed back to the present by the sound of Nate calling my name. "Time to unhook 'em and take 'em back out," he said.

Poof went my steed, cowboy wardrobe, and lasso. With no resistance, and needing almost no help from me, the docile animals lumbered slowly to their pasture. Then I went inside to get ready for school.

Over the next few weeks I tried to get into the rhythms of farm life. But inside I longed for my old life, my family. I managed to go through the motions of living, but my heart wasn't in it.

A month after I arrived, I developed painful boils all over my body. The largest and most painful was on the back of my neck. The doctor came and lanced and drained it. An old village doctor, he offered his theory: "The boils are from the change in water you have experienced."

Somehow, even as a child, I knew the boils were outward symptoms of my inner distress.

Mrs. Johnson told me parental visits were discouraged because it was thought to unsettle the children. So I was surprised, after my sixth week at the farm, when my parents showed up.

My mother took one look at my pustule-covered body and gasped. Then, in words I would never forget, she announced, "You're coming home. If we are going to be blown up in this war, then we will be blown up together, at home in Liverpool."

Mummy and Dad's Sunday best

CHAPTER TWO
—— Embracing Family ——

I was three years old and a goat. Or so I was pretending to be. Mummy was bent over her washtub in our small kitchen, and her behind looked like a bull's eye. I shuffled my feet, building up steam, raised two fingers on either side of my head for horns, and ran straight at Mummy, head-butting her and nearly knocking her over.

She turned, hands on hips, her large green eyes burning holes in me. I stood still, staring back. Then suddenly, bold as brass, I laughed. Her right hand shot out to give me a swat, but I was too quick for her. Besides, she was laughing now.

Mummy returned to her washtub, and I toddled over to the pile of laundry nearby. Grabbing my favorite blanket, I dragged it next to our coal-burning kitchen stove. As I lay down on my blanket, I felt the warmth radiating from the sputtering fire my father had built earlier that morning. I fought to keep my eyes open, the repetitive sounds of clothes on washboard a lullaby. Eyes closing against my will, I drifted off to sleep.

That is my earliest memory, and my boldness still surprises me. My mother, born Eva Hillman, 1905, in Liverpool, England, was a strong woman. She carried herself with dignity, and she commanded respect. Even my mother's close friends addressed her as Mrs. Green. Years later I heard my mother referred to as "a ship in full sail."

My mother's family were coal merchants, and as such considered modestly affluent. This afforded my mother the luxury of completing high school, uncommon for women in the twenties.

My father, born Thomas Green, in Liverpool, 1902, was the eldest of five children. He quit school at age twelve to work in the coal mines and help support the family. His job was to feed and care for the ponies that hauled the coal carts. His father was a cooper by trade, making and repairing wooden barrels. Unfortunately, his greatest passion was the alcohol that went into those barrels. Perhaps in reaction to my grandfather's alcoholism, my father never took a drink, at least not that I ever saw.

My parents were quite different from one another, in size, shape, and style. Mummy was short and plump, yet moved with grace. There was beauty in her large, luminous, green eyes; the symmetry of her face was always comforting. Her brown wavy hair, like Mother herself, had a mind of its own.

My father, showing his Welsh ancestry, had black curly hair, bright blue eyes, and an easy smile. His five-foot-ten-inch frame was lean, well-muscled, and athletic. He was a quiet man, but at ease with himself. My father rarely spoke, and when he did, it was never to explain himself. As a young child, I found the lack of explanations confusing. Later I understood: He taught by example, not words.

My mother was just the opposite. The family disciplinarian, she was full of explanations.

Despite my parents' differences, or maybe because of them, their household roles were clearly defined. Typical of the times, my mother took care of the house and children while my father went off to work. For years he mixed paint in huge vats at Clare's,

Pop at 55

a paint factory near our house. This arrangement seemed to suit both my parents.

Brother Thomas, age 7

Mum and Pop dressed for the beach in Cornwall

My brother Thomas was three years older, and we had our disagreements. Before my birth, on May 12, 1931, Thomas was the sole recipient of all my mother's and grandmother's attention. Born premature, he was a small and sickly child. In consequence, he was, to a large degree, spoiled and coddled. As the new baby, I was given momentary celebrity status and all the attention that goes with it. Thomas was not happy to be upstaged by me, something I only understood years later.

My brother was not fond of sharing his things with me. One day when I was seven, I walked into our bedroom and saw a book about radios lying on the patchwork quilt that covered Thomas's bed. Intrigued, I picked it up. Just then Thomas came into the room. "What are you doing?" he yelled.

"I just wanted to look at—"

"It's mine and you can't read it," he said, a scowl on his face. He stomped over and snatched the book from my hands. He left the room and headed for the parlor; I followed, sputtering helplessly. He put the book in a small wooden cabinet that sat in the corner of the room. He reached in his pocket, pulled out a key, and locked the cabinet, returning the key to his pocket.

Then he turned, stared at me, and stuck out his tongue. I stormed out. Back in our room, I threw myself on my bed. Angry thoughts swirled through my mind. I hated being the little brother! I began plotting ways to get even.

When he walked into our room, a triumphant smile on his smug face, I ached to jump up and knock away that smile. But I knew better. Though often sickly, he was still bigger than me— and better with words. He could explain things to our parents that made any problem seem like my fault. But not forever, I thought . . . someday . . . someday.

But I didn't want to wait for years. The more I thought about it, the more determined I became to get my way—now! I hatched a plan. "It could work," I muttered. The beauty of it was that it didn't take physical strength or verbal ability. It required only imagination, sneakiness, and stealth.

That night as we were going to sleep, I stayed awake, listening carefully to my brother's exhalations. When his breathing became deep and even, I reached under my bed, my fingers feeling for the screwdriver I'd put there earlier. Tiptoeing out of our room I headed for the parlor. Once there, I quietly closed the door and switched on my torch (flashlight). Careful not to make any noise, I pulled the small cabinet away from the wall. Then I set the torch on the floor behind the cabinet and quickly set to work.

After taking out the four screws on the back of the cabinet, I removed the back panel and set it against the wall. I grabbed the book and set it next to me on the floor. I then reassembled the cabinet and pushed it back into place. I crept back into our room and hid the coveted book under my bed. Once back in bed, I smiled. I'd done it! I'd gotten what I wanted and outmaneuvered my older brother at the same time.

Over the next few weeks I read the book whenever Thomas wasn't around. When I finished it, I returned it to its original hiding place, without anyone the wiser. I was wiser, though, and not only about radios. I realized I'd been successful because I'd thought of a way to get the book that had never occurred to my brother. His key had been in his pocket; my key had been in my head: my imagination.

What I didn't understand then was how often and how well my imagination would serve me throughout my life.

* * *

I was born ambidextrous and didn't speak until I was three years old. My parents were concerned, and the doctor had no explanation. My mother came to her own conclusions: one, I was slow; two, Thomas was not. I once overheard her call him "the clever child."

As a young lad, I didn't understand the roles Thomas and I were being cast for, but I sensed its unfairness. And I believe it gave me resolve throughout my life to prove myself.

Years later, when my eldest son David was born, I found out why I'd been so slow to speak. He too is ambidextrous, and he too was a late talker. Our doctor cited studies that found a connection between speaking skills and which hand a child favors. The doctor urged us to encourage our son to use one hand predominately. We did and it worked almost immediately. David's speech and language skills were soon within the normal range for children his age.

* * *

My father, though quiet, was a man of principles. Once, when I was fifteen, I asked him which party he was going to vote for in the next election.

"I don't vote for the party," he said. "I vote for the man, no matter which party he belongs to."

My father attended church every Sunday, though not necessarily the same church. He was truly ecumenical in his Christian beliefs. He belonged to an interdenominational association for Christian social service, known as Toc-H, originally Talbot House. The mission was to ease the burdens of others—say, by visiting veterans in nursing homes.

Sometimes my father took my brother and me with him when visiting one particular nursing home located a couple miles from our house. I remember the first time. The morning had been full of summer showers, and Thomas and I had been stuck indoors. Sitting on my bed, I scanned the room, looking for something to do. My eyes fell on the encyclopedia set that lined the top of my dresser. I walked over to the set, chose one at random, plopped back on my bed, and started to read.

I wasn't in the mood, though. After only a few minutes, I slammed the book shut in annoyance. I normally found something to catch my interest in the encyclopedias, but today I wanted to be outside playing cricket.

Equal parts annoyed and bored, I headed to the kitchen to hunt up the biscuits that had been left over from breakfast. As I entered the kitchen I saw my brother taking the last biscuit from a plate on the kitchen table. He looked up, saw me, smiled, and shoved the whole biscuit in his mouth.

I ignored this taunt, not wanting to give him any satisfaction by admitting that he had anything I wanted. We groused about the cancellation of our cricket match due to rain and agreed that we were bored. My back had been to the kitchen door, and when I turned I saw my father standing there. He announced, "Okay, you two, be ready to go by nine tomorrow morning. You're coming with me to the nursing home." And with that he turned and walked away.

A little before nine the next morning, my brother and I were sitting on the front steps of our house, waiting for our father. The sun had already dried up yesterday's puddles. I turned to my brother, sighed, and whined, "I don't want to go to the nursing home today. I want to play cricket."

For once we were in agreement. He yanked up a daisy growing next to the steps. As he pulled the petals off one by one, he said, "We missed our match yesterday because of rain, and now, with the sun out, we have to spend the day indoors, listening to some old codgers. It's not fair!"

The front door opened and out came Father. As we walked down the street, I tried to imagine the nursing home. I conjured up pictures of bandaged, sad-looking men in hospital beds. Involuntarily, I shuddered and slowed my pace.

I was brought back to the present by my father's words: "Almost there, just around the corner." As we rounded the corner, I stood for a moment, puzzled, thinking my father had made a wrong turn. Before us was a large estate house, an expanse of lush, green lawn surrounding it.

My father started up the stone path that bisected the front lawn. He stopped and called over his shoulder, "Come on, lads," and resumed walking. As I followed, my head swiveled from side to side, trying to take it all in.

To the left, men were playing cards at small tables scattered about the lawn. On the right, one of four men playing croquet waved and called out, "Hello, Thomas." He was wearing an army uniform, with the left sleeve pinned up where his hand and forearm had once been.

My father returned the wave, started walking toward him, and called back, "Hello, Colonel Parker, how are you?"

The colonel grinned and said, "Can't complain." My brother and I hurried to our father's side. My father said, "Colonel, I would like to introduce my sons, Thomas and Donald."

The colonel peered at us through the prince-nez perched on his long nose, smiled, and said, "They look like fine boys, Thomas."

My father thanked him, then turned to Thomas and me and said, "Say hello, boys."

I said, "Hello, sir," my brother echoing me.

Colonel Parker pulled a large watch from his pocket, looked at it, and gestured toward the house. "Thomas, these lads look like they could use some refreshments. How about a spot of tea and seed cake in the billiard room?"

My father, smiling, said, "Thank you, Colonel. That would suit us just fine."

With the Colonel and my father leading the way, we walked up the path and through an enormous, carved front door with long windows on either side of it. We entered a room with a high ceiling and a wide staircase leading up from its center. Multiple doors lined the left and right walls.

The Colonel opened the second door on the right, turned to us, and said, "This way, gentlemen."

As we entered the room, we saw two men standing next to a billiard table, deep in conversation. Others sat smoking, playing cards, or reading. Atop a table, in the far corner of the room, sat cakes and several pots of tea. My gaze returned to the billiard table. This "nursing home" and the people in it were not as I imagined.

After tea, Colonel Parker invited my brother and me back to the lawn area to play croquet. While we were playing, my father glided among the groups of men seated at card tables on the other side of the lawn. He spent several minutes visiting with each group. When he finished, he turned and walked back to us. He shook Colonel Parker's hand, thanked him for his hospitality, and said, "Come on, boys, it's time to go home."

We walked in silence for several minutes, lost in our own thoughts. I was still trying to make sense of what I'd just seen. I asked, "Daddy, why wasn't Colonel Parker sad about losing his arm? And why didn't the nursing home look like a hospital?"

He stopped walking. Looking down at me, he said, "Well, son... you see, millions of people died in the war, and I think Colonel Parker, like a lot of other men, is just grateful to be alive."

He glanced at Thomas to make sure he was listening; we both were. He continued, "The place we just visited had originally been someone's home, but the owner donated it and allowed it to be converted to a nursing home, to help the veterans. There are other nursing homes that take care of bed-ridden and very sick veterans, and they do look more like hospitals. Do you understand, son?"

I nodded. "Yes."

He looked at Thomas, then back at me. "Why haven't either of you boys asked why we visited the nursing home?" He paused, waiting for one of us to answer. When neither of us did, he told us about Toc-H and its mission. He asked, "Do you both understand?"

I thought I did, so I said, "Is it because the veterans fought for us in the war, and God wants us to pay them back by visiting them?"

My father smiled at me. "That's close enough."

As we walked on, I thought: This day has been full of surprises. My father gave an explanation. Not only that, it was the most I'd ever heard him say at one time.

By the time we got home, my mind was chewing on a new question: "What else does God want me to do?"

I was still thinking about that question the next morning as I got ready for Sunday school. By the time I got to the kitchen, my brother was already seated and halfway through his porridge.

My mother, standing at the sink, turned and asked, "Donald, what took you so long? Your father is ready and waiting in the parlor." She always called me Donald when she was unhappy with me.

My mother was wearing her favorite blue cooking apron; she was not dressed to go to church. Though my father went nearly every Sunday, Mother never attended. While my father, brother, and I were at church, she set about cooking a roast beef dinner with all the trimmings: Yorkshire pudding, gravy, peas, and a steamed pudding for dessert. This typical English menu was a much-loved tradition in our family.

While I quickly ate my porridge, I told my mother about the nursing home and the question haunting me. She walked over, hugged me, and said, "I think your Sunday school teacher, Mr. Jensen, will have some answers for you."

CHAPTER THREE
Surviving the War

Though I was only nine years old in 1940, I listened to the radio and to grownups when they spoke of the war. And I learned things. The first phase was called the "phony war," when neither side fired a shot. In Britain, though, the people prepared for a real war. The Germans would begin bombing England any day, some said.

Most of the British activities were defensive, aimed at minimizing casualties. The alleyways, which ran through our neighborhood of row houses were turned into bomb shelters by adding blast walls and reinforced concrete roofs. Before this, those dark, cold, wet alleyways were used mostly to provide access for dust bin collection and coal delivery.

I watched as tank traps were built and installed, blocking all the streets leading to the port and docks. Tank traps, two-foot-high concrete pyramids, never had to block any actual tanks, but they were ideal for small boys playing cowboys and Indians.

One day while playing on one of the blocks, I slipped and fell and sliced my knee on a concrete edge. I cried out in pain, alerting a policemen on guard at the dock gate. He bent over me, took one look at my knee, and yelled back to another policeman, "This is a hospital case! Call an ambulance!" That made me even more scared.

The ambulance came, and men in white coats loaded me into it. Four hours later I had sixteen stitches in my knee. I had to wear a cast for six weeks to keep the wound closed. When the cast was removed, the doctor turned me over on my stomach, put one hand on either side of the damaged knee, and squeezed. I screamed so loud, the sound is probably still echoing off the hospital walls seventy-five years later.

A few days later, a truant officer knocked on our door. He demanded to know why I hadn't been in school. I told him about my knee, which at this point was covered by a large bandage. He insisted on examining the wound. "Not bad enough to keep you out of school," he declared.

I wanted to say, "And this is based on all the medical knowledge you've picked up as a truant officer?"

* * *

People were encouraged to build shelters in their backyards, places to retreat when sirens warned that German bombers were approaching. It turned out that many Brits preferred the risk of being blown up to spending a night in a coffin-like bomb shelter. The shelters were mostly simple sheets of corrugated iron with dirt piled around them. Even as a kid, I doubted they would do much good.

For those with no yard, factory-built shelters were distributed. Designed to be used in the bedroom, they consisted of two sheets of steel, an upper and a lower, separated by steel posts. They were meant to protect people from collapsing buildings.

Elswick, the street I lived on, butted up against a dry dock, where merchant ships were repaired. My pals and I often wandered down there. We saw first-hand the damage that had been inflicted on our ships by German submarines. I couldn't help but imagine the terror of being on a torpedoed sub. Anxiety rose in my chest, a cold sweat bathed my skin, and I felt real claustrophobia, as though I were on a sinking submarine.

One day my best friend, John Evans, and I walked down to the dry dock to see if any new ships had been brought in. It was a bright spring day, but still so cold our breath came out in vaporous clouds.

As we walked, John said, "My dad told me that a British ship torpedoed and sank a German sub two days ago. It was brilliant!" he exclaimed.

But I could only think of the men trapped in that sub sent to the bottom of the sea. Again I felt small bubbles of dread rising in my chest and, despite the cold, sweat on my brow. When I failed to join him in his patriotic fervor, John stopped and stared at me, his pale blue eyes showing concern. "Don, you're as white as a sheet. You all right?"

On the verge of hyperventilating, I needed a moment to find my voice. Finally, I asked, "Don't you ever think about how terrified you'd be if you were trapped in a sinking sub?"

John looked out at the docks and said, "You know, I never thought about it before . . . but I guess it would scare the heck out of me."

By now my anxiety had ebbed. I smiled at John and said, "Come on. Let's go to your house and play with your train set."

John returned the smile. "Okay, but I get to be the guard this time."

John's train set was coveted by every boy in the neighborhood, but I was his only friend allowed to play with it. John's father loved trains himself and knew how easy it was for nine-year-old boys to damage them.

When we were almost to John's front door, he turned to me and said in an excited voice, "Oh yeah, I almost forgot to tell you. I just checked out the newest Biggles book at the library."

Biggles was a fictional literary character, an ace pilot and hero of World War I. He captured the imaginations of us young boys with the daring feats he performed in his single-seat biplane fighter, the Sopwith Camel. Like thousands of other young boys throughout Britain, I'd adopted Biggles as my hero, and I wanted to be just like him.

John added, "You can look at the new Biggles book while I get the train set up."

"Thanks." As we walked in the house and headed for his room, I felt a warm flush of friendship.

* * *

My home on Elswick Street was a small row house among countless lookalike others. On one side, fuel tanks; on the other side, the docks. Both should have been prime bombing targets. Yet the nearest bomb explosion was never closer than a mile away.

Still, when we kids walked the neighborhood, we could see signs of war everywhere. Every window was blacked out, and at night air raid wardens inspected every house for light leakage. There were shortages of every kind, and a black market developed for luxury goods. What had once been considered ordinary food items—meat, tea, eggs, butter, milk, canned goods, dried fruit—became luxury items.

Rationing became an inescapable part of war and a way of life for all Brits, including us. I remember the day it hit me. My father, brother, and I were walking home from Sunday services. The cold damp air seeped through my jacket, causing an involuntary shiver. But I was warmed by visions of our traditional Sunday roast beef dinner. My stomach growled in anticipation.

"Almost there," I muttered, as we rounded the last corner and headed down our street. I quickened my stride, passing my father and brother. When I opened the front door, I felt the warmth of our house wrap around me like a blanket. I removed my jacket and went to my room to change and wash up for dinner.

As I dried my hands, I realized that something wasn't right... something was missing. Then it hit me: "The usual glorious smell of roast beef—that's what's missing."

I ran to the kitchen just in time to see my mother placing the fourth and last plate of beans-on-toast on the table. I was roused from my confusion and disbelief by my mother saying, "Don, what's the matter? What are you staring at?" Not waiting for a reply, she added, "Sit down and eat before your food gets cold."

"But Mummy, it's Sunday. Why are we having beans-on-toast instead of roast beef?"

My mother looked at me sympathetically. "Because of the war and food rationing. I'm afraid it will be a long while before any of us have roast beef again. Don't you remember last week when we all received our ration books and you asked me what they were for and I explained it to you?"

The memory of that conversation came swimming up from the depths of my mind. Feeling sad, I said, "I guess I forgot about that, Mummy, but I remember now."

At that moment rationing was no longer just a topic of conversation whirling and buzzing out there somewhere; it had just landed on our kitchen table with a thud.

* * *

During the war, public parks were divided into sections, ten feet by thirty feet, called allotments, and given over to people for growing food. Those citizen gardens produced large quantities of food, no doubt fending off starvation all over Britain. After the war, people resisted giving back the allotments for park restoration.

With shortages so widespread, some people would get in any queue they saw. Jokes circulated about those queues. In one, a man asked the woman in front of him, "What are we queuing for?"

"Brassieres," she said.

"Well, I might as well try them," he said. "I've smoked everything else."

The bottom of Elswick Street was a gathering point for neighborhood children. Often they played soccer with a tennis ball. Many were young teens, and I was too young for most games. Only occasionally, when numbers were low, did they let me play.

One day an older boy named Reggie called me over, handed me a sixpence, and said, "Hey Shorty, go up the street to Wall's and get me a chocolate ice cream cone."

I did as I was told, but on the way back temptation got the best of me and I took a bite of ice cream. "Yum," I said, and took more bites. Soon all the ice cream was gone.

As I trudged back, I tried to think it through. I knew I'd done something wrong by eating the ice cream, but it only seemed fair that I should have some of it. When I returned with chocolate smeared on my face and no cone in my hand, the other boys broke into laughter. Reggie's face blushed with embarrassment when the boys teased him. He glared at me, unsure what to do next. His fingers curled into fists, and I knew he badly wanted to give me a good thumping. But he couldn't hit a little kid in front of the others.

I learned a lesson that day about risk and reward; I wonder if Reggie did.

CHAPTER FOUR
Self Schooled

When I returned to Liverpool from the farm, I learned that the schools had been converted to fire stations. Shut out of public school, and with two parents who did not prize education, I was left to fend for myself. I turned to the bookshelf in the parlor and fell upon a formidable set of books with a friendly title: The Children's Encyclopedia.

For the next two and a half years, those heavy 800-page volumes became my constant companions. For hours, while my brother followed his interest in horses, I sat by the bookcase and read . . . and read.

Each volume was divided into about twenty sections or "Groups." Groups were not titled "Astronomy," "Zoology," and "Botany," but rather "Earth and its Neighbours," "Animal Life," and "Plant Life."

Almost every page included graphics: maps, charts, drawings, and photos, some in color. Besides offering traditional encyclopedia fare—articles on, say, volcanoes or fish—the books were rich with poems, nursery rhymes, and music. Forgot the words to "Rub-a-dub-dub"? It's in volume 1, page 231. Need the lyrics to "Who Killed Cock Robin"? Turn to page 606.

My favorite section in each volume was "The Book of Wonder," in which The Wise Man answered questions by children. In each book, about a hundred far-ranging questions were asked and answered.

How do fish live in a frozen pond?

What makes us hungry?

Will frogs and fishes someday turn into animals like horses?

Why is it dark at night?

What is beauty?

What are our eyebrows for?

What is electricity?

In 2013, I found a set of The Children's Encyclopedia on E-Bay and bought ten volumes for $307. As I look at them some seventy years later, two things are clear:

First, my attraction to the Book of Wonder section fed my natural curiosity about how and why things work and the science behind the explanation. While the section quenched my curiosity, it also fueled my imagination, generating a hunger to use science to create something new. This would eventually have a direct bearing on my career choices.

Second, I now see gender and race biases that escaped me as a child. In volume 1, for example, an article entitled "The Inexhaustible Matchbox" begins: "Every boy (why not a girl?) has a yearning to be a conjurer . . ." The accompanying drawing is captioned "The Magic Matchbox That Any Boy May Make."

Moreover, articles brazenly reflect the moral views of the authors. More than just offering information, they aimed to develop character and a sense of patriotic duty. Thus, Britain was the paragon of civilization . . . Christianity was the only true religion . . . the white race was superior to all others.

On the other hand, the authors made clear that although people of color were inferior, they should still be treated with respect. And, not insignificantly, The Children's Encyclopedia supported evolution, though it dodged any discussion of contradictions between religion and science.

After spending countless hours poring over those encyclopedias, I'd filled my head with an array of information. Though some was trivial, I knew enough to pass the Eleven Plus examinations. The Eleven Plus was the state's way of dividing children into three streams—those with 1) college potential, 2) tradesmen potential, 3) artistic potential.

By some wondrous methodology I was lumped with the artists. Shortly after beginning school, however, it was clear that I was misplaced. In short, I had no artistic talent. I requested and was granted a transfer to the college stream, a better fit.

CHAPTER FIVE
—— *Finding Shrapnel* ——

I sat at the kitchen table thinking about Christmas, less than a month away. Just the day before, while passing a department store, something in the window display had caught my eye. As I peered past the protective sandbags, which were common in store windows during WWII, I noted dozens of items on display, but they all faded into the background when I spotted the most smashing cricket bat I'd ever seen.

I tried to reason with myself. "We are in the middle of a war and money is tight. You can't start dreaming of finding that bat under the Christmas tree."

But dream I did. I saw myself making the winning play with my glorious new bat. I was rudely blasted out of my reverie by the shrill screams of air raid sirens. My father immediately appeared in the kitchen doorway and commanded, "Everybody to the bomb shelter—NOW!"

My brother came running from our bedroom. My mother entered the kitchen, grasped my arm, and pulled me from my chair. As we headed out back to the shelter, I could hear the bombers coming and the loud booming sounds made by anti-aircraft guns launching their shells.

Our air raid shelter was situated in the alley that ran behind the houses on Elswick and Draycott streets. Whenever I think of the shelter, I think of the three D's: dark, dank, dusty.

As we entered the shelter, I saw that four of our neighbors were already inside. Even in the dim light, I recognized everyone.

There was Mr. Howard, Mr. and Mrs. Broadmoor, old Mrs. Gimble . . .

Mrs. Gimble, small and frail, slid down the bench and gestured for me to sit next to her. In the dim light provided by a few candles, I noticed she was shivering inside her worn, thin cotton coat.

My mother, who kept shelter essentials by our back door, had grabbed some blankets, bread, candles, and matches on her way out. She now handed Mrs. Gimble a small woolen blanket and said, "Here, dear. Use this."

Mrs. Gimble smiled weakly. "You are so kind, Mrs. Green. Thank you."

As my mother continued to hand out blankets and help my brother and me get situated, Mr. Howard produced a large Thermos of hot tea and some cups. The frigid damp air penetrated my coat and blanket, causing me to shiver, too. Mr. Howard, seeing this, handed me a cup of tea and said, "Hot tea, that's the ticket, my lad!"

I thanked Mr. Howard and leaned back with a sigh. I savored the hot liquid as it slid down my throat. A moment later I saw a newspaper on the ground and picked it up. I squinted, looking for the date. My mother, ever attentive, handed me a lit candle.

"Thanks, Mum."

With the aid of the candle, I saw that the paper was two weeks old. Soon an article on page three caught my eye. Entitled "Beware of Falling Shrapnel," it detailed the dangers of being hit by those jagged metal fragments from exploding antiaircraft shells.

The second half of the article was a plea for people to gather shrapnel and take it to collection sites. Shrapnel remnants could be melted down and used again. In this way, anyone could contribute to the War Effort.

I was excited and inspired by the idea that even a young lad could come to the aid of his country. I vowed to start collecting first thing tomorrow morning.

Just then, as if on cue, we heard a loud explosion. Then came the deafening clatter of metal raining down on the roof of our shelter. Mrs. Gimble began to rock back and forth, her lips moving in silent prayer. Shivering more from fear than cold, I pulled the blanket tighter around my shoulders and closed my eyes. I told myself, "Don't be afraid . . . think about something else . . ."

I remembered an old shoebox under my bed . . . the perfect receptacle for shrapnel . . .

BOOM! Another explosion, followed by the sharp metallic sounds of shrapnel hitting the roof.

Mr. Broadmoor, a small man with a large handlebar moustache, had been silent to this point. Now he said in a hearty voice, "I brought some jolly good English cheddar—would anyone like some?"

There were quick affirmatives all around, and my mother began to pass out bread to go with the cheese. It struck me even then that everyone's rapt attention on food had less to do with physical hunger than with the need to focus on anything other than the danger, destruction, and death outside the shelter.

Mr. Howard, doing his part to divert our attention, launched into a story about his days as a news correspondent stationed in India. Lulled by Mr. Howard's masterful storytelling and, eventually, the receding noises outside, I began to relax. For the next hour, we listened and ate as the sounds of war continued to diminish.

Mr. Howard was nearing the end of one of his stories when the all-clear siren blew. With a collective sigh of relief we all said our goodbyes and left the shelter.

Outside, my father said to my mother, "Eva, take the boys in the house. I'll walk Mrs. Gimble home."

With a grateful smile Mrs. Gimble took my father's arm and said, "God bless you, Mr. Green."

I'd taken only a few steps outside when my foot struck something hard. I reached down and my fingers contacted warm metal. I brought the object close to my eyes and squinted through the darkness. "I have just collected my first piece of shrapnel—and it's still warm!" I announced to no one.

When we got inside the house, my brother and I helped our mother refold the blankets and stack them by the backdoor. As my mother filled the tea kettle, she said, "Boys, go wash up and get your pajamas on while I make us some tea."

Moments later, the four of us were seated at the kitchen table, enjoying our tea. My father started listing the chores he had in mind for my brother and me the next day. My mind drifted back to the newspaper article and my new plan. Though I could hear my father's voice, his words were lost to me.

"Don, are you listening?"

"Sorry, Father. I was thinking about a newspaper article I read while we were in the shelter."

"What about?"

I explained about the shrapnel and about my plan to contribute to the War Effort.

A slight smile crept across my father's face. "Son, I am proud of you for wanting to do your part for England. But I need you to pay attention to what needs doing around here tomorrow."

"Yes, Father."

Still smiling, he said, "You can go out and look for shrapnel in the morning, but be home by ten to do your household tasks."

My brother, silent until now, brightened and said, "I'll go with you, Don. We'll see who can find the most shrapnel."

I stared at my brother and thought, not this time! "I'll take that challenge," I said.

"All right, boys," my mother said. "Time for bed."

Moments later, as I snuggled under the covers, I thought, "Ahhh, this feels good . . . I am so tired."

But sleep eluded me, my brother's challenge still buzzing about my mind like an annoying insect. "I know what I'll do," I murmured. "I'll get up before my brother and get a head start on the contest."

Smiling, I drifted off.

Elder Brother Thomas

CHAPTER SIX
Fleeing to the Bomb Shelter

It was late November 1940, and as I stood at my bedroom window, I noticed a pale boy with blond hair outside. He reminded me of someone, but who?

Fat raindrops began to pelt the glass, blurring my view. My thoughts drifted back . . . to before the war . . . and my best friend, John Evans.

"That's who he reminds me of," I said. I hadn't seen John in fourteen months, since the day before we'd both been evacuated to the country. After I returned to Liverpool, I went to John's house; his mother told me John was staying away until after the war . . .

I was yanked from my daydreaming by the sound of the front door opening and my brother calling, "Hello." I glanced at the clock on the dresser: 3:00. Time for tea.

On my way to the kitchen, I passed Thomas taking off his wet shoes and coat. "I was going to make some tea," I said. "Do you want some?"

"Yeah. Any biscuits left?"

"I don't know. I'll check."

I went to the kitchen table, lifted the lid of our old blue biscuit tin, and slowly peered inside—empty. Disappointed, I filled the kettle with water, placed it on the stove, and turned on the gas. I struck a match and held it to the burner until it sputtered to life.

On the counter sat a loaf of bread and a dish of margarine. As I sliced the bread and spread it with margarine, I wondered if there was any sugar left for our tea. I opened a tin of canned milk and set it on the table. Steeling myself for another disappointment, I removed the top of the sugar bowl and peeked inside. A sigh of relief escaped my lips. I counted eight lumps nestled in the bowl. Once the kettle whistled, I made the tea, placed our old knitted cozy over the pot, and set it on the table to steep.

Just then Thomas entered the kitchen, headed straight for the biscuit tin, and lifted the lid. "You ate the last one, didn't you?!" he snapped

"No I didn't. There weren't any left."

I was missing my friend John, generally feeling out of sorts, and didn't feel like arguing with my brother. Thomas studied my face. Perhaps he saw the anguish I felt. "I'm sorry, Don. I'm just so tired of all this food rationing. I wish things could be like they were before the war."

"Me too," I said. We both sat down, and I poured the tea. "The other night I dreamt it was a Sunday and we were all sitting down to our usual roast beef dinner. You remember the kind we used to have before the war. Anyway, just as I was about to put a forkful of roast beef and gravy in my mouth, I woke up."

We heard the front door open, and a moment later Mum came into the kitchen, pulled out a chair, sat down, and said, "I'm done in. I could sure do with a cup of tea. Any left?"

She had started work at a bomb factory four months earlier, and just been promoted to supervisor.

"You're just in time, Mum," I said. "It just finished steeping."

I poured her tea. As she cradled the hot cup in her hands, she closed her eyes and sighed. "Thank you, I needed that. It's been a long day."

I had other things on my mind. "Mum, since you and Daddy are both working now, do you think we could afford to buy a beef roast and have it on Sunday like we used to?"

"No, Don, we can't. I'm sorry. It's not a question of having enough money. There isn't enough meat available for any one family to have an entire roast. Before the war, England imported half of all its meat, cheese, sugar, fruits, and grains. They came by ship. But since the war started, the German navy has been stopping the supply ships from getting to England."

She paused to sip her tea. "And with so many of our young men away fighting for our country, we don't have as many people to do the farm work. If that weren't enough, there is no feed for the animals. "Lastly, and maybe most importantly, we have to feed the men fighting for us. Do you understand, Don?"

I was silent for a moment. A picture of a faceless English soldier on a battlefield, cold, tired, and hungry, flashed through my mind. Looking at the floor, I said, "I hadn't thought about what our soldiers had to eat. I understand now, Mum."

Thomas, who had been silent until now, said, "One of my friends was telling me yesterday how his rich uncle said a person could get things like sugar and even steak if you knew the right people and had enough money to pay the high prices."

I looked at Mum. She was frowning, and when she spoke her voice was low but steely. "That is unfortunately true, and what you were just describing is known as the Black Market. Those involved in it are scoundrels, disregarding the laws that govern food rationing. They do a grave disservice to England by profiting off the hardships of war and the sacrifices of others." Her voice rose as she went on, "Not only is it illegal and morally wrong to sell on the Black Market, it is illegal and wrong to buy as well." She looked at my brother and then at me. "Can either of you tell me why it would be wrong to buy things on the Black Market?"

I thought I knew, so I said, "Is it because England is at war and we have to do our part to support the war effort and the soldiers by only buying and eating our fair share of the food?" The picture of the hungry soldier again flashed through my mind.

Mum smiled at me. "You are absolutely right, Don. I don't think I could have said it better myself."

We sat around the table for a while longer, finishing our tea in silence, each of us lost in our own thoughts. After a few moments my mother got up, put on her favorite blue apron, and began to clear away the tea things. "Boys, get going on your work," she said. "I'll get dinner started."

That night I dreamt my friend John had come to Liverpool to visit me. We were sitting on my bed when I asked him about his life in the country. When he spoke, I realized he didn't sound like John. His voice was deep, more like a grownup's. Looking closer, I saw that I was talking to the faceless soldier who had flashed through my mind earlier.

I asked, "But why are you here? What happened to John?"

The soldier opened his mouth to speak, but all I could hear was a loud, mournful siren. As the sound continued, the soldier faded away. Someone called my name and I opened my eyes.

My brother was standing over my bed. "Come on, Don—wake up! It's an air raid, and we have to get to the bomb shelter."

I got up quickly and threw on my coat. Father appeared in the doorway, saying, "Hurry, boys! Get to the shelter!"

When we reached the back door, Mum was already there, her

arms full of blankets and other shelter supplies. She handed my brother and me a blanket each. Outside we carefully picked our way through the darkness, following our practiced route to the shelter. The sirens continued to wail.

My father was last into the shelter. He closed the door, latched it, and lit a candle. In the dim light I could see we were the first to arrive. My mother set her supplies on the bench just inside the door and lit another candle; she handed it to me, and gestured toward the far wall. "Please put it in the candle holder," she said.

As soon I put the candle in the holder, someone pounded on the shelter door. Father opened the door, and Mrs. Gimble came rushing in, followed by Mr. Howard.

My mother sat down on the bench and pointed to the spot next to her. "Come sit by me, Mrs. Gimble."

Mrs. Gimble smiled at my mother, pulled her grey wool blanket tightly over her bony shoulders. "Thank you, Mrs. Green. I think I will."

Mr. Howard sat on the opposite side of the shelter, next to my brother. He pulled out his pocket watch and peered at it in the dim light.

"What time have you got, Mr. Howard?" I asked.

"A little after midnight," he said.

My father started to speak to Mr. Howard, but his voice was drowned out by the loud cracking noise of the antiaircraft guns launching their shells, followed by a deafening clatter as metal shards pelted the roof of the shelter.

BOOM! A loud explosion shook the shelter, knocking the candle out of its holder, and provoking a terrified shriek from Mrs. Gimble.

My mother, one arm around Mrs. Gimble, handed me a box

of matches. "Don, relight the candle and put it back in its holder."

I did so, then sat back down. "No more explosions," I quietly pleaded. Ack, ack, ack went the British antiaircraft guns. But this time, to my relief, they sounded farther away as they tracked the retreating German bombers.

Everyone was silent, listening, hoping, waiting for the next sounds. And feeling relief as they continued to recede into the distance. Mr. Howard spoke first, to my father. "Is it true, Mr. Green, that you are now a fireman for the Auxiliary Fire Service?"

My father smiled. "News travels fast. I only started last week."

My father and Mr. Howard chatted a bit about the Fire Service. Mr. Howard was in the middle of a sentence when the all-clear siren blew.

It was still dark when we returned to the house. Just as my mother set the kettle on the stove, we heard a knock on the door. My father went to answer it. When he returned, he solemnly addressed Mum. "The explosion that shook our shelter was from a bomb that hit a building not far from here. I gotta go."

He bent over, kissed my mother goodbye, and dashed off to gather his gear. At the front door, he turned to us and said, "Put out the lights, so I can open the front door." My brother flicked the switch, and in the darkness my mother followed my father to the door. In almost a whisper she said, "Be careful, and come home safe."

Once my mother closed the door, we turned on the lights. After hearing my mother's last words, I studied her face as we went back into the kitchen. Her brows were knitted tight, and worry clouded her green eyes. I had a jumpy feeling in my stomach. My mother was not easily alarmed, and I wasn't used to seeing any trace of worry in her face.

In a tentative voice I asked, "What's wrong, Mum? Will Daddy be all right?"

My mother stood up ramrod straight, turned to me, her eyes clear and focused, and said in a calm voice, "Of course. Your father will be fine. It's just that firefighting is very dangerous. But your father is a careful man. He will take care of himself."

My mother, brother, and I sat at the table, sipping tea and talking about Mum's new job as a supervisor. Then we all headed to bed.

My father had still not returned by breakfast time. Just as I was about to ask Mum about it, we heard the front door open and close. My father appeared in the kitchen doorway, his face and hands smeared with dirt and sooty ash. A strong smell of smoke surrounded him like a cloud.

His right hand clutched a large canvas sack that had once been white, but was now streaked with black and grey. Seeing my father through new eyes, I asked, "What's in the sack, Daddy?"

A mischievous light glowed in his eyes and a smile crept across his face. "Dinner."

I could barely contain my excitement. "But what is it?"

My father carefully set the bag down, grabbed the bottom end with both hands, and turned it upside down. With a loud clatter, the contents of the sack rolled out onto the kitchen floor. Staring in amazement at the pile of tins, I picked one up. "But Daddy, I still don't know what we're having for dinner. They don't have any labels."

"That's the fun of it, lad. Whenever we open one of these tins for dinner, it will be a surprise."

I smiled weakly. "Well, maybe. But where did you get them and why don't they have labels?"

My father's face lost its smile. "Rubble—and these tins were all that was left of the building bombed last night. We worked for hours trying to get the fire under control, but couldn't save the building." He brightened a bit. "We were able to stop the fire from spreading to the building next door. Anyway, the water from the fire hoses dissolved the glue that held the labels on."

I smiled. "I have an idea. Let's see who can guess what's in the tins before we open them."

My brother, who'd been busy shoveling in his breakfast, spoke up for the first time. "Oh, I bet I can guess better than you, Don."

I smiled confidently. "I'll take that bet and win, dear brother."

CHAPTER SEVEN
—— *Sinking the Bismarck* ——

By 1941, the war was two years old and I was ten. I'd heard on the radio that the German navy was sinking Allied merchant and supply ships. Before sinking the ships, the Germans usually took the sailors as prisoners. The prisoners were then transferred to a German supply ship.

One of our Liverpool neighbors, Mr. Jones, had worked as a stoker, feeding and stoking fires on various ships in the British Merchant Navy. His ship had been attacked by a German battleship, *Tirpitz*, sister ship to the more famous *Bismarck*. He and the crew were taken prisoner. For a long time that's all I knew.

Mr. Jones lived three doors down from us on Elswick Street, but I'd never talked with him. In fact, I don't think anyone on our street knew Mr. Jones well, if at all. Not only was he often at sea on a merchant ship, but he seemed a quiet, shy man who kept to himself.

Then one day I rounded the corner of Elswick Street and saw Mr. Jones standing on his front steps, addressing a group of people. As I got nearer, I recognized Mr. Howard, Mr. and Mrs. Broadmoor, Mrs. Gimble, and five other neighbors. Mr. Howard was leaning forward slightly, a look of rapt concentration on his face. Getting closer, I saw that Mr. Jones had everyone's attention.

Curious, I quietly edged through the crowd, until I could make out Mr. Jones's words.

". . . I was sleeping in my bunk below decks, when I was

startled into wakefulness by the sound of an exploding shell. I rushed on deck to find that a large battleship had fired a warning shot across our ship's bow. Suddenly a voice came over the loudspeaker informing us that we were now prisoners of war.

"If we had any thoughts of resisting, they were quickly dashed. In seconds, armed German sailors were boarding our ship from both sides. While some of our captors remained on deck, acting as guards, others went below deck to gather up the rest of the prisoners . . ."

Mr. Jones paused, looked down at the ground. "I have to admit, at that moment, standing there surrounded by German sailors, I was mighty scared. My stomach began to feel queer, like my insides were turning to liquid. I said a quick prayer under my breath . . ."

I glanced around at the others. All eyes were on Mr. Jones. He continued: "Once the Germans had gathered all of our crew on deck, they began to load us into lifeboats. They took us to a nearby supply ship.

"Before we were taken below, the German officer in charge addressed us. 'First, gentlemen, there is something I want you all to see.' He shouted some orders in German, gestured toward our now abandoned ship, and said, 'Watch this, gentleman. I would not want you to miss it.'

"He shouted another order in German, and a second later we heard several loud explosions. Our ship began to sink before our eyes. As I stood there, forced to watch, I felt any hopes for my life and my future ebbing away and sinking along with the ship.

"The ship slipped completely from sight in less than ten minutes, then we were all taken below deck. Part of the ship's cargo hold had been turned into jail cells. Since we were in the bowels of the ship, there were no portholes, and the only light came from a few dim bulbs hanging from the ceiling. As I was shoved into a cell, I uttered another silent prayer and told myself, 'Keep your chin up.'

"Next morning we were assembled on deck, and the senior German officer addressed us again. A smile spread across his fat pink face as he began to speak. 'I have good news to report . . .' He paused, walked closer to us, and continued. 'The pride of your English Navy, *HMS Hood*, was struck by several of our shells yesterday and quickly sank.'

"His piggish little eyes were full of merriment as he went on. 'Your beloved *HMS Hood* was not the only casualty yesterday. Four other ships from your British fleet are also lying, crushed and broken, at the bottom of the sea. Soon all of your fellow countrymen will be subjects of the Third Reich . . . I wanted you all to have something to think about while you are sitting in your cells.'

"Then he gestured for the guards to take us back to our cells. Once behind bars, I scanned the faces of my fellow prisoners. Most reflected the hopelessness I felt. But one man, Jake, was an exception. He said, 'Chin up, boys. They very well could be lying to us. Think about it: they want us to feel defeated, 'cause it makes us easier to control.'"

Mr. Jones paused, became thoughtful, and then with a look of wonderment on his face, said, "It may seem silly, but until Jake's suggestion, it never occurred to me that the Germans could be lying." He continued, "From then on I clung to that hope, and I began to feel stronger.

"A week or so later, as I lay on the floor of my cell, we heard explosions nearby." Mr. Jones's face was animated now, his eyes glowing. "All of a sudden we felt a strong jolt. We knew the ship had been hit . . . Do you know what happened then?"

I looked around: everyone was hanging on his every word, but no one spoke. Excited, I said, "Oh, Mr. Jones, please tell us what happened next!"

Mr. Jones smiled down at me. "What is your name, son?"

"Don Green, sir. Please finish the story."

After murmurs of agreement, Mr. Jones went on. "Only a moment later, footsteps approached our cell. Our cell door was flung open, and there stood the most lovely sight any of us had ever seen—a British sailor. Our floating German prison had been captured by the British navy. I immediately asked the sailor what everyone wanted to know: 'Was it true that Hood and four other ships had been sunk by the Germans?'

"The sailor said, 'Partially true. The Hood was sunk, but not four others.'"

Mr. Jones paused, and the neighbors began firing questions at him. I was interested in hearing the answers, but I was even more anxious to get home and tell my parents about Mr. Jones.

As soon as I walked in the house, I heard the radio on. When I went into the kitchen, my mother looked up and put her finger to her lips. My parents and my brother were seated around the kitchen table, listening intently to a BBC broadcast. I sat down.

"I repeat, the German battleship, *Bismarck*, was hit and sunk in the Atlantic Ocean late last night . . ."

We all cheered. A moment later my mother got up and turned off the radio.

I said, "I have some war news, too." And I related Mr. Jones's story.

Lying in bed that night, I thought, "What a powerful thing information can be. We all make decisions based on the information we have, but what if it's not true? What would happen if, like Mr. Jones, I was given some truths and some lies—how could I tell the difference? And make the right decision?

I later came to realize that merely asking that question, even though I couldn't answer it then, made me aware that the decisions we make are only as sound as the information on which they are based. I vowed to get the best information I could.

CHAPTER EIGHT
— Returning to School —

I was excited when the schools reopened. I was to attend Childs Hill Elementary School. As back-to-school day approached, I grew more jittery.

As I lay in bed Sunday night, my brain was crowded with unanswered questions. I sighed, closed my eyes, and thought, "What if the other kids don't like me? . . . What if I don't like them? . . . Will I like my new teacher? Will it be a man or a woman? . . . Will I ever have another best friend like John Evans?"

Unable to sleep, I sat up in bed. "This won't do. You need to quit worrying."

I went to the kitchen for a cup of tea. As I was filling the tea kettle, my mother came in the kitchen and said, "You have fifteen minutes, and then it's off to bed with you, my lad. You don't want to be tired for your first day of school."

I nodded. "Mum, what if the other kids don't like me?"

My mother, who never seemed afraid of anything, replied, "Nonsense. You are a nice boy, Don. Of course they will like you."

It seemed like a stock answer for a mother, but it did make me feel better. I sat drinking my tea and talking to Mum and soon forgot my worries. I finished my tea, walked over to the sink, rinsed out my cup, and headed for bed.

I fell asleep immediately and didn't wake until early morning when my mother's voice invaded my dream and pulled me from slumber. "Time to get up and get ready for school."

School! I stayed in bed for a moment, trying to imagine what the day held for me. I was no longer worried. In fact, I was excited about my new adventure. I missed school and friends. And I'd practically memorized our entire set of Children's Encyclopedias.

I was nearly dressed when I heard my mother's voice booming from the kitchen: "Boys, hurry up. You don't want to be late for your first day. Porridge is on the table. I have to leave for work... see you tonight."

I heard my brother groan from his bed. He lifted his head, looked around, and then snuggled back under the covers, pulling them over his head. He was decidedly less thrilled by our return to school.

I finished tying my shoes, grabbed my jacket, and headed to the kitchen. Over breakfast I worried that the paperwork informing me of my teacher and room number hadn't come in the post yet, but I figured someone would tell me once I got there.

After a short walk to school, I headed for the main office. Behind the counter stood a thin woman, her dark hair pulled tightly into a bun. As I stepped forward, she lifted her gaze from the stack of papers lying on the counter, peered at me over her glasses, and demanded, "Why aren't you in class, young man?"

Feeling some of my excitement fade, I answered, "My class assignment didn't come in the post, and I don't know where to go."

Staring bullets at me, she leaned forward, her beaky nose just inches from mine, and said, "Didn't get your assignment? That's impossible. I prepared them all myself and sent them out over two weeks ago." Then she crossed her arms over her chest and said, "Your mother probably got the notice and forgot to tell you about it."

"Maybe it went to the wrong address," I said timidly.

Frowning, she demanded, "What's your name and address?"

I hesitated for a second, too long for this woman. She barked, "Well, get your skates on, lad. I haven't got all day. Out with it!"

I recited my name and address, then waited while she ran her bony finger down the first page, then the next. Halfway down the third page, she had me repeat my address. "Aha," she exclaimed. "Just as I thought, someone else made the mistake. When they entered your address into the rolls, they transposed the numbers." Then she looked up at me and said in a triumphant voice, "I knew I hadn't made a mistake." Suddenly she stopped smiling and announced, "You're in Miss Bennington's class, room 26. You better be swift . . . you're already fifteen minutes late."

As I headed for the door, she said, "It's upstairs, third door on the left."

I hurried up the stairs and down the hall, found the room, and peeked in through the small window on the door. All seats were filled except one, right next to the door. Maybe I could sneak in . . .

Barely breathing, I quietly opened the door, closed it behind me, and slid into the vacant seat. Unfortunately in my haste, my foot hit the desk causing it to screech along the floor a few inches. I sat down and slowly looked up; all eyes were on me, including Miss Bennington's.

Flushed, I started to explain, but I wasn't three syllables in when she interrupted me. "You're Donald Green, aren't you?"

"Yes, Miss," I managed to say.

"Welcome, Donald," she said with a weak smile. "As you can see, we've already begun our English lesson, so please open your

English book to page seven and study the poem, "Daffodils," by Wordsworth. We will have ten more minutes of study time. When I point to you, it will be your turn to recite. Do you understand?"

I nodded and set about reading the poem. Then I read it again, trying to memorize as much as possible. After ten minutes Miss Bennington announced, "Time is up. Everyone please close your books." Then she pointed at a blond-haired boy sitting in the second row and said, "Please stand up, Joseph, and recite the first part."

He stood and spoke in a clear, confident voice, then sat back down. I was impressed.

Then Miss Bennington pointed to the girl sitting next to me and said, "Your turn, Susan."

The girl stood, took a moment to straighten the bow on the front of her dress, recited the next verse flawlessly, smiled at Miss Bennington, and sat down. Four more students gave their recitations, and after each seemingly perfect performance, I could feel my nervousness grow. My heart pounded in my chest and beads of sweat dampened my upper lip. Incoherent thoughts raced through my mind.

I thought I had to memorize the whole poem, but each student had recited only one verse. How did they know which one? Now, in near panic, I could remember only the first verse.

Through a loud whooshing noise in my ears, I faintly heard my name called, as if the voice were coming to me from a great distance. I looked up to see Miss Bennington staring at me. "Donald, it's your turn."

A bead of sweat rolled down my face and dripped onto my desk. I stood, swallowed, and stammered out the first line. As

I began to stumble through the second line, Miss Bennington stopped me.

"Donald, I'm sorry. I forgot you weren't here when I gave the full instructions. The desks are numbered, and you need only recite the line number that corresponds to your desk number." She glanced at the clock on the far wall and said, "We'll try again tomorrow. You may be seated."

I sat down, feeling like an idiot.

Though that happened decades ago, I've never forgotten those feelings, the intense fear that accompanies speaking to others when unprepared. I vowed never to let it happen again.

CHAPTER NINE
House Bomb

One morning on my way to school, I saw that a crowd had gathered a few houses ahead and across the street. I crossed the road to investigate.

The day was cold and overcast, and people were bundled in heavy coats and hats, making it hard for me to see past them. As I slipped through the crowd, I heard someone crying.

Once at the front of the crowd, I stood stunned, staring at what lay before me. Two partial walls and a large pile of rubble were all that remained of the house I'd seen there just yesterday.

To my right a woman was wringing her hands and wailing. The sound reminded me of the time Farmer Johnson's steel trap caught a rabbit. The woman's worn, lined face was contorted in pain, her lips pulled back in a grimace. Though her eyes were clamped shut, tears escaped and rolled down her cheeks. Her grieving sobs sounded as though ripped from deep within.

A moment later, another woman came through the crowd and put her arm around the crying woman. "Oh Mary dear, please come in out of the cold. I know how much you cared for Millie and little Amy." With that, her voice quavered and her own tears began to fall.

Mary turned to her friend and cried, "They were like family. Amy was like a granddaughter to me. With all of my own family dead, Millie and Amy were all I had left . . ."

As those last words escaped her lips, Mary's rigid body slumped, and she allowed her friend to lead her away.

On my left, an old man with wiry grey hair was explaining to a woman what had happened. I heard only snatches. "A bomb . . . hit the house . . . middle of the night . . . mother and daughter in bed . . ."

Stunned, I backed away and headed for school. Fearing I'd be late, I quickened my pace.

But then my thoughts returned to the scene I'd just witnessed, and I slowed, thinking, someone could be alive, sleeping peacefully one minute, blown to bits the next.

It boggled me. Even at age twelve, I'd been aware of the war, but only as a distant, theoretical thing. I'd never experienced anything firsthand—until now.

I hurried on for another block, then slowed again, lost in thought and swirling emotions.

The injustice, I thought. An innocent mother and child murdered in their beds. Anger welled up inside me. "Hitler, you rotten, bloody coward. Why don't you pick on somebody your own size?"

I began to fantasize about joining the Royal Air Force, becoming an ace pilot, protecting my country—just like Biggles.

The fear of being late jolted me back to reality. I ran the rest of the way to school, making it into my seat just as the starting bell rang.

CHAPTER TEN
— Joining the Boy Scouts —

In 1943 my father was offered a better-paying job at a London factory that made truck parts. So we packed up and moved from Liverpool to London. My mother got a job at an ordnance factory, making bombs and antiaircraft shells.

Though the move from Liverpool to London improved my family's financial status, it was at first a tough adjustment for me. But then I found a Boy Scout troop to join, made some new friends, and began to feel more at home. The troop was called the 14th Willesden Troop, and the Scoutmaster was Jim Bishop. He was only about five foot three, but he was fit and muscular, and seemed to radiate power. And he could fix anything. His motto: "If I can't fix it, it isn't broken."

Jim Bishop, Scoutmaster

I still remember the first time he introduced himself to our troop. "First," he said, "I want you all to call me Jim. Second, I would like to tell you a little about my background and training.

I served during the war with a group of commandos from the Indian Army. We were parachuted behind Japanese lines to disrupt communication links and supply lines. Training for those dangerous missions was extremely rigorous, but it paid off. When we finished, we were a capable fighting force that could be used in many different situations. We learned how to forage for food in the jungle, and sometimes had to survive on just roots and berries."

Jim went on to recount the exploits of his Special Forces team, called the Chindits. His story inspired me, and I asked hopefully, "Will you train us to be Chindits, Jim?"

Jim seemed pleased with the question. He smiled at me. "What is your name, son?"

I sat up, ramrod straight, pulled my shoulders back. Then, trying to look and sound like a Chindit, I answered, "Donald Green, sir."

"That's a fine name, but what do your friends call you?"

I grinned. "Don, sir."

"Well, Don, we will incorporate some of the principals of the Chindits into our Scouting activities. Of course, we will modify the training, making it suitable for teenage boys."

Jim scanned the room. He had our full attention, each of us, I imagined, with visions of being a Chindit warrior dancing in our heads.

"There are three important Chindit principles I hope to instill in all of you," he continued. "One, sound ethical reasoning. Two, moral integrity. Three, discipline . . ."

Jim had a huge influence on us boys. He taught us how to find our way in the wilderness, how to pay attention to the terrain we passed through. He also taught us to spot and name various bird species, and this became one of my favorite activities. I quickly earned a Boy Scout patch for my bird-watching skills.

Because of our dedication to Jim and his principles, our troop was successful in various competitions. We won something called the Pioneering Competition, a race to see which troop could build a bridge across a stream first, without getting wet. We also won the signaling competition, which required Scouts to stand on top of a hill and successfully send messages using flags.

More than victories, though, I received important lessons that helped me later in life. Jim was a good and careful communicator. After we had completed a task, he would ask us what we had learned from it besides technical skills.

One day our troop met in a large country house, which was on loan to us for meetings. The house itself was in good repair, but dead and potentially dangerous limbs hung from some of the trees surrounding the house. Jim taught us how to safely prune those limbs by using ropes, pulleys, and a chainsaw.

When we had finished, he gathered our troop together for a discussion. After we were seated on the lawn, Jim looked out at our sweaty, dirty faces and smiled. He thanked us for our hard work and for remembering to work safely. Then he paused and asked, "Boys, why do you think I suggested we prune the trees?"

Robert, a small dark-haired boy, raised his hand. "Is it because it gave you a chance to show us how to prune trees safely?"

"Yes, that is one reason," Jim said, "but can anyone think of another?"

I raised my hand, and when Jim called on me, said, "Well, since the owners of the house were kind enough to let us use it for our meetings, then we owe them a kindness in return."

Jim's face brightened. "That's right, Don . . . but can anyone think of another reason?"

The troop was quiet. A moment later George began waving his hand frantically. "Oh, I know, I know."

"Tell us, George," Jim said.

"Is it because we are Scouts and we should always try to be of service to others?"

Jim's eyes seemed to fill with pride. He scanned his audience and said, "What do you think, boys? Do you think that's a good reason?"

We all cheered and shouted, "Yes."

Jim said, "One good deed deserves another, so I'm treating you all to ice cream. Let's go!"

Cheering wildly, we all rose and headed down the street toward the ice cream shop.

* * *

I continued to see Jim long after I was directly involved in Scouting. An excellent photographer, he taught me the craft. Jim praised my "natural ability for taking pictures," and soon we were in business together, photographing weddings, babies, and doing family portraits.

Because film was expensive, we had to be careful not to take too many unwanted shots. When photographing babies, the challenge was to get the tykes to smile. Parents typically spent the first fifteen minutes trying to cheer up the child, and then, after much wasted film, bought an unsmiling photo. I learned to pretend that I was snapping dozens of photos during the first part of the session, but actually I saved my film until after the parent had moved away from the child. That way I was able to capture the child in a more natural state.

I learned two things from this: First, don't argue with the customer about what they think they want, and be willing to offer them alternatives. Second, keep overhead costs down by taking only photos likely to sell.

My partnership with Jim was successful because we each had complementary skills and strengths. We relied on Jim's skill as a photographer and my ability to interface with customers and keep the business on a firm financial footing.

We remained close until I left for Canada in 1956. As the years went by, my contacts with Jim became less frequent, but I never forgot the lessons he taught me. Jim was a firm believer in "clean living": no smoking, drinking, or swearing, and he practiced what he preached. From him I learned the importance of listening to my conscience and how to conduct my business affairs with moral integrity.

These principles have guided me throughout my career and helped me sleep well at night.

A soccer team with a checkered outlook

Boy Scout leader

CHAPTER ELEVEN
—— *Confronting Two Bullies* ——

I was cycling to school one bright September morning when I heard an ominous buzzing sound coming from the sky. We all knew what that meant: a V1 rocket, a pilotless bomb, was headed our way. The Germans had killed thousands of Englishmen with their "buzz bombs."

We had learned that after the buzzing came ten seconds of silence, then explosion. I skidded to a halt, threw down my bicycle and scrambled behind some trees. As I crouched there, the bomb exploded! "About a mile away," I murmured.

Only then did I take stock of my situation. I was hiding behind a copse of saplings that would have provided near zero protection.

I got back on my bike and raced to school. Thanks to the V1, I hadn't missed any lessons. My classmates, who had been hiding under their desks, were only now emerging. Just then the all-clear siren sounded.

Miss Peabody approached me, a concerned look on her face. "Donald, are you all right? I was so worried. You're white as a sheet."

I sat down at my desk and told the class of my brush with the buzz bomb, embellishing it only a little.

Miss Peabody walked over to my desk, ruffled my hair, and said, "I'm glad you're all right, Donald."

I decided right then I liked Miss Peabody.

* * *

The teachers seemed nice and I quickly made some new friends. One day at lunchtime I saw a kid with mousy-brown hair push another kid to the ground, apparently for no reason. I soon learned his name was Rupert.

During our afternoon recess, I got involved in a game of dodge ball.

And there was Rupert, louder and more obnoxious than the other kids. When it was his turn in the middle, he taunted whoever had the ball. "You throw like a girl . . . you can't hit me!"

"Stupid bugger," I muttered.

He was still at it when the ball bounced toward me. I'd been throwing with my right arm, so no one knew what I knew: I was nearly as good with my left. I had to dart to my right to catch the ball. Without thinking—or aiming—I spun clockwise and threw as hard as I could left-handed—and hit Rupert right in the head. He staggered backward and fell to the ground. The sound of laughter filled the air.

Rupert jumped to his feet, face flushed with anger, and rushed toward me. I sidestepped him, pushed him to the ground, then pinned him with my knee on his chest. "I don't ever want to see you bully anyone again!" I said. "You got that, Rupert?"

Through his tears, he bellowed, "I'm going to tell! You can't do this to me!"

"Ha." I got up and said, "Remember, Rupert, no more bullying."

He struggled to his feet, snot and tears streaming down his face. I curled my fingers into fists, waiting for another attack. But just then the playground monitor put a stop to it and sent us to the headmaster's office.

When we entered his office, the headmaster ordered us to sit down. Scowling, he looked first at me, then at Rupert. "Okay,

Rupert, what happened?"

Rupert pointed at me and said, "He started it. He hit me when my back was turned. He's just a bully, picking on somebody smaller."

I was set to give my version when the headmaster ended the conversation. "Two strokes of the cane on the palm of the hand for each of you."

"But—"

The headmaster raised his hand to silence me. Still looking at me, he asked, "Are you left-handed or right-handed, boy?"

I hesitated. "Neither . . . both."

That seemed to confuse him, though only briefly. He told me to hold out my left hand, palm up. Slowly I did so, then without warning—for I had not seen the wooden cane in his hand—he smacked my fingers hard; then he did it again. Pain shot to my brain. The blows left my hand red and swollen, but I showed no expression.

I left the headmaster's office serenaded by Rupert's yelps of pain.

I don't know if it was fear, humiliation, or a budding conscience that prompted the change in Rupert, but I never saw him bully or taunt anyone again. If nothing else, I'd shown the other kids that Rupert wasn't as scary as he wanted to be.

My basic transportation, London

CHAPTER TWELVE
Winning Maureen

A boy in my Scout patrol, Peter Eustace, had a sister, and one day she walked into the St. Andrews church hall, where our Scout meetings were held. About five foot two, she was trim, her features delicate. She looked serenely composed, and I couldn't take my eyes off her. She was the most beautiful girl I'd ever seen.

She seemed shy, avoiding eye contact, perhaps because I wasn't the only boy staring. She found her brother and spoke briefly to him. Conversation over, she quickly glanced around the room and exited, leaving me sputtering silently, helplessly.

I learned her name—Maureen Eustace—and that she was seventeen, two years older than me. No wonder she had ignored my moonstruck glances. Only later did I consider that my "struck dumb" look, mouth agape, may not have been the most seductive pose.

Muscle Beach

After that I thought about her all the time. In moments of intellectual clarity, I realized that although our brief encounter had exerted a dramatic effect on me, it hadn't touched her at all. How could it? I was just one of a dozen boys ogling her, much to her discomfort.

Maureen decorating Brighton Beach

Over the next few months, I occasionally saw her at the local park, strolling with girlfriends. Sometimes I went out of my way to make sure I passed her. We nodded politely to each other—at least she knew who I was!—but I couldn't work up the nerve to talk to her.

Maureen, 16, at the far right with girlfriends

Over the next few years, I saw her only at Boy Scout fundraising activities. Then one day she joined the amateur drama group I belonged to. I'd recently been given the male lead in Thornton Wilder's play, "Our Town," but I hadn't been nervous until now. Casting appraising looks at Maureen during our first rehearsal, wondering if she remembered me, I repeatedly fumbled my lines.

Eventually I recovered some composure and got through rehearsal. Walking home, I decided that, yes, she had noticed me, was in fact giving me appraising looks, too. Maybe she was drawn in by the role I was playing, but I didn't care; I'd take anything I could get.

King's Hall theatrical

A week later I went to the mailbox and found an envelope addressed to me. The return address told me it was from Maureen! I tore it open, and inside was an invitation to her twenty-first birthday party.

Elation flooded my soul; I pumped my fist in the air. Only later did I wonder: Why did she invite me? We had barely spoken, and my few attempts at artful conversation had come out as mumbling monosyllables.

I arrived at the party and immediately had my answer. She greeted me with a peck on the cheek. "I'm glad you could come," she whispered. "Me too," I said.

The party was as lively as it could be without alcohol. After the first guests left, Maureen took me by the hand and led me into an empty bedroom. She closed the door and approached me. Rising up on her tiptoes, she kissed me on the lips.

"Can we go out sometime?" I asked. "Without all the party guests?"

She smiled and kissed me again. It was the beginning of a love affair that has not yet ended.

* * *

We began dating after that, and I soon learned that during the war Maureen and I had experienced some of the same things—with some major differences. We'd both been evacuated from our homes to the countryside. But whereas I'd spent six weeks on a farm before returning to my family in Liverpool, Maureen had stayed almost four years with a family in a country house. The family had two younger children, and as the oldest, Maureen had more than her share of household jobs and baby care to do. I thought of Cinderella.

During the war, my parents both worked and I was left on my own a lot. I became independent and self-motivated and—I believe—strengthened by the war years. Maureen, on the other hand, was damaged by those years, especially by the death of her father, Walter, whom she adored.

* * *

I came to admire Maureen's array of skills. We shared an interest in choral music, but after hearing her voice I decided it wasn't fair to call what I did singing. She was also a better writer than I could hope to be. But my greatest admiration was reserved for her people skills.

Only six months after we began dating, I had it fixed in my mind that she and no other would be the mother of my children. We were strolling through King Edwards Park one cold November day when I suddenly stopped, took her hands in mine, and blurted, "Will you marry me?"

She stood on her tiptoes, and I lifted her off the ground. "Yes," she said. This time it was no whisper.

Wedding day: registry office, Willesden

Wedding day, 1951

CHAPTER THIRTEEN
Maureen: The War Years

Maureen wrote a short memoir of the war years, entitled, "A Child's View of World War II," which filled in some details previously unknown to me. She captured my attention with this provocative opener: "I was eight years old when the shadow of war fell on my bright world . . ."

Growing up in a working-class area of London, Maureen was typecast by the neighborhood kids as "rich." That appears to be because 1) her father, Walter, a master cabinet maker, made the grand salary of five pounds per week, 2) she was one of the few kids who had a bicycle, and 3) every year she had a birthday party and wore a new satin or rayon dress made by her mother.

Maureen and her mother Addie

Walter, indulgent father

Yet it was hardly an opulent upbringing. Maureen: "Our bathing was done in a galvanized iron tub before the kitchen fire, once a week. Each evening other than bath night, my brother and I were hoisted to the kitchen table, stripped and scrubbed by my relentless mother, who believed that cleanliness actually came before Godliness."

The family relied on an outhouse, and one of her great terrors was having to go to the backyard toilet in the middle of the night. "To reach it," she wrote, "I had to negotiate our passage, through a doorway, down a dark stairway, through the outside door, then along about twenty feet of dark, paved path. The toilet was clean, but there were always lurking spiders, and of course the darkness terrified me. I was not permitted to carry a candle since I might set myself on fire. My hopes for a flashlight were dashed because batteries, like everything else, cost money."

Maureen's greatest desire was to have long, curly hair, but hers was clipped in a bob just above her ear lobes. Her mother believed that long hair encouraged fleas and lice, and indeed Maureen never received the "dread notice" from the school nurse who regularly inspected the students' heads.

Nearby was a playground, called "The Rec," where the neighborhood kids hung out. Even as a child, Maureen knew she was lucky to have a bike. "The bike was forcibly taken from me a couple of times," she remembered. "But my mother always went out and somehow found and retrieved the bike. I assumed she was all-powerful in the business of finding and returning stolen property."

Waiting for her turn to play

One day on the playground, one of Maureen's classmates fell from the top of a slide and landed on his head. He lay on the asphalt, not moving, while adults rushed about. "He was carried off in an ambulance, and we never saw him again."

The Rec featured a banked racetrack, and Maureen often stopped to watch older, more daring riders speed by on their bikes. For her it was the stuff of dreams.

Her home entertainment was dominated by books and "a large family of dolls meticulously washed and dressed and bedded by me, each with its own name and personality."

She was a voracious reader with an impressive library. Some of the books were prizes for academic achievements; others were gifts from parents or relatives. Since she had been labeled "overactive" as an infant, she was not allowed to read newspapers or see any but the most innocuous films. Shirley Temple was occasionally allowed.

Maureen attended the local public school, calling it "a place of forbidding appearance. Its sooty black exterior contained classrooms 'warmed' to sixty degrees in winter by tepid water flowing through the radiators. We sat at worn wooden desks with benches. Our playground was bounded by a high chain fence, also sooty, and our comings and goings were commanded by whistles and handbells."

Despite this Dickensesque upbringing, Maureen excelled in school, earning "top girl" ranking.

Early in 1938, Maureen saw dozens of young boys marching through the streets carrying signs that said "War" and "We Want War."

Maureen ran to her mother. "What is war?" she asked.

"It's not something for you to worry about," she said. "Besides

I have good news. We are going to send you on a little holiday, with Connie."

Connie was Maureen's best friend, and the news succeeded in diverting Maureen from an unpleasant subject. That was her mother's way. She believed her children should know only what she thought good for them. Maureen later recalled another of her mother's efforts to protect her. "Until I was ten and became enlightened by my knowing peers, my vision of human birth was composed of glorious angels surrounded by piercing light, descending beautifully into hospitals, each bearing a rosy, smiling bundle of infancy. The reality, gloatingly related by a friend, left me sickened and repelled."

In summer 1938, Maureen and Connie were sent to the southeast coast of England to live for three weeks. They stayed with Connie's aunt and uncle, who treated them well. Later, during the war, the area would be bombed, but at the time it seemed a safe place, far from the perils of London.

Even in the placid village of Willingdon, Maureen found things to fear. Many a morning, Connie's aunt woke the girls early and led them in search of mushrooms. Having been alerted to the dangers of toadstools, Maureen remained unswayed by the aunt's assurances and refused to eat them.

Just before Maureen's ninth birthday, her family moved to a better part of London. The single-family homes had gardens front and back, enclosed within iron-railing fences. Maureen liked the new, larger house. Although there was a bedroom for her, she continued to sleep in her parents' room. "I was reckoned to be highly strung and was still subject to nightmares, fears of the dark, and a horror-producing imagination."

Maureen's first day at her new school fell on her ninth birthday. Facing a sea of unknown faces in the classroom, she burst into tears, shakily explaining to the perplexed teacher that it was her birthday.

Maureen had skipped a grade and was younger, smaller, and smarter than most of her classmates. It was a challenge making friends. She became further alienated from her classmates when her mother decided to take a stand on the school's approach to religion. Although Maureen attended a public school, it was "sponsored" by the Anglican Church next door.

"This proved to be too much for my mother. A Roman Catholic, she would not have her children involved in any high-church form of worship. So, when the main body of the school went to prayers and mass each morning, I was obliged to stay back with the Jewish students and read quietly."

In August 1939, Maureen's mother announced that she and her classmates would be evacuated to somewhere in the English countryside. A week later, the teachers, students, and parents were gathered at the bus station. Before her daughter boarded the bus, Maureen's mother thrust into her hands a bunch of bananas. For years, bananas became a symbol of departure for Maureen. "It's only temporary," her mother said. "Even if there is a war, they say it will be over by Christmas. Then we'll all be together again."

Weeping softly, Maureen found a seat next to her friend Betty. As the buses lurched into motion, she tearfully waved goodbye to her parents and five-year-old brother.

Soon Maureen, Betty, and the other kids were distracted by a guessing game: Where were they going? Apparently not even the parents knew. "We were enjoying quite an adventure," Maureen remembered. "We were with friends, with teachers we liked. Nothing had happened in our short lives to shake our faith in the future."

Their destination was Northampton, in England's Midlands. They were herded off the bus, onto a train, then onto another bus, eventually taken to a distribution center of some kind. There they were handed a bag of emergency snack foods before being led out into the streets. It was late afternoon, cold and drizzly.

"At each house where the occupants had agreed to accept children for wartime care, the line halted," Maureen remembered. "The teacher talked a moment with the residents, checked her list, and selected a child or two, who then disappeared into the house. The line walked on, our number getting fewer the further we walked."

Maureen and Betty were selected to live with two maiden sisters, the "Misses Berman." Two days later they heard on the radio that England and Germany were at war. "It will all be over by Christmas," said Misses Berman.

The next night, the howl of an air raid siren blasted everyone from sleep. The sisters gathered the children and took them to what they imagined was the safest place—a brick tunnel between their house and the next. Even there Maureen shook uncontrollably. Together they waited, listening for bombs, but there were none. Still, Maureen shivered. "The wail of a siren forever after caused my heart to leap from its confines and into my throat."

Misses Berman had apparently underestimated the effort required to care for two spirited young girls. They soon asked to have the girls reassigned.

Maureen and Betty were separated, though both stayed in Northampton. Maureen moved in with a couple and their two baby girls. The house sat on a hillside, with a view of open country and distant farmland.

She lived there for three years, mostly protected from news of the war. Her mother had alerted the couple that Maureen was "highly strung" and should not see newspapers, the wrong movies, or hear anything "exciting" on the radio. Still, she couldn't miss overhearing adults talk about the war.

Though her mother sent weekly letters and care packages of candy, comics, pencils, and notebooks, her parents rarely visited, and then stayed only a few hours. Her mother had taken a job in a shoe-polish factory that had converted to war work. She was making fuel tanks for Halifax bombers and clearly proud of it.

One day at school, the students were all fitted for gas masks. Maureen recoiled in horror at the ugly black rubber contraptions. To add to her terror, the masks were tested weekly by a volunteer team, and the children were obliged to put them on and try to breathe while a cap was closed over the intake end. This tested the leakproof qualities of the rubber part around their face—and struck terror in Maureen. "I have a fear of enclosed places, and this caused me to suffer claustrophobic nightmares."

Northampton lay on route between Germany and Coventry, a prime bombing target, and so Maureen endured frequent air raid warnings and heard countless bombs explode. One day the body of a pilot whose parachute failed to open landed in the city park. Everyone, including Maureen, went to see. "His body made a deep indentation in the turf, which we viewed with awe and reverence. We felt little animosity that this was a German, a man sent to drop bombs on our country. Rather, we discussed whether he was dead before his body hit the ground."

Despite her fears and phobias, Maureen continued to excel in school. Whenever the class read aloud, she grew impatient and read ahead. Eventually she was taken out of the reading group and "turned loose in the library." The principal, a mythology buff, introduced her to classical mythology, which became a lifelong interest. She worked her way through all the translations of Greek classics the library could produce.

In April 1941, Maureen came home from Sunday school and found her parents there. She especially lit up around her father. "To me he was all that was tall and handsome and kind and good in the world."

She leaped into her father's lap, ignoring the gifts they'd brought. She asked about them and her little brother, and stayed close to them for the next three hours. "I walked down to the bus, clinging tightly to my father's hand, and waved them off with tears running down my face."

Walter and Maureen (middle) before the war years

As she walked home alone, she mournfully announced to the heavens, "I will never see my father again."

She didn't mean it, but in fact she never did see her father again. Preparing to enter the Air Force, he developed an abscessed tooth. Like Maureen, he had a mortal fear of dentists. He put off the work, saying, "The Air Force will fix my teeth."

He then contracted the flu. Trying to fight through it, he insisted on finishing some woodwork outside—and developed pneumonia. Only 34, and never sick a day in his life, he died within a month. Penicillin, developed a year later, probably would have saved his life.

Maureen was told nothing of his month-long illness, a result of her mother's protectionist policy. Then suddenly, like a bomb exploding closer than the others: "Your father has gone to Jesus."

Maureen's world fell apart. She screamed uncontrollably for hours. A concerned neighbor, a nurse, arrived with brandy; some of the burning liquid was forced down Maureen's throat. Still crying, she retreated to her room and didn't come out for three days. "I sat and hugged the last doll my father had sent me, and sang—much to the disgust of my foster parents who couldn't see how I could possibly sing when my father had died."

Maureen stayed out of school for weeks. When she emerged sufficiently from her trauma to return, she immediately caught German measles.

She had recently discovered the Church of England, and every night had prayed for her parents and brother, and for an end to the war. And yet the war raged on, and now her beloved father was dead. "My faith was shattered . . . the God I had prayed to each night had deserted me. My outlook on life changed drastically. The sad world weighed heavily on my frail shoulders."

CHAPTER FOURTEEN
GPO Apprenticeship

In 1947, I turned sixteen and started work for the General Post Office (GPO). At the time Britain's telephone system was owned and operated by the postal branch of the government. I was excited about my apprenticeship as a Telephone Repair Technician, and not just for the paycheck.

One advantage of the program was that it allowed me time off to study for the Higher National Certificate in Telecommunications. But most of all, I was thrilled to have a chance to work in a field that had fascinated me since I was a small boy.

Hired on a Friday, I was told to report for work the following Monday. That weekend the minutes dragged. At last it was Sunday night. At ten o'clock, I carefully laid out my clothes for the next day, set my alarm clock, checked it twice, and crawled into bed.

Twenty minutes later, I was still awake. I tried counting sheep, but gave up when I hit two hundred. I went to the kitchen, warmed some milk, downed it quickly, and headed back to bed. I tossed and turned for another two or three hours before lapsing into a fitful sleep.

When my alarm sounded, I sat bolt upright in bed, rubbed my bleary eyes, smiled, and said, "Well, Don my boy, you're on your way."

My first week of orientation was mostly spent touring various GPO buildings and central offices. I was overwhelmed by the complexity of the seemingly endless switches, bundles of wire, banks of relays, and confusing technical jargon. Would I ever be able to understand it?

GPO training school

On Friday I was told to report for a relay-repair course on Monday morning. There I would learn about relays, the building blocks of the automatic telephone network.

The two-week class was taught by grizzled veterans who knew all the tricks required to adjust and repair a relay. "A relay is an electrical mechanical device that provides the basic logic elements in an automatic telephone exchange," we were told. "A relay consists of a magnet, a copper wire, and a series of springs. At the end of each spring is an electrical contact. When current flows through the copper wire, a magnetic field is generated, overcoming the magnet. The magnetic field allows the contacts on the springs to make their connections."

We were given a tool bag containing a set of spring-adjustment tools. We were also given a malfunctioning relay and told we had one hour to fix it. When the instructor came by to see how

I'd progressed, he examined my work, declared it satisfactory, put a checkmark on his clipboard, and then re-bent the springs. "Do it again, Green," he said.

This went on for more than a week. Having quickly mastered the process, I was now officially bored out of my mind. My fellow apprentices were equally bored, and that's when the practical jokes began.

It started when someone loosened the screws on one of the worktables—with predictable results. The first time a trainee leaned on it, it collapsed, scattering the contents onto the floor. I laughed, along with everyone else.

More practical jokes followed. One day I'd just come in from lunch when the phone at my workstation rang. I answered it and said hello. Silence. "Hello, is anyone there?"

GPO technician

Suddenly I became aware of two things: snickering in the background and a wet sensation on my ear. As I held out the receiver to inspect it, several drops of a special lubricating oil used in our shop landed on my pants and shoes. I felt the side of my head—the oil was in my hair, too.

Glancing around the room, I saw that all of my fellow apprentices were snickering. But one, Ron Brown, only twenty, was nearly in convulsions. My eyes rested on the can of lubricating oil perched on my desk, and I had to fight the urge to pour it over Ron's head. Instead, I would play it cool. "Very funny, Ron. You got me."

Still laughing, he sputtered, "You . . . you should have seen your face. It was priceless!"

Gathering my composure, I smiled and set off for the bathroom to clean up, all the while plotting my revenge.

The next day I wolfed down my lunch and returned to the workroom before everyone else. I removed all the tools from the tool bag sitting next to Ron's workbench. Then I drove several nails into the bag, pinning it to the floor, and returned the tools.

When my fellow apprentices returned, I watched as Ron headed for his bag. I held my breath, barely able to contain my glee. Then Ron did the unthinkable: he walked right past his bag and picked up another bag nearby.

Big bold letters etched themselves in my brain: "YOU FOOL, YOU NAILED THE WRONG BAG!"

Seconds later the true owner of the bag bent to pick it up. He was a surly ex-army sergeant, a boxing champ, with a flattened nose and a slight under-bite. Appropriately, he went by the nickname Buster. I shuddered.

When he yanked at the bag and it didn't budge, he roared in

anger. His fiery eyes darted about the room, searching for the guilty party. Then, abruptly, he turned and left the room.

Sighing in relief, I went back to work. A moment later Buster returned with a hammer and pried loose the bag, not even looking in my direction. By the end of the day I was almost confident my guilt would remain a secret.

But the next morning, as I sat working at my station, Buster approached, planted his face two inches from mine, and shouted through clenched teeth, "You think you're a funny guy, don't you, Green?! Well, I got news for you. I'm gonna catch you alone one of these days and beat the bloody daylights outta you. Then we'll see who has the last laugh!"

Buster stalked out of the room. With an audible swallow, I stole a glance around the room to see who had witnessed this threat. Everyone was staring at me. I noticed Mr. Wick, our manager, standing in the doorway. I stood, intending to go talk to him, but next time I looked, he was gone.

What I lacked in strength I made up for with stealth, speed, and an acute awareness of where Buster was at all times. Those tactics worked for about a week. Then one day my tormentor was absent. At lunchtime I approached Ron Brown and said, as casually as I could, "I wonder where Buster is."

Ron smiled. "I heard through the grapevine that Mr. Wick had him transferred to one of the Central London Exchanges. You're one lucky bugger, Green!"

I felt the weight of the world lift from my shoulders. Giddy with relief, I found myself humming and smiling for the rest of the day.

My high spirits were dampened the next morning when Mr. Wick stepped into the workroom, asked for our attention, and made an announcement: "It has come to my attention that playing practical jokes on one another has become a favorite pastime around here. I am giving you all fair warning: anyone caught behaving in this manner in the future will find himself commuting to our Central London Exchange. Have I made myself perfectly clear?!"

We all nodded, and I for one vowed that my days of playing practical jokes were over. I certainly didn't want to face a two-hour commute to one of the London exchanges, where Buster might be lurking like a junkyard dog. Some of my fellow apprentices were not so easily deterred.

One Friday afternoon I left the office, only to find that my motorcycle was not where I'd parked it. Theft had never been a problem, so I routinely left my keys in the ignition. I was mentally kicking myself for being so trusting when out of the corner of my eye I saw my coworker, Joe Stanton. He was leaning against his car, staring at me with a sheepish look on his face.

"Okay Joe, out with it. Do you know where my motorcycle is?"

Studying his shoes, he murmured, "I'm sorry, Don. I told them not to take it, but they wouldn't listen. Ron said they were going to park it in the driveway of our school principal, Mr. Franklin."

Mr. Franklin was Mr. Wick's boss. He lived about a quarter-mile away; with any luck I could retrieve my bike before he saw it. Without saying another word, I started running. I rounded the final corner in time to see Mr. Franklin emerge from his car, which was parked half on his driveway and half on the street.

A few inches from his bumper was my motorcycle.

Hearing my approach, Mr. Franklin turned and glared at me. He went over to my motorcycle, started it up, and moved it to the far side of the drive. Then he took my keys out of the ignition, held them up, rattled them, and said with a sneer, "See these? I'm keeping them until Monday. I'm tired of all these childish pranks, and I'm going to teach you a lesson. You can walk home."

"But Mr. Franklin, I didn't park my bike there," I pleaded. "Someone else did, as a joke. My friend is getting married tomorrow and I'm the best man and the ceremony is fifty miles away. How will I get there?"

Heading for his front door, he stopped and said, "Not my problem, Mr. Green. Now be on your way. We have dinner guests arriving soon, and I don't want them to see you skulking around here." Then he disappeared into his house, slamming the door behind him.

Spotting a low garden wall on the side of the house, I trudged over and sat down. After studying my shoes for a while, I looked up and realized I was staring directly into the Franklins' dining room. There on a table sat my keys. As I gazed longingly at them, the dinner guests arrived.

Void of ideas, I continued to sit. I could tell from the laughter and glances directed my way that the guests inside had been told of my plight. When they sat down for dinner, Mrs. Franklin faced me. Her hard blue eyes darted around the room, but always came to rest on me. Obviously she was not amused.

This went on for about ten minutes. Finally she rose, snatched the keys from the table, went to the front door, opened it, and threw my keys as far as she could. "Bugger off!" she yelled, "and don't come near our house again!"

I let out a sigh of relief, retrieved the keys, and was on my way.

* * *

I was sure I hadn't heard the last of it; I fully expected to receive a P55 asking me to explain my behavior. For the next month I waited and worried, but I heard nothing.

"Well, no news is good news," I concluded. "The principal

probably wants to forget that incident as much as I do."

Basic transportation

CHAPTER FIFTEEN
Missing Dial Tone

It was my second month working as a Night Tech for GPO, and I felt confident with my routine. As I completed the last task on my checklist, I yawned and stole a glance at my watch: 12:15 am. I'll just pull out the roll-away cot and have a nap, I thought.

Lulled by the ever-present hum of the phone lines, I was soon fast asleep. When I awoke, I checked the time, 2:00. I sat up, rubbed my eyes, and decided to have a cup of tea. As I walked to my locker to get my thermos of hot tea, I realized something was wrong.

I found my clipboard and began to go through my checklist when it hit me—silence! Gone was the comforting clatter of a call going through the central office.

I dashed to my phone and—no dial tone! I checked the other phone—silence. It's possible, I thought, that 10,000 people are now without telephone service.

Suppressing an upwelling of panic, I ran down to the parking area, found my bicycle, and pedaled off to the adjacent central office, a mile or so away. I pounded on the door, rang the bell, and waited for what seemed an eternity. Finally the Tech on duty opened the door. I rushed by him, grabbed the nearest phone, and let out a whoosh of air when I heard the comforting sound of a dial tone.

I called my supervisor, apologized for waking him, and told him all our phone lines were down.

"Oh, that," he said with surprising calm. "It happens from time to time. Here's what you need to do to fix it. Get two buckets, fill them with water, and take them down to the lower basement. Pour them into the grill in the basement floor."

I expected him to explain what seemed a decidedly bizarre way to get a dial tone. When he didn't, I asked why.

"Your office was built without adequate ground structure. During the dry season, the ground is too dry to maintain an adequate ground connection."

"Why hasn't this been fixed before?"

He lowered his voice, as though sharing a secret. "The needed copper mesh wasn't installed in the foundation, as it should have been, and management is reluctant to admit the mistake."

In my report for the night, I detailed the problem and offered some suggestions. The solution could be as simple as installing a standpipe in order to test for ground resistance, I concluded. That would allow the Night Tech to test and then add water if needed, ensuring a connection is maintained.

After finishing my report, I sat and pondered the events of the evening. I recalled the adage: "Measure twice and cut once." This incident, though uncomfortable at the time, offered me an invaluable lesson: A key to success is proper planning.

CHAPTER SIXTEEN
—— More GPO Battles ——

I handed my adjusted relay to the instructor for his critique. He barely glanced at it. "You're done, Green," he said. "I sent your paperwork to the personnel department."

"You mean I don't have to look another relay in the face?"

A month later, I received a P55 form from the company asking me to explain my absence from class on Friday, June 14. I remembered the day well. Having mastered the material and bored stiff, I'd slept through the alarm. The only reason I didn't call in sick was fear of having to repeat the course, which, along with meeting Buster again, was at the bottom of my wish list.

In the space provided I replied that I'd not been absent. Rather, I had arrived at the training center at 11:00 am. I added that I'd completed the course requirements.

Back came another P55 form, repeating the demand for an explanation for the missing day. I wrote back, asking that the missing hours be put in the "Medical Leave" category.

I received yet another P55 form—same request. I returned it, asking that it be called "Leave of Absence." Back came another form explaining that "Holiday Leave" requires two weeks' advance notice.

This went on for weeks until I wrote requesting a meeting with someone in management to see if we could find a way off this endless loop. Meeting granted.

I arrived at the appointed time and was shown into the meeting room, where I waited for 45 minutes. Finally, Mr. Jackson entered, shrouded in a cloud of smoke emanating from his pipe. He dropped a file on the table. I was stunned to learn that it was my file—several inches thick.

"Most P55s I've ever seen," he said.

Turned out, Jackson wasn't a bad fellow. He conceded my point. "You just got caught up in the bureaucracy," he said sympathetically.

After we chatted a while, I suggested we place my P55 forms at the bottom of my file and "let them die of old age."

He nodded. "I'd just as soon not see them for the next six months—or ever."

* * *

I leaned back in my chair and let out a sigh of satisfaction. I'd completed my GPO apprenticeship and was now a full-fledged Technician. Nearing the end of my first week on the job— the night shift—things had gone well, I thought. The biggest challenge was staying awake.

My tasks included making a few checks and being ready to respond to any unusual situations. One of my duties was to start and cycle a large diesel engine that provided the standby battery for the telephone exchange. I had not performed this duty before, but how hard could it be?

As I scanned the sheet of instructions, my confidence grew; it seemed easy enough. I'd been told to go through the test procedure each Saturday night, 2:00 a.m. At the appointed time, I went downstairs, where the generator was housed, and started the engine. It came to life with a deafening roar. I then proceeded cautiously with the tests outlined in the instructions.

Just then I heard someone pounding on the front door. Who would be rapping on the door of the Telephone Exchange at two in the morning? When I opened the door, I came face to face with two young, determined-looking constables. Behind them swarmed a mob of irate neighbors, dressed in robes and pajamas. The only things missing from the scene were torches and pitchforks.

Before I could speak, the constables pushed past me, and I closed the door, shutting out the angry mob. "Turn off the noise-making machine!" one constable shouted.

Ah, so that was it. As I later learned, the noise from the generator had awakened everyone within a three-block radius. I motioned for the men to follow me to the still roaring generator.

Once downstairs, I shouted, "It will take about fifteen minutes to complete the shut-down procedure, but I'll work as quickly as I can."

Once the task had been completed and the roar of the offending machine had ceased, the constables went back outside and took credit for solving the problem. A few minutes later, crowd dispersed, the constables came back inside. They were friendlier this time, especially after I thanked them for saving me from a lynching.

They introduced themselves as Jerry and Joe, and I invited them for tea. I told them it was my first week on the job and that I was just following company instructions. "It is obvious that this test should be removed from the nighttime duties list, and I will include that suggestion in my report," I assured them.

After we shook hands and said our goodbyes, I sat down and wrote my report.

It was brief; I suggested three actions:

Never turn the generator on during normal hours of sleep.

Equip the generator with a better noise suppressor.

Issue a formal apology from GPO senior management to the sleep-deprived neighbors.

I eventually heard back from my supervisor. The company agreed to implement my first two suggestions, but my last suggestion was ignored.

* * *

I was 19 and had been working for GPO for three years when someone in upper management got the bright idea to tap into the expertise of the company's technical workforce, which included me. And so one day suggestion boxes appeared around the central office. We received a memo, a promise that management would "evaluate and respond to all suggestions."

I quickly decided that those boxes offered me a great opportunity to demonstrate my capabilities. After all, I subscribed to technical journals . . . I was familiar with the latest thinking on some important technologies and issues . . . I had ideas.

I began to drop suggestions in the box—one every week or so—and soon realized the company's response time was glacial. Within weeks the system was hopelessly backlogged. Still, I kept submitting suggestions.

One morning I had an idea while wiping soot off my desk, a daily ritual. Kings Cross train station was nearby and copious amounts of smoke and dust belched by the trains wafted into our central air system, and onto virtually every surface throughout the office.

Inspired by the insanity of it all, I sat down and wrote out a suggestion, really two suggestions: 1) protect office equipment from dirty air, and 2) add filters to our central air system.

More than a year later, I received a response from management. In a 20-page report, they detailed the research that had been done and explained why my suggestions could not be implemented.

Shortly thereafter, the suggestion boxes were quietly removed. I never knew if the whole episode helped or hindered my career.

But the experience did give me a closer look into the world of management. I developed a new appreciation for the importance of thinking through proposed systematic changes. Implementation of such changes requires cooperation between departments and between different levels of management. That was sorely lacking in many organizations.

CHAPTER SEVENTEEN
Our First Child

With the sun on my shoulders and the wind whipping past my ears, I pressed harder on the accelerator, urging my Jaguar even faster. The curves of the narrow road came rapidly now, and I gripped the wheel, in great concentration . . .

Something was wrong . . . someone was calling my name. It was Maureen, and when I took my eyes off the road to see where she was, the car began to spin out of control. With a death grip on the steering wheel, I shut my eyes and waited for impact . . .

When I opened my eyes, I was home in bed, with Maureen bent over me gently repeating my name. Ah, a dream. I let out a sigh, but my relief was brief. "It's time, Don. I think I'm going into labor!"

I stole a quick glance at the bedside clock: 2:25 am. Still groggy, I rolled out of bed, went to the washbasin, and threw water on my face. Five minutes later, we were in the backseat of a cab, wearing pajamas and overcoats. Maureen sat beside me, a worried look on her face. "It'll be all right," I said. "We'll make it."

In 1953, almost a third of births in England happened at home. But Maureen and I had decided to have our first child in a hospital. So far everything was going according to plan, and I felt confident as I guided Maureen through the hospital doors. Before we reached the admitting desk, a large nurse with steel-grey hair recognized Maureen's condition and rushed to her side.

The nurse barked an order to a clerk, "Call for a gurney and a doctor, quickly!" As an orderly wheeled Maureen away, the nurse said to me, "Have a seat, sir. I'll be back in a moment to update you on your wife's progress."

I sat down, picked up a magazine, put it back down, and fidgeted. Searching for some peace, I closed my eyes, feeling tired and nervous all at once. When I opened my eyes, I saw the nurse coming toward me, clipboard in hand.

"You're wife is fine, sir. I just need to get some information from you." She sat beside me, asked a few questions, copying my answers onto a form. Then she handed me the clipboard and said, "Please complete the rest of this form, Mr. Green . . ."

I looked up to see her eyes resting on my slippers. She smiled at me and went on. "As I said, your wife is doing just fine, but her labor has only just begun. It will probably be hours yet." I nodded and a yawn escaped. "Mr. Green," she added with some warmth, "why don't you go home and get some sleep. We will call you when your wife gets close."

Exhausted, I completed the forms and left the hospital, confident that Maureen was in good hands. Five minutes after arriving home, I was dead asleep.

Up at dawn, first thing I did was call the hospital. A nurse came to the phone. "Congratulations," she said. "It's a boy . . . eight pounds, seven ounces."

"Whaaat?!" I said with a whoosh of air. "You were supposed to call me—"

"You're a father," she said.

Both relieved and annoyed, I rushed back to the hospital. Soon I was standing with three other fathers, each of us waiting for our first look at our newborn. Then four nurses brought the babies to the window. Three of the infants were about the

same size—maybe six pounds—bald, looking like tiny Winston Churchills.

Then there was my son, David, nearly twice the size of the others, with a mop of black hair. Much as I tried to deny it, my son's head looked lopsided, squashed on one side.

The happy new fathers were chattering and boasting and making goo-goo eyes at their offspring. First one, then the others, noticed my son. The men stopped talking and just stared at David. One muttered, "My god, look at that one."

David, number one child born on my birthday

I bit my lip and thought, "My son might be ugly, but he's all mine." Later I realized that because my infant son did not look perfect, I felt all the more protective toward him.

Sunscreen salesmen's
day off

The obstetrician explained that forceps during delivery caused the odd-shaped head and it would soon return to normal. He added that black hair was not uncommon and that it should fall out in the first few weeks.

The doctor was right on both counts. David's head soon took on a more symmetrical shape, and his black hair was replaced by golden curls. In less than three weeks, he looked, at least to his parents, like the Gerber baby.

"If only I could reach the pedals"

Four Generations

As of this writing, 2016, David is sixty-three years old. He is an accomplished photographer, artist, and father—with a perfectly shaped head.

Just captured an escapee

Enjoying an English summer

The apple doesn't fall far from the tree

CHAPTER EIGHTEEN
Time to Leave

Maureen and I had just finished dinner. As she cleared the dishes, I sat staring out the kitchen window into the darkness, lost in thought.

"Don, are you listening to me?"

"What? Oh sorry, Maureen. I was just thinking."

Maureen laughed. "I can see that. What's on your mind?"

I blurted out what I'd been contemplating for weeks. "What would you think about leaving England, emigrating to Australia, or Canada, or maybe the U.S.?"

Maureen's eyes clouded with concern. "But what about my mum and stepdad, and your parents? We can't just pack up and leave them."

Maureen's mother and stepfather

Eva and Thomas on holiday in Cornwall

With more intensity than I intended, I said, "I'm not responsible for our parents!" After a slow, deep breath, I reached over and gently patted Maureen's swollen stomach. "But I am responsible for my family, you and David and our new baby. It's 1956, and Australia, Canada, and the U.S. are making new technological advances, while Britain is still trying to recover from the war. The Labor Party has nationalized everything, the coal mines, steel mills, railways . . . and all these industries are running at a loss . . . in fact, the whole country is running at a loss. The shortage of capital is showing up in places like the GPO. I now realize my advancement in the GPO will take years. In order to jump start my career, and boost our income, I think we have to take a calculated risk and leave Britain."

The mechanic

Maureen sat silent for a moment, then lifted her eyes to mine and said, "I trust your judgment. If you think emigrating would be best for our family, then that is what we'll do." She sighed and added in a tremulous voice, "But it's going to be hard to leave behind our families and friends, our country, all that's familiar."

"I know, I know. Difficult and a little frightening. But also a new adventure, and the chance to explore new places together."

Next day I went to the Australian Embassy to gather information. Posted on a bulletin board was a job listing that caught my attention: telephone technician for Australian Telecom. I applied for it.

The Canadian Embassy was close to my office, so on my lunch break I went there to apply for a technician job with IT&T Canada.

Two weeks later I heard from Australian Telecom, asking me to call for a phone interview. But as I read the detailed job description, my enthusiasm faded. Applicants had to be at least twenty-five years old; I was only twenty-three.

As the search continued, Maureen and I decided we had to tell our families about our decision to emigrate. So one Sunday over dinner with my parents, I introduced the subject. I talked about how my job with the GPO offered few advancement opportunities. "I don't want to end up a complacent government employee in a dead-end job," I said.

Sneaking glances around the dining room table, I plowed on, "That is why Maureen and I have decided to emigrate, probably to Canada or Australia."

Another birthday passes

Play time with Granny

100

The room fell silent except for the rhythmic ticking of the old grandfather clock in the corner. For a few moments my mother said nothing. Then, in a dismissive tone: "Don't be daft, Donald. Of course you'll do no such thing."

Maureen and I silently exchanged glances, and I let the subject drop. While lying in bed that evening, I pulled Maureen close and said, "You know, my mother won't believe we're leaving until we've actually gone." With a chuckle, I added, "And maybe not even then."

Family gathering, London

The next day I received a letter from IT&T Canada, telling me I had a telephone interview the following week.

Two weeks after my interview, I walked in the house and Maureen called out, "You received a letter today from Canada."

I found the envelope. Holding my breath, I ripped it open and read it. A moment later, I came up behind Maureen, wrapped my arms around her, and said, "They've offered me a job, and they want me to start as soon as possible. Looks like we're moving to Canada, Mrs. Green!"

Maureen outside the Liverpool's ferry terminal

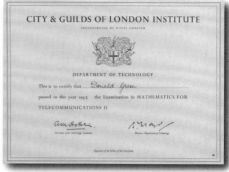

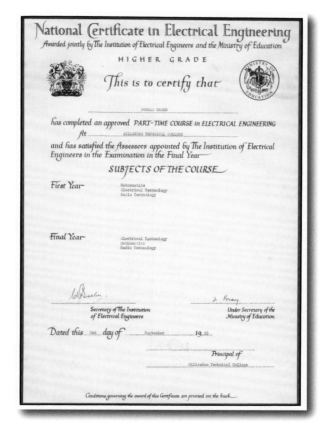

Electrical engineering certificates, the product of
nine years of day and night school

PART II

CANADA
(1956-1960)

CHAPTER NINETEEN
Leaving Home Again

As I sat on my suitcase, I had serious doubts about the seaworthiness of the ship moored before me. The year was 1956. Sitting there on the dock in Southampton, I recalled what I'd just overheard: "That ship is forty years old." Like a woman trying to camouflage her age with makeup, she had a fresh coat of white paint. Despite the cosmetics, the ravages of age were clearly visible: ribbons of rust showed through the hastily completed paint job.

Neptunia on a sunny day: Day 1, Mid-Atlantic

The sun was comfortably warm, and I tried to relax. But I couldn't take my eyes off the ship, couldn't stop worrying. I imagined that only the paint was holding her together. I tried to think of something else—my new life in Canada.

Questions roiled through my mind: Would I like Canada?... Would I succeed at my new job?... Would I like my new coworkers?... Would they like me?...

"All aboard!" came a voice over a loudspeaker.

Jettisoning my worries, I stood, picked up my suitcase, and headed for the gangplank. Once on board, I found a map of the ship's layout, complete with cabin numbers. When I located my cabin on the map, I realized it was situated on the lowest level of the ship, near the engine room.

The hallways and stairwells were crowded with my fellow passengers, but as I descended into the dank bowels of the vessel, the crowd began to thin out. When at last I reached my cabin, I saw the door was open. Four of my five roommates were already there. They were busy transferring the contents of their suitcases to the tall, narrow lockers lining the wall just inside the door.

I entered the small, cramped cabin, set my suitcase on the floor, and introduced myself.

A stocky young man with dark hair and eyes held out his hand. "Hi, I'm Frank. This here is my mate Stephen." He gestured toward the blond man standing next to him.

The others introduced themselves as Ian and Nigel, their accents revealing that they were fellow Brits. We all shook hands, and I realized that at age twenty-four I was at least five years older than any of them.

Introductions out of the way, my roommates returned to their unpacking. I headed for an unoccupied lower bunk and began to do the same. When I'd finished, I lay on my bunk and gazed about my new home.

Walls, ceiling, and floors were all made of steel and painted grey. On opposite walls hung six bunks. The cabin's only light was provided by a single bulb surrounded by a metal cage.

I thought, "Well, I paid for the least expensive ticket I could get, so I can't expect the Ritz." Just then the heavy odor of motor oil wafted through the cabin, and I remembered that we were right next to the engine room. This may be my bed for the next ten days, I thought, but I don't have to spend all my time here.

I hopped off my bunk and said, "Think I'll go up on deck and have a look around. See you blokes later."

Once up on deck, I leaned against the rail, closed my eyes, and inhaled the cool, briny air. I opened my eyes, looked out at the calm water not yet disturbed by the open Atlantic swells, and let out a contented sigh. After a few moments, I noticed an older couple standing near me at the rail. I smiled at them and they smiled back.

The man said, "Please allow us to introduce ourselves. We are the Coburns."

"Glad to meet you. My name is Don Green."

Mr. Coburn, a short, slender man, looked me up and down, taking in my tweed coat and grey flannel trousers. "We thought you were English . . . got to stick together, eh what?" He looked around conspiratorially. "So many damn foreigners on this ship."

Mrs. Coburn nudged her husband. "Charles, you mustn't say such things!" Clutching the string of pearls around her neck, she added, "Don't take what my husband says too seriously."

I smiled politely and changed the subject. "Why are you going to Canada? Do you have family there?"

"No," Mrs. Coburn said. "My husband just retired—he's been an accountant for forty years—and now we would like to see something of the world, enjoy ourselves. That is, if my husband can learn to relax." She nudged him again.

Mr. Coburn smiled. "You're right, old girl. I do need to relax more." With a wink, he added, "In the spirit of relaxation, how about we go to our cabin for a drop of Scotch before dinner. What do you say, young man?"

"Why, thank you. I'd like that." I didn't drink, but any excuse to stay out of my cramped quarters.

Mr. Coburn took my arm and led me down the deck. Mrs. Coburn, following close behind, said, "You must call us Mary and Charles."

"You must call me Don."

Upon entering their cabin, I saw immediately that the Coburns had paid a lot more for their ticket than I had. Their cabin was large, well lit, and didn't reek of motor oil. A small table with two chairs sat under the porthole at the far end of the cabin. Twin beds with matching dressers filled out the rest of the room.

They had a makeshift bar on top of one of the dressers, and Mary went to it and began to make drinks. I'd have preferred lemonade to alcohol, but I didn't see any among the bottles of gin and Scotch. Not wanting to be rude, I said nothing.

When we all had our drinks—mine a gin and tonic—Charles gestured for me to sit at the table with Mary. Perching on the edge of the bed, Charles asked, "What takes you to Canada, Don?"

I explained that I'd spent the last nine years as a telephone technician for the British Post Office while attending school in engineering. "I have my degree now, and I'm going to Canada, to a new job in the expanding field of telecommunications."

Mary and Charles were both nodding appreciatively, so I went on. "I have a wife and two small children who will be joining me once I get settled."

"That sounds very exciting," Mary said. "Do you—"

Charles, downing the last of his drink, abruptly stood and pointed at me, "Ready for another?"

I looked into my still-full glass and said, "No thanks. Still working on this one."

Charles went to the bar and poured himself another two fingers of Scotch. Looking at his watch, he announced, "It's half past five."

As if cued by a director, my stomach growled, audibly I was sure. I smiled sheepishly. "I haven't eaten since breakfast. I must be going."

I set my untouched drink on the table and said my goodbyes.

"We will do it again soon, young man," Charles called after me as I left the cabin.

After washing up, I went upstairs to eat. The large dining room was already crowded, and a savory aroma filled the air, causing my stomach to growl again. As I looked around for my roommates, I heard someone call my name. Following the voice, I saw Frank and the other roommates sitting at a table nearby.

As I headed for an empty chair at their table, a tall, lanky, red-haired man rose and stood between me and the chair. His face was inches from mine. We were roughly the same height, but he was years younger and, I reckoned, lacked my solid build and natural confidence.

I said, "What can we do for you, old chap?"

With a sneer, he replied in a heavy Irish brogue, "It's English, are ya? I hate the English."

I looked deep into his eyes and asked, "Does anybody care?"

His gaze immediately left mine, and he began to study the floor. After a moment of silence, he raised his eyes to mine. His face was flushed. "I . . . I didn't mean it. I don't know why I said that. I'm sorry." For a moment he was silent again, his eyes staring into the distance. Then he added, "Me Da always said that all of Ireland's problems could be laid at England's doorstep, but now... I don't know..."

Ian stood up and patted the man's back. "Don, this is Patrick, our other roommate."

I appraised the man. Young... probably a teenager... insecure... tries to mask it with bravado. I held out my hand to Patrick. "Let's start over, mate."

Patrick shook my hand vigorously. "Glad to meet you."

As we ate, we shared our immigration stories. Eventually I asked, "So Patrick, tell us what brings you to Canada?"

He shoveled a heaping forkful of Shepherd's Pie into his mouth and gulped it down before answering. "Me uncle has a horse ranch in Calgary. I'll be helping out around the place. Don't know what exactly."

"What about you, Don? Do you have a job lined up?" asked Nigel.

I got no further than telling them about quitting my job with the GPO when Frank interrupted, his dark eyes wide in disbelief. "You had a secure civil service job and gave it up? You're a braver man than me, mate."

I smiled. "I know it sounds a bit risky, but I wanted to work for a company that could offer opportunities in my field. So I got a degree in engineering, then applied for a position with IT&T in Canada, as a field support engineer. I got the job. Nine long years of night school and day school has finally paid off."

As it turned out, Patrick and I were the only ones who had jobs. The rest were driven by the emotion that had long propelled immigrants—hope.

* * *

I spent much of the next day exploring the ship. I was determined to get some exercise and to spend as little time as possible in my small, dark, airless cabin. By afternoon, I'd walked dozens of laps around the ship. Ready for a rest, I found an open chair on deck. For the next hour, I sat looking out at sea and thinking about Maureen and the kids.

The wind began to gust, and with it came cold, damp sheets of fog. Visions of hot tea and shelter danced in my head. With new purpose I headed for the bar.

Once inside, I removed my coat and scarf and took inventory of the pub and its occupants. The room held two large round tables and several smaller ones. An ornately carved bar of dark wood ran almost the entire length of the back wall; it spoke of the vessel's younger and more elegant days as a cruise ship. The bones of the bar were still there, vestiges of a once proud lady of good breeding. A closer look at its surface, however, revealed gashes and water rings.

I grabbed the last empty stool at the bar. I noticed that a number of my fellow passengers were Canadian soldiers. I counted fourteen in all. Eight were perched on stools at the bar; the others were playing poker at one of the larger tables. At the other large table sat a group of Englishmen, also playing poker.

At some of the smaller tables sat clusters of young Irishmen in farm clothing. Their thick Irish brogue was difficult to understand, but their boisterous manner made it clear they were having fun.

The bartender, an older man with white hair and a large nose, sidled up and I ordered lemonade. Once he left, I couldn't help eavesdropping on the two soldiers sitting to my left.

My lemonade was set in front of me. As I drank it, the soldiers began discussing the Dieppe Raid, which I had read about.

The Dieppe Raid, also known as the Battle of Dieppe, was an Allied attack on the German-occupied port of Dieppe, on the northern coast of France, August 19, 1942. It involved 5,000 Canadians, 1,000 British troops, and 50 U.S. Army Rangers. It was a disaster from the beginning. In ten hours, almost 60 percent of those who made it ashore were either killed, wounded, or captured.

The soldier closest to me noticed my interest and stopped talking. Looking at me kindly, he extended his hand. "Hi, I'm Sergeant Graves . . . this is Sergeant Blake."

As I took Sergeant Graves's hand in mine, I noticed the skin was discolored and scarred in several places. Sergeant Blake soon left for the loo, and I noted the deep scar under his right eye.

I said to Graves, "Please forgive my eavesdropping, but I heard you mention Dieppe and it caught my interest."

Sergeant Graves was a nice bloke and we talked for a while. I got the impression of a man who had seen too much and aged too fast. His grey hair was closely clipped, deep worry lines creased his forehead, and his blue eyes looked weary. And yet, for some reason, I didn't think he was over forty.

"Sergeant Graves, do you mind if I ask you a question?"

He took a long pull on his pint and said nothing. I waited, then plunged in. "Were you at the Dieppe Raid?"

He was silent a moment longer, then looked me in the eyes. "Yes . . . yes I was. In fact, both Blake and I were there."

"The reason I ask is, I recently read a magazine article about it . . . it said two thirds of the five thousand Canadian soldiers were wounded, captured, or killed. It suggested the high losses suffered by the Allied troops were at least partly due to poor planning."

That got his attention. "It was poor planning, all right," he said. "And because of it, Sergeant Blake and myself, along with thousands of others, were either killed or stranded on the beach and captured." He signaled the bartender and continued. "Don't get me wrong, son. I'd do it all over again for my country and the Empire. I am a dedicated soldier, willing to risk my neck and follow orders, but I'd like to think those orders had been based on real intelligence."

Sergeant Blake returned, and we all clinked glasses. The soldiers downed their beers. I gestured to the bartender and said, "Please give these men another round, on me."

When the beers arrived, Sergeant Graves stared into his glass and said, "You know, there are times when I lose track of where I am. Suddenly I'm back on that beach in Dieppe, surrounded by explosions and gunfire, and when I look around all I can see are the bodies of my comrades, wounded and dying, scattered on the sand. Sometimes at night I dream I'm back there. I can hear my buddies calling for help and there's nothing I can do. I wake up in a cold sweat. Some days are harder than others, but a pint now and then sure helps."

He raised his glass and drained it. Sergeant Blake followed. I ordered two more pints. I felt out of place, sipping lemonade while those damaged vets relived their harrowing war experiences and mourned their dead comrades.

I finished my lemonade and said, "Speaking for all Englishmen,

I'd like to thank you both for your sacrifices in the line of duty."

Sergeant Blake raised his hand and saluted me. "At your service, sir."

"You're welcome," said Sergeant Graves.

I gestured to the bartender, paid my bill, said goodbye, and headed for my cabin. Looking forward to some peace and quiet, I hoped my roommates were still out. When I reached my cabin, I opened the door slowly and peeked in—nobody.

I removed my shoes, lay down on my bunk, and thought about my latest encounter. I hadn't the heart to tell the sergeants—though they probably already knew—that the article had also suggested the Dieppe raid had been an experiment, a test run for the invasion of Normandy.

I wondered, "How could those in power risk the lives of so many soldiers in such a seemingly cavalier fashion?" Agitated, I got up from my bunk and began to pace the length of the small cabin. My thoughts raged. "Those in charge had chosen to use those men as guinea pigs, and their justification? The ends justified the means."

A wave of sadness washed over me. Though Sergeant Graves was still alive, he was trapped in a recurring nightmare, forced to relive the horrors. I understood that "the ends justifies the means" kind of thinking could cause much harm.

I vowed always to consider the ramifications my decisions could have on others. Then I lay on my bunk and wrote Maureen a letter.

Over the sea and far away

T.S.S Neptunia

At Sea: 27th June, 1956

Dear Maureen,

I have discovered that we stop at COBN (Eire) and can post some letters, so I hope this will be a pleasant surprise.

We have been at sea 24 hours and have only just lost sight of land. We are now crossing the Irish Sea, which is very calm. There is only a slight movement of the ship to indicate we are moving.

The crew of the ship and about a third of the passengers seem to be German. They make some attempt to speak English, recognizing that they are going to a country with few German speakers.

The occupants of my cabin are mostly English and very friendly. One of them used to work at the GPO in the NW area, but we had never met. He's already half Canadian in his talking and his dressing, but apart from that he's OK. One of the others, Patrick, ought never to have left his mum. He's like a lost soul and has picked on me as his protector. I haven't been able to get rid of him for five minutes yet, but there's still plenty of time for me to push him overboard.

Cigarettes and drink on board are cheaper now that we have left England due to the absence of taxes, so I can get drunk every night quite cheaply.

The two meals they have given me up to now were really nice and I'm hoping they will all be as good. If I'm not too seasick to eat them.

I'm breaking off now for lunch—continuing later . . .

Following morning. The meals are very good and you can have as much as you want. I have developed an enormous appetite and can do justice to the supply.

It may all sound like I'm enjoying myself tremendously, but all the time I keep wishing you were here with me. I keep thinking of things to tell you, then I remember it has to be written down and posted a week before you can answer me.

It's a pity in a way that you won't be sailing. I think you would enjoy it. But I'm selfish, so I'll make you miss this 10-day cruise.

I have sent a postcard separately with a picture of the ship.

I'll close now, but don't forget I'll be thinking of you all the time, and already I'm missing you all terribly. Give David and Rebecca a kiss for me, and ask David to kiss you for me—if you can sort that out. I'll be writing again tonight, but you won't receive it for some time.

All my love,

Don xxx

---

* * *

I was on my third lap around the deck, walking fast enough to work up a sweat, which sent a cold shiver down my back. I stopped, pulled up my coat collar, and adjusted my scarf in hopes of keeping out the damp sea air. After five days on the ship, I was ready to get off. I had too much time to think, and too little to distract me from missing Maureen and the kids.

I began walking again at a brisk pace, determined to stay busy and expend as much energy as possible. Then something caught my eye. Attached to a bulletin board was a piece of paper fluttering in the breeze. I moved closer and saw that it was an announcement.

"Show your skill and win a prize," it said. "A Table Tennis Tournament will be held tomorrow at 1:00 pm in the Games Room . . ."

At the bottom of the flyer was a signup sheet and a pencil dangling from a string. Fifteen people had already signed up, with only one slot left. I grabbed the pencil and added my name to the list, then headed for the Game Room to get in some practice. I was a pretty good club player, but I hadn't picked up a paddle in months.

Practice would be impossible. Most days there was a long line for the one table, and today was no different. I hadn't played once since I'd been aboard for that reason. Disappointed but not surprised, I went back on deck and continued doing my laps.

Next morning, full of pent-up energy, I headed for the Game Room. My match was scheduled for two o'clock. I had no idea who I would play until game time. Across the table stood a slim reed of a girl, maybe fifteen, a shy smile on her face.

I felt the killer instinct drain out of me. How was I supposed to try to beat this sweet little girl without feeling guilty? My resolve to go easy on her lasted about two seconds. Assured that I was ready, with determination in her eyes, she hit a spinning serve that barely cleared the net and landed deep on my side of the table. Caught off guard, I swung at it—and missed!

Embarrassed, but also liberated from constraint, I played aggressively, and well, and won easily.

Throughout the tournament I enjoyed some close games, but with careful playing and a little luck, I made it to the finals.

When my final opponent stepped forward, I was struck by his appearance. With his blond hair, blue eyes, and broad shoulders, he personified the Arian ideal. He held out his hand. As I shook it, he asked in a thick German accent, "Are you ready to lose, Englishman?"

I glanced at his name tag and smiled. "Ready when you are, Hans."

My serve. As I fingered the ball, I glanced at the crowd. The spectators had separated into two groups: Germans on one side, Irish and English on the other. As I prepared to serve, all chatter stopped.

The German was a good player and the game was close. I mustered all of my concentration, and not just because I was playing a tough opponent. The sea swells were getting worse and just keeping my balance was a challenge.

My serve, match point. I spun a serve to Hans's backhand, well-placed. Indeed, the ball hit Hans's side of the table. He was ready for it. As he drew his paddle back, the ship suddenly rocked upward. The table flew up and hit Hans under his jaw, sending him flying backwards.

He lay on his back, arms and legs splayed out, eyes closed. I rushed to his side, knelt down, and felt for a pulse. "I think he's okay, just knocked out. Someone get a doctor."

The doctor arrived a moment later. As soon as he held smelling salts under Hans's nose, he groaned and his eyes fluttered open. The doctor asked him a few questions, then declared that Hans was fine.

A moment later a small man wearing a red bowtie and wire-rim glasses called for quiet. He beckoned me to his side, handed me a bottle of whisky, and announced, "Let's hear it for Don Green, our tournament champion!"

I was soon surrounded by well-wishers pumping my hand and patting me on the back. Ian snatched the bottle from my hands, opened it, and took a pull. He wiped his mouth with his sleeve. "You don't mind sharing with your mates, do ya lad?"

I smiled and gestured for Ian to pass it around. Five minutes later the bottle was handed back to me, empty.

Smelling of whiskey and full of good cheer, Ian grabbed my hand and raised my arm above my head. "Don Green," he bellowed, "world champion wins by a knockout!"

That night as I lay in bed, I remembered Ian's proclamation and my lips curved into a smile.

CHAPTER TWENTY
Hello, Canada

The sky was cloudless and a light breeze ruffled my hair as I stood on the dock in Quebec City. I smiled; my journey was almost complete. Tomorrow, when we docked in Montreal, I would begin a new chapter in my life. Still smiling, I joined the line of passengers waiting to go through Immigration.

Suddenly I felt dizzy and nauseated. Was it something I ate? I wondered. Then it hit me. "It's the stillness that's making me feel strange, I've been ten days at sea," I said aloud, making heads turn. I'd become used to the constant movement of the ship, and now, on terra firma, my equilibrium was off.

Beads of sweat dotted my forehead. Afraid I might throw up, I headed back to the ship. I fought through the crowd of passengers disembarking, found a chair on deck, and sank into it. I figured I'd feel better within minutes, but an hour passed before I felt well enough to try again. As soon as the immigration process was complete, I found a nearby café and wrote to tell Maureen the news.

Dear Maureen,

There is not an hour that goes by that I don't think about you and the kids. I miss you all terribly. I get through it by reminding myself that it won't be long before we will all be together again.

Tonight is the last night of the voyage. Today in Quebec City, I completed the immigration process, and tomorrow we arrive in Montreal. So you see, we are one step closer to our reunion.

I just had to send you a quick note to let you know. I have to close for now, because the ship will be leaving soon, and I still need to find a post office. Kiss David and Rebecca for me. I'll write tomorrow night and keep you informed of my progress.

Be my brave girl for just a little longer.

All my love,

Don

I placed the letter in my pocket and dashed out to find a post office. I walked briskly, heading in the direction I'd been told I'd find one. After searching for fifteen minutes without any luck, I asked a pedestrian.

"Excuse me, sir, do know where the post office is?"

"Yes," he said, and kept on walking.

The next person I asked was more helpful, and I found a post office in the next block. I posted the letter and just made it back to the ship before it sailed.

* * *

The disembarkation process in Montreal took longer than anticipated, and I fought my impatience. By the time I walked off the ship, it was two in the afternoon. With the dizziness and nausea of the day before behind me, I quickened my pace. I stopped at the first newsstand and bought a newspaper and a local map. I turned to the want ads and found Rentals. One caught my eye: "Rooms for rent, gentlemen only, apply in person at Mrs. McDonald's Boardinghouse, 1703 Jeanne–Mance Blvd."

Opening my map, I quickly found the street I was looking for—just a few blocks away. Loaded with heavy luggage, I took a cab. The house was a large, brown Victorian that had seen better days. Two large oak trees flanked the gravel path that lead to the front steps, and an ugly wire fence surrounded the yard.

I set my suitcases on the sidewalk and stood for a moment, staring at the house. "This place certainly doesn't look very welcoming," I muttered. I glanced at my watch. It was getting late, and I needed somewhere to stay the night so I'd be ready for my first day on the job tomorrow. I picked up my bags, headed for the front door, and rang the bell.

As I waited, I noticed a sign hanging to the right of the door, announcing in large black letters: "NO WOMEN ALLOWED!"

A dowdy-looking woman opened the door and said sternly, "Yes, young man? What is it? I'm in the middle of cooking supper, so state your business and be quick about it."

I tried to smile. "My name is Donald Green and I saw your ad in the paper. I was wondering if you have a room for rent."

For a moment she said nothing, just stood there looking me up and down. I did my own analysis, though more discreetly. Her faded dress, topped by a starched white apron, looked as though it had been in fashion some thirty years earlier. Her iron-grey hair was pulled into a bun, and her face was lined and creased with age. I guessed her to be in her mid to late sixties, and they had not been easy years.

I must have passed her inspection because her face softened. She gave me a quick smile and said, "My name is Mrs. McDonald. Why don't you come in and we can discuss the terms."

I followed her inside and was immediately assailed by the smell of baking bread and furniture polish. In the entryway I took a moment to examine my surroundings. Directly in front of me was a staircase, and on the right was a room with a long dining table and eight chairs. On the left was a parlor, filled with chairs and a large sofa. Everything was old, but the place was clean and tidy.

In a businesslike manner, she spelled out the terms, "The rent is fifteen dollars a week, due in advance every Monday. Dinner, bagged lunches, and breakfasts are included, every day of the week except Sunday. In addition, I will do one load of laundry for you per week."

I stood silent for a moment. I was stunned by all I would get for only fifteen dollars per week. "I'll take it," I said.

She smiled, but then caught herself and added in firm voice, "Wait a moment, young man. You haven't heard the rest of the terms yet. There will be no drinking, no smoking, and, without exception, no women. The doors will be locked promptly at ten every night, and if you are locked out, no refund for that night. Now, do you still want the room?"

Undeterred, I reached into my pocket, withdrew fifteen dollars from my wallet, and handed it to her. "I have no problem with your rules, Mrs. McDonald."

Her gaze narrowed. "You're a nice-looking young man. Are you sure my rule about female visitors won't be a problem?"

"Oh no, Ma'am. I have a wife and two small children in England. I start my new job tomorrow, and as soon as I can save enough money, I will get a flat and send for them."

My explanation seemed to satisfy her. "Very well, Mr. Green. Come this way." As she led me up the stairs, she said over her shoulder, "I'll show you to your room. I expect you're tired and would like to unpack and rest before supper, which is served at six on the dot. The two bathrooms upstairs are shared by your fellow lodgers. There are six of you at the moment."

She stopped at a doorway, reached into her pocket, withdrew a key, and handed it to me. Then she hurried back down the stairs.

I inserted the key and stepped inside. The room was small, containing only a single bed, a chest of drawers, desk and chair, and a tiny closet with three hangers. There were two windows, lots of light, and not a speck of dust in sight. As I looked around I thought, well, it's certainly not fancy, but the price can't be beat. And meals included!

At 5:58 I headed down for dinner, ravenous. When I entered the dining room every chair was already filled except one. I sat there and said, "Hello, everybody. My name is Don, and I'm the new lodger."

I received mumbled hellos in return. Just then Mrs. McDonald entered, carrying a large cast-iron pot. As she set it on the table, she said, "Beef stew tonight, boys. Bread and butter are already on the table, so dig in."

A line quickly formed, plates were filled, and soon the only sounds were of six hungry men wolfing down their food. The stew was plain but plentiful, and Mrs. McDonald's bread, still warm from the oven, was light as a cloud. I couldn't believe my luck.

After about fifteen minutes, conversation picked up again, and I began to get acquainted with my fellow lodgers. Everyone, except one other fellow and me, held entry-level labor positions. It was this other fellow, Horace Lamboski, who seemed especially interested in getting to know me. He was a tall, gangly young man with thick glasses, a slight lisp, and eyes that seemed to be constantly darting around the room.

"I'm a clerk for Jacobson & Meyers, the largest accounting firm in Montreal," he said proudly. "What do you do?"

"I start work tomorrow at Standard Telephone & Cables. I'm a communications engineer."

"Forgive my ignorance, but what exactly will you be doing?"

"I'll be repairing and installing phone equipment. And teaching customers of STC how to install and maintain their equipment."

Apparently that satisfied his curiosity, so I changed the subject. "Why does Mrs. McDonald charge so little for room and board? Are all rentals in Montreal so cheap?"

Horace nodded. "I wondered the same thing, so I asked her. Turns out Mrs. M—that's what I call her—didn't turn her home into a boarding house for the money. Her voice cracked as she told me the story.

"She said, 'My husband and I were never blessed with a child, and when my husband died five years ago, I found I missed having someone to take care of. Sounds silly, I know, but I like to think of my lodgers as my boys.'"

Horace and I eventually got around to hobbies and we discovered our mutual fondness for stamp collecting. Horace brightened. "I've got a great stamp collection in my room. Would you like to see it?"

"Sure."

His room was furnished like mine, except he had a small bookshelf. Among his volumes were four large leather-bound stamp albums. He pulled one off the shelf, plopped it on the desk, opened it, and said, "Have a look."

As I turned the pages, a chill ran down my spine. Every page was filled with stamps—but the very same one-cent Canadian stamp. I glanced at Horace, searching for some sign that this was a joke, but his face was blank. He gestured toward a second and a third album. Again all the pages were filled with the same one-cent stamp.

"Well, what do you think? Wonderful aren't they?" he asked in a childlike voice.

I stared at the corners of his mouth, looking for a slight smile, a twitch of irony, some indication that he was kidding. Nothing. Instead, I saw a serious, confused face.

Feeling confused myself, and not wanting to hurt his feelings or make him mad, I mustered some false enthusiasm and said, "That's a great collection you have. Thanks for showing it to me, but I better get to bed now. Don't want to be sleepy my first day on the job."

To my relief, he said nothing about my going to bed at 7:15 in the evening. I thanked him again and left, fleeing to my room.

That night as I lay in bed, I thought, if I can just avoid talking about stamp collecting with Horace, I'll get along here just fine."

CHAPTER TWENTY ONE
Reunited

I stepped out of the taxi and onto the curb in front of the Montreal Airport. It was late October and a cold wind made me shiver. This was it, today was the day: Maureen and my children were arriving. It had been over three months since I'd seen them, and I could barely contain my excitement.

I found the arrival gate and took the last available seat in the waiting area. I checked my watch: they weren't scheduled to arrive for another twenty minutes. As I sat wondering how Maureen had managed with two small children on the flight, I couldn't help but overhear the woman next to me. She was talking about her new washing machine, and it was almost enough to put me asleep.

I was yanked back to the present by a booming voice over the airport loudspeaker: "Flight 309 from London now arriving at Gate Seven."

Moments later the doors opened and the first passengers from Flight 309 emerged. I scanned the crowd as passenger after passenger filed past me. After ten minutes the parade had come to an end, and still no sign of Maureen. I noticed my palms were sweaty. Where were they?

Spotting an airline employee, I started toward her to inquire— when I saw Maureen! Although clearly tired, she was as lovely as I remembered. Holding her left hand was three-year-old David, and in her other arm she held six-month-old Rebecca. What a beautiful family, I thought as I hugged and kissed them all.

"How did the children do?" I asked.

She smiled and patted each child on the head. "They did fine. But it was an eight-hour flight and I'm exhausted." She yawned and laid her head against my shoulder.

In the taxi on the way home, I chatted nonstop, anxious to tell Maureen everything. Only after I asked her a question and got no response did I realize she was fast asleep. I smiled, kissed the top of her head, and thought, I guess our reunion will have to wait a little longer.

Rebecca, a cute little thing

CHAPTER TWENTY TWO
The Plymouth

Soon after starting work as an engineer for Standard Telephone Cables (STC Canada), I became friends with a coworker, Ron Doyle. Ron, a kind man, and a third-generation Canadian, was always available to answer my questions about my new country. He told me what to expect when I ordered eggs "over easy."

During a chat over morning coffee, I mentioned to Ron that I was looking for an affordable used car. Ron said he'd keep his eyes open. Then he added, "How'd you like to learn to drive? I could teach you."

I was touched by his generosity. I did note, however, that he chose a company car for the lessons, not his own. Generous but not stupid, I thought.

The lessons went well once I remembered to drive on the right side of the road. A few weeks later, Ron approached me at the office, waving a company memo. Smiling, he handed it to me. "This might be your chance to get a car," he said. "Read it."

The headline, in big bold font, read: "Used Company Cars For Sale!" According to the memo, the company had purchased a fleet of cars for a particular project. Now that the project was completed, the cars were no longer needed. Interested employees could buy them at a discount.

I thanked Ron and headed off to talk to my manager about the cars. En route, I fretted over the numbers. How much discount? Could we afford it?

My manager, Dave Denby, waved me into his office. I sat in

the hard metal chair that was offered, handed him the memo, and said, "I'm interested in buying one of those cars."

We talked for a moment, then Dave said, "Okay, I'll phone over to the motor pool and let George know you're coming. Once you pick out a car, bring me the check and we'll transfer ownership."

I thanked him and, my feet barely touching the ground, headed over to the motor pool. George was outside his office waiting for me. He gestured to a line of cars. "There they are. No extras on 'em, like air conditioning, radios, or rust protection. But at five hundred each, they're a good deal. In fact, I was thinkin' of gettin' my wife one."

As I slowly walked toward the cars, I felt my hopes fading. They were more expensive that I'd hoped for. We didn't have five hundred dollars. Still, I inspected each car. The last model was a light-blue 1956 Plymouth. Unlike the others, its interior was clean. I checked the odometer and saw it had the lowest mileage. I headed back to tell George that I wanted the Plymouth.

Back in Dave's office, I swallowed audibly and plunged in. "I can't pay for the car all at once . . . but I could pay for it over time."

He smiled, the first time I'd seen his teeth, and said, "Tell you what . . . how about we take a hundred dollars out of your pay each month. Can you swing that?"

Beaming, I said, "Yes, sir. Thank you!"

That evening I drove the Plymouth home at the speed of a funeral procession. I was still getting used to driving on the right side of the road. Besides, I didn't yet have a Canadian driver's license.

Pride of ownership

The following Monday I went to the Quebec Motor Vehicles Department to apply for a driver's license. I was nervous about taking the test and relieved to find the office nearly empty. I was given a short form to fill out. It could have been completed by a small child, which encouraged me. Twenty minutes later, a man in a blue uniform called me for my driving test. I recalled Ron's advice that it was easier to drive a car if you sit on the side with the steering wheel.

My instructor told me to start the car and exit the parking lot. For the next fifteen minutes, he periodically gave me directions. But he showed no apparent interest in what I was doing with the wheel, brake, or gas pedal. I made all the turns, stopped at all the red lights, and felt fine about my performance.

After I pulled back into the parking lot and turned off the engine, the inspector scanned his clipboard holding my paperwork, signed the bottom of the form, took it off the clipboard, and handed it to me. "You should shift to a lower gear when you go around turns," he said curtly.

Then he got out of the car. Thus ended my driving test.

* * *

I decided, with some trepidation, to teach Maureen how to drive. I started with the basics—how to hold the steering wheel and what each control did. Then I asked her to turn on the engine, put the car in gear, and slowly drive down a country road.

She looked over at me with uncertainty. I said, "Don't worry, you'll do just fine."

Maureen shifted her gaze forward. Clutching the wheel tightly, she said, "But Don, what if I'm not ready? What if I make a mistake?"

I reached over, patted her knee, and repeated my reassurances.

At first it went well. Then we came to a T-junction. "Turn right," I said gently.

She glanced at me, then back at the road. She eased her foot onto the gas and pulled the steering wheel to the right. But once the turn was completed, she failed to let the wheel slide through her hands and back to the normal position. Instead, she gripped the wheel tightly—and we continued to turn. Before I could say anything, we had made a near u-turn, gone off the road, down a hill, and stopped in some brush.

Neither of us was hurt. I turned off the engine and looked at Maureen, who shot me a look that seemed to say, "I told you so."

In case I didn't get the message, she added the words: "I told you I didn't think I was ready!" A tear escaped and rolled down her cheek. I offered the most comforting words I could manage, while thinking, "Maybe husbands and wives shouldn't teach each other to drive."

Maureen, David and the blue Plymouth

* * *

Winter in eastern Canada is brutal on cars. The city of Montreal salts roads to melt snow and ice, and rust never sleeps. I'd overheard many heated discussions on the merits and demerits of an antirust coating available for the underside of cars. One local swore by the concoction, a slurry of oil and tar. Another man argued vehemently that the slurry actually created small pockets that captured the salt sprayed on the road and thus increased rust damage.

In the end I decided against using the coating. It cost $200, which no doubt influenced my decision.

Near the end of winter, Maureen and I went for a drive in the country. I took the wheel, and after a while I noticed Maureen hunched over, searching for something.

"What are you looking for?"

"My scissors. I just dropped them, and now I can't find them anywhere." She bent down and continued the hunt.

When she sat back up, she had a surprised look on her face. "Don, did you know there is a hole in the floorboard? I can see the road rushing by. And I think my scissors fell through the hole."

I pulled the car to the side of the road and stopped. For a moment Maureen and I just sat there looking at each other. Then we both burst into laughter. Still chuckling, I made a u-turn to go back and look for the scissors. "Well, I guess we don't have to wonder anymore about the merits of slurry coating."

CHAPTER TWENTY THREE
Montreal Winters

Because Montreal winters see an average of 10 feet of snowfall, the city is highly efficient at clearing snow from the most-traveled streets. We lived in an apartment right on a bus route, so the snowplows gave us priority. Of course, the plows don't make the snow disappear; they push it aside, into piles that often block driveways.

Rebecca's new sled dog

One evening I parked in the sloping driveway of our apartment building. Next morning the driveway was blocked by ice and snow, and I knew I'd have trouble gaining traction. I decided to

try a trick I'd heard about. I took a stick and wedged it between the seat and the accelerator, adjusting it so that it pressed lightly on the gas pedal. Then I opened the driver's door, leaving it ajar so that I could slide quickly into the driver's seat. I started the car, put it in reverse, got out, and began to push. But I hadn't taken three steps when I slipped on the ice, bumping my head against the door. As I lay there, the car slowly drifted away from me.

Verging on panic, I watched the door swing open and catch on a snow bank at the end of the driveway, stopping the car but damaging the door.

"I'm tired of winter," I muttered.

* * *

While driving home from work, I made a sharp turn, hit an icy patch, stomped too hard on the brakes, and went into a skid. The Plymouth slid sideways and banged into a parked car. Seconds later the owner of the other car rushed out.

He examined his car—not much damage—then eyeballed me in disbelief. "What's the matter with you, can't you drive?"

I looked at the ground, then at him. "I'm sorry about your car. I can give you my insurance information or pay for the damages myself." I looked at the ground again. "I'm new to the area and haven't gotten the knack of driving in the snow yet."

Even before I'd finished my explanation, I saw his face soften. He looked at my car and said, "Well, looks like your car was damaged a lot worse than mine." He bent down and pointed to a puddle forming under my car. "You got yourself a leaking radiator. Better take care of that right away."

I thanked him and offered him money, but he waved it away. "I can knock the dent out of my car all right, don't worry about that. You better hurry and get your car home while it still has some radiator liquid in it."

Back home I examined the damage. Besides the leaking radiator, the only problem was body damage. Next day I filled up the radiator and drove to a shop, where they replaced it. Then, using a crowbar, I straightened some parts of the body, but still drove the rest of the winter with a crumpled front fender. It surprised me how people gave me clearance because of that fender. Apparently I looked like a dangerous character.

* * *

When I came home from work each winter evening, I'd plug in a heater and place it near the car to keep the engine from freezing. Then I'd remove the battery and take it into the apartment. In extreme cold, internal resistance of the battery goes up and reduces voltage.

As I covered the car with a tarp, I thought, "Maintaining a car in this weather sure takes a lot of planning and effort . . . I'm tired of winter."

* * *

One Sunday morning in early spring, I got an urge to fix the crumpled fender. With some difficulty I removed the hood and began to pound out the larger dents with a wooden hammer. Soon, people in apartments all around me were shouting for me to be quiet.

"Sorry, sorry," I mumbled. I packed up my tools and put the hood back on the car. I didn't secure it, figuring it was heavy enough to stay put and I'd be going slowly and only a short ways. I found a field two miles away and started banging away.

An hour later I'd done all I could. The best I could say was that most of the dents were less visible. When I went to secure the hood, I found it stuck tightly to the frame. No matter how hard I pulled, pushed, or yanked, the Plymouth refused to give up the hood.

I had a larger crowbar at the apartment—that might do it. On the way home, although I was driving slowly, a sudden wind came up and dislodged hood from car. It sailed over me like a big blue Frisbee, landing with a crash in the middle of the road. Exhaling with relief, I pictured the bloodbath if other cars had been behind me.

CHAPTER TWENTY FOUR
Nova Scotia

It was late May and winter was a memory, though not a distant one. The afternoon sun felt warm and welcoming as Ron and I walked out of the STC building. "Where will you take the family on vacation this summer?" he asked me.

"We don't have enough money to go far," I said. "We'll probably do day trips, maybe explore greater Montreal."

A sudden warm gust ruffled our hair. Ron said, "My family has a coastal house in Nova Scotia. We don't use it much. It's eight hundred miles from here, but if the idea appeals to you, you are welcome to it."

I imagined exploring the coast with Maureen and building sand castles with the kids. That night I told Maureen of Ron's generous offer. She shared my enthusiasm, and soon we had reserved a week in July.

In preparation I bought a luggage rack for the car and built two storage boxes to fit snugly into it. I attached the luggage rack to the car with four straps and placed my custom-made boxes on the rack. Then I drove the car around the block to test my invention.

I quickly discovered that the lids of the boxes were loosened by vibration. This was easily fixed by rotating the boxes.

Before setting off on an 800-mile drive, I wanted one more test, to be sure our belongings didn't end up on the motorway. This time Maureen and the kids came along. Everything seemed secure until we hit 55 miles per hour and heard a loud hum.

I accelerated to sixty—and the sound grew louder, almost deafening.

David clamped his hands over his ears and shouted, "Make it stop, Daddy! Make it stop!"

I rolled down the window, reached up, and put my hand on the rack. The noise stopped. I removed my hand, slowed to fifty—the noise stopped. I sped up to seventy and it came back. "If we drive under fifty-five, it's quiet," I said. "I'll have to fix it."

Back at the apartment, I removed the luggage rack and took the Plymouth for another test drive. No noise. After further study and several more test drives, I secured the luggage rack with additional straps. "It worked," I announced to Maureen. "At last we're ready for our journey."

I'd been looking at the map for several days prior to our trip, trying to figure out the best route from Montreal to Nova Scotia. The quickest way, I decided, meant crossing the border into Maine, then into Nova Scotia. When I revealed our route to Maureen, she shared my excitement about seeing even a little bit of the United States.

The Plymouth held up fine on the long drive, as did the luggage rack. We passed easily into Maine. At the Maine-Nova Scotia border, an immigration officer approached us, peered inside the car, looked at little David in the back seat, and asked, "What's your name, son?"

David, four years old, stared at the large looming face of the uniformed officer and said nothing.

"His name is—" But the officer held up a hand to silence Maureen. He repeated the question, his eyes not leaving our son. David remained mute, just staring up at the man, eyes wide, lips clamped shut.

The officer repeated the question in French. Silence.

Suspicion etched in his face, the officer politely but firmly demanded that we all get out of the car and follow him into the office. There a poster on the office wall greeted us. It had photos of many children beneath a headline that read: "Have you seen these children? They may have been kidnapped."

David looked up at me and asked, "What does that say, Daddy?"

Ignoring David's question, I asked the officer, "Are kidnappings common around here?"

The officer looked at me grimly. "It happens. Kidnapping rings like to use small border crossings like this one to try to smuggle in kidnapped children."

After a few more questions, he decided we were clean and sent us on our way.

We had to take a ferry across the Bay of Fundy. When we got to the ferry terminal, dozens of cars were waiting ahead of us, in multiple, merging lines. As we inched forward toward the ferry, a high-pitched squeaking sound suddenly pierced the silence. After a moment, Maureen said, "That's us."

The unrelenting noise was of such a pitch as to make dogs whine and people cover their ears. I looked over at the car next to us; the passengers were glaring back at me. I knew I could do nothing until we parked. Embarrassed, I slid down deeper in my seat.

At the end of the boat ride, near the ferry building, we found a garage. The mechanic quickly diagnosed the problem. "Rust has eaten a hole in the exhaust pipe," he announced. "That's what's causing your noise."

He fixed it by welding a piece of metal to the rusted exhaust pipe, and we were soon on our way.

* * *

The Doyle house sat majestically on a bluff, thirty feet above the high-tide mark. It was built in the traditional Cape Cod style, and similar houses were scattered around the small town of Clam Harbor. A gas station had just opened to handle what we were told was a growing tourist trade, though we saw none of that. Until just two years ago, Clam Harbor had been a "fishing outport," which meant no access by road, only by boat.

We were met at the Doyle house by a weathered old fisherman named Walter. Walter turned out to be a local storyteller of some renown, and over the next ten days he regaled us with several of his best tales. He told us about the time the Mormons came to town on missionary work. In entertaining detail, he described the machinations employed by the locals to appear friendly to the Mormons while not allowing them to use their parish hall for meetings. Walter brought the colorful local characters to life, and the kids enjoyed his stories as much as Maureen and I did.

Walter came to visit us every day. He liked to borrow my binoculars and for long stretches would gaze at things near and far. He always paid for their use with another story. We appreciated Walter even more because it rained relentlessly; we saw maybe an hour of sunshine in ten days.

The relentless dampness damaged the electrical parts of the Plymouth. I had to remove and dry the distributor cap every time we wanted to go out. When I told my tale of woe to a local garage owner whom I barely knew, he offered to come by every day to see if I needed help starting the car. Struck by his generosity, I tried to hand him money, but he refused. Small-town hospitality, I thought.

* * *

It was a fine day and I decided to go bird watching by myself.

144

I drove onto a small deserted beach, then grabbed my binoculars and climbed up and over some rocks to a lookout spot. From there I could look down on the Plymouth, and I soon realized the tide had risen a good deal just in the past hour. I suddenly feared losing the Plymouth to the Atlantic Ocean.

Clamoring down the hill, I got to the car in time—the highest waves were lapping at the tires—but then another fear jolted me. What if it didn't start? I hadn't dried the distributor in two days.

Sliding into the driver's seat, I said a silent prayer and turned the key. It roared to life, prompting another silent prayer. I shifted into gear, stepped on the accelerator, only to feel the tires spinning uselessly in the sand. I feathered the accelerator, but still the tires spun.

I uttered a silent curse, then stomped on the gas—same results. Looking out the window, I could see the waves inching higher. I jumped out of the car and searched for rocks or branches to put under the tires, but found nothing.

Spotting a nearby storage shed, I ran over to it. I rattled the doorknob—locked. Feeling panic lapping at my shore, I saw something out of the corner of my eye. Next to the shed lay a bundle of old newspapers. I grabbed them, ran back to my car, and shoved newspapers under both rear tires.

Mumbling yet another silent prayer, I got in and eased my foot down on the gas pedal, and held my breath. The tires began to spin—then caught! The car lurched forward, and I shouted in delight. Pressing harder on the gas, I sped away, vowing to learn more about tides.

CHAPTER TWENTY FIVE
Little Cabin in the Woods

My friend Archie and I were sitting in a coffee shop in downtown Montreal. Archie suddenly changed the subject. "I have a piece of land, four acres on a lake, about eighty miles north of here. I'd like to sell it."

In the middle of the property, he said, sat the framework of a cabin. He shook his head. "I bought the property intending to finish the cabin in my spare time. That was five years ago. I never got around to it and probably never will."

I liked the idea of owning something as substantial as land, but money was short. "How much?"

After some back and forth, we agreed on a tentative price: $2,000.

When I got home, I immediately told Maureen about it. "It could be our weekend retreat," I said, and she quickly joined me in my enthusiasm.

The next weekend, imbued with a sense of adventure, Maureen and I loaded the kids into the car and headed out to inspect the property. We knew only that the land was adjacent to one of a chain of lakes and the nearest neighbor was half a mile away.

The land was beautiful, just as Archie described. But what he hadn't captured were the delicious smells of the deep woods. In fact, the four acres was mostly birch forest, with a clearing in the middle for a cabin. At least it used to be a cabin; now it was little more than rows of studs.

Years earlier the woods surrounding the property had been

burned in a fire, and the result was a densely packed forest of six-inch-diameter birch trees. The lake frontage consisted of round rocks worn smooth by the action of ice and water over countless years. As we stood on the shore, I heard the slap of a beaver's tail on the water. "Look, kids." Across the lake we could see the workings of a beaver dam.

We all stood there, stock still, even the children quiet, taking in the sights and sounds. Birds and squirrels darted here and there. The squirrels, untroubled by our invasion, came quite close, as though inspecting us. The plunk of fish jumping could be heard from time to time, and I thought I might try my hand at fishing. I pictured fresh trout piled up on a platter.

Ten minutes later we decided to buy the property.

* * *

A few weeks later I vowed to spend a Saturday at the property thinning out some of the smaller birches. "It will open the place up a bit," I told Maureen. "And we can burn the wood for heat."

So I drove up there and chopped down a dozen small trees. Then I laid them out to dry. When I returned the following weekend, my birch logs were gone. My first thought—that someone had stolen them—was ridiculous. Then I noticed little paw prints and drag marks in the dirt. Following those prints led me to the lakeshore. "Oh," I said aloud. There before me sat a beaver dam! Near the top were my birch logs.

"Okay," I said. "You win this round. But this isn't over. I'll make the necessary adjustments."

That night when I told Maureen the beaver story, I said, "I bet they think we're going to be their favorite neighbors."

* * *

Buying the land opened up new opportunities for me to be

creative, to learn new skills, and to discover new ways to make mistakes. First I had to learn how to use a hand saw, so I could cut in a straight line. I also needed practice driving a nail in straight.

My plan was to straighten out the framework of the old cabin. This required twisting old wood into new shapes. After hours of frustrating labor, I concluded that it would have been cheaper and easier to burn the place down and start afresh. But stubborn to a fault, I pressed on.

One of my goals was to make the cabin rainproof. I bought large plastic sheets and tacked them all over the cabin. Next I set out to deal with the smoke problem. When the wind blew in our direction, the dirt-floored cabin filled with smoke from the campfire.

I visited the local dump and found a functional potbellied stove. Perfect, but heavy. I needed help lugging it back to the property. Time to call on our new neighbor.

Maureen and I had met Dan earlier, when he came by to see how I was progressing on the cabin. A good-natured fellow, he was happy to help. At the dump we loaded the stove into the trunk of my Plymouth, drove to the property, and moved it to a corner spot in the unfinished cabin.

"Need a stovepipe," Dan said.

I got in the car and headed, yet again, to the local hardware store, fifteen miles there and back. Since I had to pass the dump again, I decided to take another look for some useful household items.

I came upon a set of windows, slightly damaged but repairable. The windows presented a new challenge—how to fit them in my car. I crammed and squeezed them in every which way. No matter what I did, they stuck out the Plymouth's side window.

So I drove home slowly, careful not to get too close to mailboxes or other unyielding objects.

To close in the cabin walls and roof, I purchased cedar sidings. They were cheap, but also easy to break, which I did often. They also burned easily, and I used broken sidings as fire starters.

Then I discovered that I had the right size pipe, but not enough of it. So I slipped cedar strips in between the sleeves to extend the pipe and make it fit. Ready to test the stove, I lit a small fire and watched in horror as the pipe got red hot and the cedar strips burst into flames.

"I'll get water," I shouted. Brushing past Maureen, I darted outside, grabbed two buckets, and headed for the lake. I filled the buckets with water and raced back to the cabin. While I was gone, Maureen had grabbed the basin of dirty dishwater and doused the flame, which was now smoldering.

I lost count of the lessons learned that day.

* * *

The local dump was five miles from the cabin. Short of money, I subscribed to the old adage: "One man's junk is another man's treasure."

I soon discovered that Saturdays offered the best selection of junk/treasures. One such Saturday I spotted an iron bed frame, complete with springs. It struck me that if I were to cut it in half, it could be used as a bunk bed for the children.

Grunting with the effort, I pushed and pulled that bed frame and crammed it into the back seat of the Plymouth. I had to drive with the back windows down and the frame sticking out a few feet on both sides. I drove slowly, hoping for no oncoming traffic.

The trip back to the cabin was incident-free. A good omen, I thought.

I'd already measured the bed frame to be sure it would fit through the cabin door. I had an inch to spare! Once inside, I took a hacksaw and began the arduous task of cutting it in half. Minutes later, I heard a loud twanging noise, and the frame sprang into a contorted shape.

I stared, mouth wide open, until it hit me: I'd cut through one of the support members that held the frame straight. Not only did I have a deformed bed frame, but how was I going get it back out the door? Because of the twist, it had a wider profile than before.

After considerable reflection, the solution came to me. I cut through the other support member, causing the frame to curl more into itself, and creating a more compact shape.

I dragged the twisted metal back outside and into the back seat of the Plymouth. I waited for nightfall, then drove it back to the dump.

On my next visit there, I noticed that the bed frame had disappeared. My junk had become somebody else's treasure.

CHAPTER TWENTY SIX
Henry Lee

I've rarely disliked anybody as much as I disliked Henry Lee, my coworker. For starters, he disagreed with everything I said, no matter the subject. It didn't have to be religion or politics; he had strong views on everything from the superiority of Chinese cinema to the route we should take to our assignments.

I soon learned that it wasn't just me; he argued with almost everyone in our office.

One morning as I drove Henry to a job site, we argued about left turns and right turns, then about politics. As I tightened my grip on the wheel and bit my lip, Henry steered the conversation to table tennis.

"I very good at ping pong," he said. "I beat anyone in our office."

This was too much. I'd watched his movements—getting in and out of the car, lifting equipment—and I was not impressed with his physical abilities; he seemed clumsy.

I looked down at him, for he was much shorter than I, and said, "I could beat you at ping pong, no problem."

In a sneering tone, he said, "Ping pong is the sport of my country. Besides, you are too big to move quickly."

I said nothing for a moment, lost in thought. I recalled all the ping pong games I'd played while working the nightshift at GPO. Working nights had allowed me to attend school during the day and play thousands of games at night, after my coworker and I had completed our tasks.

Now I had a feeling that all those sleepless nights were about to pay off.

Henry must have mistaken my silence for weakness, because he said, "What's a matter, you change your mind? You afraid I beat you?"

A mirthless laugh escaped my lips. "Tell you what, I'll not only beat you, I'll do it left-handed." I was, in many ways, ambidextrous; could in fact hammer a nail equally well with both hands. Plus I'd often played the kids using my left hand.

Glancing over at him, I thought I detected a glimmer of surprise. But he quickly found his usual confrontational tone. "I accept your challenge . . . but don't cry when I beat you."

We arrived at our destination, an RCAF airbase. I'd been there before and knew they had six ping pong tables. Once we'd finished our assignment, we retired to the cacophonous recreation room, where we found one available table.

As we warmed up, I hit a few balls with my right hand, then shifted to my left. I was a little rusty, and Henry wasn't a bad player. The game was close—I won 21-17. Henry was, predictably, seething. "You cheat," he whined. "I remember you sign something at work with your left hand. No fair! That game no count!"

"Okay, I'll play you again, this time right-handed. How about we make it interesting and bet, say, twenty dollars."

He hesitated, but only for a moment. His pride was at stake. "Okay, but do not cry when I take your money."

"Arrogant little pipsqueak," I mumbled under my breath.

Turned out I was much better with my right hand. That plus my heightened intensity made for three easy victories. When he handed me the money, I smiled but said nothing.

After that we continued to argue, but we never mentioned ping pong again. I went out of my way not to boast of my victory. Instead, on those days when I found him particularly annoying, I'd recall my victory and smile to myself. It was enough.

CHAPTER TWENTY SEVEN
A Trip from Hell

It was early Monday morning, and I was grateful to have some quiet time to tackle the mound of paperwork on my desk. The pile had grown at least two inches higher in the past week, while I'd been out of the office on service calls.

I'd barely made a dent when the phone rang. It was Owen, the Canadian Pacific Railway technician I'd trained to maintain the telephone equipment we'd recently sold to his company.

He had bad news: The equipment had failed and he was unable to restore it to service. The equipment had been installed in a small mining camp called White River, some 200 miles west of my office. I'd been traveling a lot, and I dreaded the prospect of heading back out into the hinterlands. My only hope was to talk Owen through the repair over the phone.

I asked him to make some measurements and check some equipment parts. I continued to guide him over the phone, but after an hour of unsuccessful probes, I concluded I'd have to go to White River.

I phoned Maureen. "I'm sorry," I said, "but I have to leave immediately. Without this equipment, the mining camp is cut off from the world." As always, she understood.

As I headed out the door, I stopped, glanced back at the unfinished pile of paperwork threatening to overrun my desk, and thought, Well, there's always tomorrow.

I went home and hastily packed a small bag, kissed Maureen and the children goodbye, and left for the main railway station.

There I phoned my boss and explained the situation. "Be sure to wire my expense money to White River," I reminded him.

He assured me he would.

To reach the mine, I first had to take a passenger train for six hours. I got off at the White River junction, found the stationmaster, and told him I needed to get to the mine head as soon as possible. "I'm here to fix the telephone equipment," I added, hoping for quicker results.

Indeed, the agent leaped into action. Soon he had arranged for an open-air track car to take me to the mining camp. This turned out to be both slow and miserable. It had been a warm day when I left Montreal, so I wore only a light summer jacket and a pair of jeans. By the time we got to the mine head twenty miles away, I was shivering, my teeth chattering like castanets.

As I stepped down from the track car, I rubbed my arms vigorously, trying to coax some warmth. I was determined to make the repair quickly and find warm lodgings.

Once inside the hut, I took a quick look at the equipment, opened the front panel, replaced a blown fuse, shut the panel, and uttered a silent curse. Two points flashed in my mind like neon signs: One, I had travelled over eight hours to make a ten-minute repair; two, the CPR tech, Owen, was not even there to watch me make the repair. Had it been more complicated, he would have learned nothing about it.

Just then I heard a noise. It took a moment to realize it was my stomach growling. I hadn't eaten for ten hours. I left the equipment hut and found a small hotel with an attached restaurant. I was greeted at the front desk by a tall woman whose auburn hair was streaked with silver.

We exchanged names—she was Mrs. Daily—and I told her I needed a room and a hot meal. "You are in luck, Mr. Green. We have one room left and the kitchen is still open. Mind you, you'll be gettin' nuthin' fancy here."

For a moment I wondered what I would've done if that room had not been available, but relief and weariness washed that away. I smiled and thanked her.

Mrs. Daily came out from behind the counter and gestured for me to follow her. She led me into the dining room, small and rustic, and then to a table near a potbelly stove. The only other diner was a grizzled old miner seated at a corner table, his head bent over his bowl, slurping soup with gusto.

Heat radiated from the stove, and I yawned. Hungry though I was, I felt as though I could fall asleep right there. Saving me from that embarrassment, Mrs. Daily arrived with a small earthenware crock, some bread and butter, and a pot of tea. She deposited them on the table, smiled, and left.

I tentatively lifted the lid on the crock, and was greeted by the aroma of baked beans and bacon. Matching the miner's gusto, I ate two servings. After downing the last of my tea, I found Mrs. Daily and thanked her profusely. She gave me my key, and I headed up to my room.

Mrs. Daily was right—it wasn't fancy, but I didn't care; I could have slept in the closet. Wanting to catch the morning train, I searched for an alarm clock, but found none. Exhaustion seeped into my bones, and I decided I'd worry about it later; I desperately needed sleep.

I awoke next morning to sunlight streaming in the window. I reached for my watch—7:30. I got out of bed and went to the wash basin. My plan was to recheck the equipment and start my long journey home.

I turned on the faucet, expecting only cold water, and I wasn't disappointed. I dipped my hands into the water and splashed my face with it. I did it again and felt a lightning bolt of pain shoot through my left eyeball. I knew immediately that I'd scraped it with a fingernail.

I tried to look at my injured eye in the mirror, but I couldn't keep it open long enough to inspect the damage. My left eye was now completely closed, and my right was beginning to flutter, as if wanting to close out of sympathy. Struggling with the pain, I got dressed, packed my bag, and checked out. Mrs. Daily wasn't at the desk, but I learned from the young clerk that the mining camp had a company doctor.

After checking the equipment—no problems—I walked to Dr. Gilbreath's office. He looked about sixty-five, his manner straightforward but kind. With his fingers, he gently opened my injured eye and peered into it.

A second later he nodded. "Scratched cornea," he said. "It will heal on its own in a week or so. In the meantime, I'll give you some ointment and we'll put a patch on it."

I told him I was also having trouble keeping my other eye open.

"That's not uncommon," he said. "That eye is moving in sympathy with the other. It should go away."

And if it doesn't, I thought anxiously, I could be blind.

After the doctor put the patch on, I collected my tube of ointment, thanked him, and left. Outside I muttered, "What else can go wrong?"

More impatient than ever to get home, I found the telegraph office and sent my boss a reminder to wire my expense money to White River—immediately! I then sought out the stationmaster, a crusty old codger. I asked him about getting a track car to take me to the main line. There I would catch the TransCanada to

Montreal.

He used his fingers to reposition the chewing tobacco in his mouth, then deftly spat brown saliva on the ground and said, "Ain't no track car available right now, but there's an ore train close by . . . leavin' two this afternoon . . . goin' to the railhead."

He pointed to a train a hundred yards away. The end of the train was closest to us; it had so many cars—maybe 100—I couldn't see the engine. The old guy gestured to the end car, where the caboose is usually located, and said, "Help yourself."

I thanked him and climbed aboard. Once seated, I surveyed my surroundings. I felt as if I'd been transported to a Western movie set, complete with swinging hurricane lamps overhead and wooden benches lining both sides of the car.

Sitting there in that sun-baked railroad car, I felt time ticking slowly. The train didn't move. Hours went by and I saw no one. The sun set and it grew dark. Lacking matches or lighter to light the lamps, I lay down on the wooden bench and slept fitfully. I was awakened by a clicking sound that seemed to be coming toward me.

Without warning, the car jerked violently—and I was thrown from the bench, landing on the floor with a thud. The impact knocked the air out of me and I struggled for breath, then slowly sat up. "What happened?" I said aloud. "Ahh, at last we're moving . . . I am on my way home."

I carefully picked my way through the darkness, back to my bench. Eventually I fell asleep sitting up.

When I arrived at the mainline junction, I walked, as quickly as one eye would permit, to the telegraph office to pick up my expense money. The clerk there, a man in his twenties, looked bored. I gave him my name, and the young man pawed through a stack of papers, looked up, and said, "Nothing here."

Panic shot through me. "Please look again... Donald Green... it must be there."

After another cursory glance through the papers, he said, "Why don't you check back in an hour or so."

Despondent and angry, I walked slowly out of the telegraph office. Maybe someone, somewhere, had a voodoo doll with my name on it. I imagined him having a good laugh at my expense.

Just then I saw the TransCanada train pull up, a passenger train going my way. I needed to get on that train, with or without a ticket. I would rely on my powers of persuasion.

I found the conductor. He was a short man with thinning black hair, permanent frown lines, and small dark eyes. I mustered a smile and told him my tale of woe. I showed him my paperwork, proving that I was under contract with his railroad. "We're working for the same employer," I added hopefully.

As his small hard eyes looked me up and down, I became aware of my appearance. How disheveled—even disreputable—I must have looked, with my rumpled clothing, my unshaven, mustached face. If that weren't enough, a patch covered my left eye.

I thought I detected a slight softening of his features. Then, without uttering a word to me, he turned and walked away, shouting, "All aboard."

Incredulous, I just stood there, paralyzed. Now what? I have no money, no ticket, and no way to get home from this one-way trip to hell! I took a deep breath and exhaled slowly. Gathering what was left of my patience, I decided to return to the telegraph office. "Maybe my luck has changed," I muttered.

It was a different clerk; I asked if the money had come in for me. "No," he said. Then, as though awakened from a dream, he looked up and asked, "What did you say your name was?"

"Green. Donald Green."

"Oh. There's no money, but there is a ticket here in your name."

I snatched the ticket from his hand and stormed out, almost banging into the door jam.

Standing outside the telegraph office, I watched my train round the bend and disappear from sight. Dejected anew, I went back into the telegraph office. There I learned that I'd have to wait 24 hours for the next train.

Exhausted, I weighed my options. I had none. There was no motel or restaurant for hundreds of miles. I lay down on a bench and tried to snatch some sleep, a futile endeavor. As the night wore on, the temperature dropped, leaving me shivering.

I noticed a vertical pipe six inches from the wall; it was warm. I leaned against it, wrapped my body around it, then buttoned up my jacket with the warm pipe inside.

And so it went, the most boring, uncomfortable, food-deprived 24 hours of my life. When I finally boarded the train to Montreal, I vowed that when I got home I'd sleep for two days straight.

CHAPTER TWENTY EIGHT
Cub Scouts Canada

The senior manager for STC Canada, Bill Henderson, called me into his office to discuss a project I was working on. Bill was a middle-aged, pipe-smoking, Oxford graduate with a Yorkshire accent and an impressive vocabulary.

Our business completed, I rose to leave. Bill pointed to a pin on my jacket and asked, "What does that represent?"

"It's a Boy Scout pin," I said. "As a young lad in England, I was the equivalent of an Eagle Scout. Later I was a Scout leader."

He nodded. "This is indeed serendipitous. I have two sons in the Cub Scouts, and their pack leader is leaving. We need a replacement. How about you?"

I asked him a few questions—size of the pack, age of the boys, frequency of meetings—then stood silent for a moment. I had work, family, the cabin—did I really want to take this on?

"Tell you what," I said. "I'd like to attend a meeting with the entire pack, to get a sense of the boys and their stage of development. After that I can give you an answer."

Bill grinned. "Of course," he said, pumping my hand in gratitude. "I'll arrange it."

The following Friday I donned my Scoutmaster uniform for the first time in years and drove to the meeting. I was met at the door by Archie McDonald, the current Scoutmaster. We talked and I asked if I could briefly address the boys. He agreed.

The meeting was held in a school gymnasium in the town of

Mount Royal. As I approached I could hear the raucous sounds of young male voices seeping through the double glass doors. It sounded like a small war, and I wondered if I was really up for this.

Inside the gym were two dozen highly active boys, ages 8 to 11. Knowing I had to take charge immediately or not at all, I walked to the front of the room and, in full throat, shouted, "You, boy! What's your name?!"

Silence. I knew that each lad would stop and wonder if he were the one being singled out. All eyes turned to me. Having successfully seized their attention, I lowered my voice to a normal volume. "My name is Don Green. Now, when my hand goes up, your mouth goes shut." I paused; I still had their attention. "Do you understand?"

Twenty-four heads nodded in agreement. "I'm your new Scout leader." Only then, as the words were leaving my mouth, did I realize that I'd made my decision.

For the next hour I engaged them in some activities designed to help expend their excess energy and prepare them for more serious activities. After spirited rounds of dodge ball and British Bulldogs, they were more subdued and able to listen to me as I gave them a lesson in knot tying.

By the end of the meeting, I found myself smiling, and some of the boys were, too. Driving home, I began planning activities for the next meeting. Of course, I was a hero to the parents, most of whom were just happy to have . . . someone, anyone. That I was an experienced Scout leader was a bonus.

We had weekly meetings, and I threw myself into preparations. I tried to make our time together both entertaining and stimulating. One indication of my success was that we never had more than one boy absent at a time.

In my new role, I got to meet people. Soon after I took over, some parents organized a dinner party to welcome me. Maureen and I attended the swanky affair. As I sat there amidst the crystal and silver, observing the Canadian upper class, I decided that I too wanted the finer things in life for my family and myself.

Although I knew I had a long way to go, I didn't feel discouraged. In fact, I felt inspired, confident in my abilities and willing to work hard.

By the time Maureen and I left the party, I felt optimistic and determined.

* * *

I enjoyed being a Scout leader. The meetings were going smoothly, and I was growing more confident in my role. That is, until one Friday evening when the phone rang.

It was Fred, manager of the local Scout area. "We have an emergency," he said.

I hesitated, mind racing. Had I done something wrong? Was someone hurt?

Fred continued. "Both of our volunteer hockey referees are unavailable for tomorrow morning's game. I was hoping you could fill in. You're my last hope, Don."

The idea was outrageous; I'd been on skates only a few times, and "graceful" was not the first word one would use to describe me on ice. Visions of pratfalls and turned ankles careened through my head. And yet, after warning Fred of my limitations, I said, "Well, I don't know how effective I'll be, but I'll do my best."

"That's fine, Don. There's a hockey rulebook among the materials I gave you. Study it tonight. Know the rules, that's the important part."

After I hung up, the phrase "temporary insanity" came to mind. After studying the rulebook for two hours, I dropped into bed. My dreams that night were filled with hockey pucks and broken bones.

Next morning I arrived at the rink, armed with my rulebook and a pair of borrowed skates. A parade of silent prayers ran through my mind. While the boys warmed up, I practiced my skating skills, concentrating mainly on how to stay upright.

As soon as the game started, I knew I was in trouble. Every time I tried to accelerate and stay close to the action, I flailed about like some cartoon character. Despite the cold, I began to sweat.

By the second period, I'd gained a little confidence. I hadn't yet fallen or been assaulted, which I counted as a personal triumph.

With only three minutes left in the game, a fight broke out between two boys. I headed that way, madly blowing my whistle, pumping my arms back and forth to build up speed. As I neared the boys, I realized too late that I might not be able to stop in time. I should've spent some time learning how to apply the brakes, I thought. With arms flailing wildly, I let the whistle drop from my lips and yelled, "Look out!"

The crowd that had gathered around the boys saw me coming and scrambled to get out of the way. The two brawlers, however, were oblivious. The only way to stop, I decided, was to sit down. SMACK, my rear hit the ice, sending a shock wave of cold pain through my body.

It was too late. I plowed into the boys, knocking them both off their feet. The boys popped back up—their fight was over—but I remained on the ice for several minutes, a new phrase flashing through my mind: body cast.

Eventually I was helped off the ice, and a father of one of the Scouts volunteered to referee the rest of the game.

For the next two weeks, especially every time I sat down, I was reminded of that hockey game. It was a rare opportunity to relive a humiliating experience, over and over.

* * *

The only popular winter game in Canada that I proved to be any good at was badminton. The game offered me an excellent way to get exercise during those long winter nights. I played often and improved. When I moved to California, where the game is also popular, I won a Northern California mixed-doubles championship, with Maureen.

CHAPTER TWENTY NINE
———— *Royal Canadian Mounted Police* ————

It was only 9:00 a.m. and already the perspiration was dripping off me. Richard Chan, a fellow engineer for STC, and I were traveling by train from Montreal to White River. Our assignment was to perform a final check on the equipment we had sold to Canadian Pacific Railroad (CPR).

Richard was fresh out of college, and it was my job to teach him his job. I figured I had my work cut out for me. He was a tiny lad, looked about sixteen, and seemed incapable of lifting anything heavier than a screwdriver. I wiped the sweat from my forehead and reminded myself to be extra patient with him.

At White River we went into the office to see about renting a truck for our trip to the mine. Twenty miles of dirt road lay ahead of us. Behind the counter sat a man who looked about ninety. I approached and said, "Excuse me, sir, we need to rent a truck for the day."

Cupping his hand behind his right ear, he shouted, "What's that you say, son? Speak up!"

I asked again, louder. He closed his eyes, as though deep in concentration. Perhaps he's a magician, I thought, able to make a truck materialize. I was about to ask if anyone else could help us, when suddenly the old man opened his eyes and said, "Follow me."

Once outside, he pointed to a battered panel truck. It looked like a survivor, barely, of a demolition derby. The exterior was pitted with dents and decorated in rust. I walked over to the truck and looked inside. It was just as discouraging, with ripped seats, exposed springs, and littered with loose papers and empty pizza boxes.

Remembering to shout, I asked the old man, "Is this the only truck available? Don't you have anything else?"

He smiled and shook his head. "This is it, son. Take it or leave it."

After I paid the man, I loaded our equipment into the back and got behind the wheel. We were about halfway to the mine when I looked in my rearview mirror and saw red flashing lights emerging from the dust. It was the Royal Canadian Mounted Police (RCMP).

The officer got out of his car, approached my window, and asked, "What kind of cargo are you carrying, sir?"

"It's telephone-measuring equipment," I said. Offering a weak laugh, I added, "No contraband."

He gave me a long appraising stare and asked, "Mind if I see for myself?"

Can an endless day get any longer? I wondered. I sighed and said, "Is that really necessary?"

He gave me another stare, and I stared back. He couldn't have been much older than twenty-one. With heightened zeal illuminating his blue eyes, he said, "Yes, sir, it is. And I would appreciate your full cooperation."

Feeling weary and wondering what else could go wrong, I said, "Help yourself."

He went around the back and opened the doors of the truck. I followed and got there just in time to hear him say, "Are these your beer cans?"

I said, "They came with the truck. It's a rental."

"Is that so?" he said suspiciously. Grunting with effort, he attempted to lift our equipment box. "What's in here?"

"I told you. It's telephone-measuring equipment. We're going to—"

Scrutinizing the Allen screws that held the box closed, he asked, "What kind of fasteners are these? And how do you remove them?"

I worked hard to suppress a mischievous grin while fingering the Allen wrench in my pocket. "They need a special wrench, which I have at the mine head."

All business, he said, "I'll follow you. We'll open the box there."

For the next ten miles, the young officer drove behind us, eating our dust, much to my delight. When we arrived, I gave a doubtful glance at my puny coworker and asked the officer to help me carry in the box.

Once inside, I disappeared into another room and quickly reemerged. "Here it is," I announced.

I gave him the tool and he quickly went to work. Screws removed, he pulled off the top and peered inside. A look of disappointment spread across his face, just as a smile swept across mine. The officer grunted and hurriedly left, both of us feeling annoyed with the other.

Richard and I completed our work, and as we were heading out to the truck, he asked in a pleading tone, "Hey, Don, could I drive back?"

I looked at him dubiously, but before I could speak he added, "I need the practice before I take my driving test next week."

Approaching exhaustion, I welcomed the relief. Maybe I could nap while Richard drove. "Okay, but the road is rough so go slowly."

With a broad grin, he vowed, "Sure thing, Don. I'll be careful."

Off we went. Richard looked like a leprechaun behind the wheel of the truck, but he seemed capable, so I soon relaxed. Resting my head against the window, I was asleep in seconds.

I woke with a start as my head hit the roof of the truck. Looking out the window, I saw that we were stuck in a ditch. "What happened?" I asked. Richard, looking sheepish, said nothing.

We struggled out and examined the truck. "Doesn't look like we did any damage." I laughed mirthlessly. "Of course, how could we tell?" The front of the truck was about three feet below road level. "Well, we can't drive it out. And we can't push it out," I said.

As we stood there scratching our heads, a familiar vehicle approached us in a cloud of dust. It was our zealous young Mounty. He got out of his car, walked slowly over to the truck, put his foot on the bumper, and with some relish said, "Well, well, you seem to have a little problem here. Is there anything I can do for you, gentlemen?"

I said softly, "Yes, Officer, we would be very grateful if you could radio for a tow truck."

The young officer, wearing a self-satisfied look on his face, said, "Of course I can assist you, gentlemen. That is my job, and I take my job seriously."

I smiled and thought, If not for Richard, how different my opinion of the RCMP would have been.

CHAPTER THIRTY
The Bear

For the past year and a half, I'd spent much of my time working on the Pine Tree line, which stretched all the way across northern Canada. Some stations were located in remote wilderness areas, accessible only by helicopter. It was at one of those stations that I discovered something new about myself.

Approaching the station in a helicopter, I was in good spirits as I surveyed the colorful autumn landscape far below me. Enthralled by its beauty, I was a little disappointed when the helicopter pilot said, "We're almost there, Mr. Green."

We landed in a small clearing near the radio station I'd been sent to repair. As I climbed out of the helicopter, the pilot shouted, "Call me when you're ready for pickup." I nodded, ducked my head, and walked off, bent at the waist until I cleared the whirring helicopter blades.

The station consisted of a radio tower and a small equipment hut, all surrounded by a tall chain link fence. I was just about to unlock the gate when I heard leaves rustling behind me. Turning quickly, I glimpsed a small rabbit darting into the forest. Inhaling deeply, I savored the fresh piney scent of Mother Nature.

Once inside the equipment hut, I found and repaired the problem in just a few minutes. I called the helicopter pilot. "I'm already finished," I said. "An easy job."

"I'm sorry," he said over the static. "I'm in the air, transporting a passenger . . . soonest I can get there . . . two hours."

Determined to make the most of my time, I decided to go for a walk and take in the scenery. I went through the gate and found the circular path that ran parallel to the chain link fence. After a few minutes, I came around a rocky outcrop—and stopped dead in my tracks. A black bear was ambling toward me. My heartbeat pounding in my ears, I turned and ran back the way I'd come.

Glancing over my shoulder, I saw that the bear had also turned and was now running in the opposite direction. If neither of us changed course, we were destined to meet again. I slowed and tried to calculate when that would be and whether I had time to get to the gate before the bear did. For a second, I thought of the word problems we had in math class: "If a bear leaves point A, traveling at 35 kilometers per hour..."

I decided to go for it. Sprinting madly, I reached the gate, ducked inside, and locked it. The bear was nowhere to be seen. For a moment I leaned against the gate, letting my jackhammering heartbeat return to normal. Soon it all seemed more amusing than scary, especially when I pictured telling the story to Maureen.

I still had an hour to wait. Looking around for something to do safely inside the fence, I spotted it: a 250-foot tower with a ladder inside the structure.

I'll climb to the top, I thought. Take in the sights, maybe spot the bear. I found the ladder and began to climb. About fifty feet up, I paused to catch my breath. Unthinkingly, I looked down— and whoa! Wobbly legs, a fluttering sensation in my stomach. I suddenly felt so dizzy, I worried whether I could get down on my own.

I tried to move my right foot down to the next rung—it wouldn't move! Was I paralyzed? Would I have to call for help? Terror threatened to grip me. Rivulets of sweat ran down my back. I closed my eyes and forced myself to breathe evenly.

 *The Bear*

"You're okay, you can do this," I said over and over.

After repeating that mantra for a few minutes, I felt calmer. Movement returned to my limbs, and I began a slow, careful descent. Once safely on the ground, I walked over to the equipment hut and sat down, determined not to budge until the helicopter arrived.

CHAPTER THIRTY ONE
French River

As a roving support engineer, I spent many nights in hotels all across Canada. I figured I deserved the best accommodations I could find.

One of the nicest places I stayed was a fishing lodge near French River. The river itself was dotted with thousands of islands, some of which sported a fishing lodge. I'd heard the best one was the French River Lodge. A friend had raved about "the gourmet food and spectacular fishing."

I had little interest in fishing, but the gourmet meals caught my attention. That and the prospect of doing some bird watching.

You could reach the lodge only by boat, and by the time I climbed aboard it was pitch dark. But the boat's powerful headlights cut through the darkness, and my pilot sped through a maze of islands. I was grateful for his expertise. I could barely see my hand in front of my face.

When I entered the lodge, the desk clerk, a woman with grey hair and a bright smile, greeted me and offered to show me the layout. As she led me on a tour of the place, she explained where the canoes could be found and what time meals were served.

Once back at the front desk, I signed in, thanked her, and headed for my room. Though not large, it had a cozy, woodsy feel. Exhausted after my long travel day, I decided to hit the sack early. As I felt myself slowly sink into the welcoming softness of the bed, a smile formed on my lips.

I awoke early, looked out the window, and felt another smile crawl across my face. Water, water everywhere. Though no doubt brisk, the river looked attractive enough for a morning swim. I pulled on a pair of shorts, grabbed a towel, and walked down to the dock. As I got there, a fisherman was stepping out of his canoe. He reached down and pulled something out of the bottom of the boat—a big fish. To keep the tail from touching the ground, he had to raise his hand above his shoulder.

I was struck by the fish's set of sharp teeth; it looked mean. "What kind is it?" I asked.

"Northern pike," he said with no elaboration.

As he gathered up his fishing tackle, my eyes remained glued to the menacing-looking pike, and suddenly the idea of a morning swim had lost its appeal. A hot cup of coffee up at the lodge—that's what I needed.

When I got to the dining room, the breakfast buffet was already laid out on a large antique sideboard; the aroma of coffee and bacon permeated the place.

My friend had been right: the breakfast spread was impressive. It included kippers, sliced tomatoes, scrambled eggs, sautéed mushrooms, ham and bacon, and muffins. A deep sigh of contentment escaped me as I filled my plate.

After breakfast I walked down to the dock. Certain that pike couldn't leap into boats, I planned to take one of the canoes and explore the area around the lodge. At the dock an older man wearing a fisherman's cap asked, "Do you need a guide? I know all the best fishing spots."

"No, thanks. I'm not going fishing. Just bird watching."

"Do ya need a motorized canoe then?"

I smiled. "No, thanks. I don't plan to go far."

The old man looked down at the ground and muttered, "Suit yourself."

I gingerly climbed into one of the canoes and found the paddle. I paddled slowly in what I thought was a northerly direction, stopping every now and then to listen for bird calls.

After about a half hour I stopped rowing and drifted, listening to nature, until the bow nudged up against a small island. I continued to sit very still and was soon rewarded: a pine martin on the shore nearby, looking straight at me. He was so close I could make out individual hairs on his sleek pelt. I was mesmerized by the beauty of this creature in its natural environment. He ducked down between some brush, then reappeared on top of a log a second later. He did this two or three times, then disappeared for good.

I was ready to paddle back to the lodge and see about lunch. I pointed the canoe in the direction from which I'd come and headed that way. After a few minutes I stopped and looked around: nothing looked familiar. I tried to recall the tips I'd learned in the Scouts for finding direction.

But here moss grew on all sides of the trees, and the current was so slow I couldn't tell upstream from downstream.

As I sat in the boat pondering my next move, I heard the sound of a motor. Soon a canoe came into view; in it, a guide and a fellow lodge patron. When they got close, I cupped my hands around my mouth and shouted, "Which way to the lodge?" and the guide pointed left.

Thirty minutes later the old man at the wharf took my canoe and asked if I'd had any problems.

"Not really," I lied.

"Because people can get lost for days out there," he said with

a wink.

Now you tell me, I thought.

* * *

That evening I had dinner with two fishermen, both executives at large financial companies. As I listened and asked questions, my interest rose. I felt an urge to learn more about big business and finance. Until then I'd focused almost exclusively on technology. It was something I needed to rectify.

Next morning, while waiting for the boat to pick me up, I picked up a financial magazine, *Money*. First page I turned to featured a Dun & Bradstreet ad for a correspondence course in basic accounting. Hmmm, I thought.

One month later I enrolled in that twelve-week correspondence course. By the end of the eleventh week I felt I'd acquired an adequate understanding of the financial side of business. I had reached my goal. And so, when I received the final lesson, The Basics of Credit, I decided to ignore it. After all, I reasoned, it's unlikely that information will ever be of use to me.

If I could have anticipated the future, I would've taken that lesson.

CHAPTER THIRTY TWO
Dynamite

We shared the dirt road to our cabin with two neighbors, Francois and Fred. One winter, storms created ruts big enough to hide a small child. We had to drive the road slowly lest we tear out the underside of the Plymouth.

Then a particularly ferocious storm dislodged a boulder that partially blocked the road. Francois worked for the Quebec Highway Department, so I asked him to have coffee with me and discuss the problem.

Francois suggested we get some dynamite and blow up the rock. Although this seemed risky, I assumed that, given his profession, he had experience with explosives. I agreed to help, and he volunteered to procure what we needed.

A few days later, he announced that he had some dynamite, blasting caps, a roll of wire, and other necessaries. We drove out to the obstructed part of the road, and I stood by as Francois placed several dynamite sticks under the boulder. Then he unreeled about fifty feet of wire, and proceeded to connect a battery to the blasting cap.

With everything in place, Francois took the two ends of the wire and put them together, creating a spark that was supposed to ignite the dynamite fuses.

When nothing happened, Francois said, "There must be a break in the wire somewhere." We then followed the wire, looking for the break. About then some questions popped into my head: Where were the ends of the wires? Were they touching? Would we step on them?

Francois quickly found the break and repaired it. "Looks good," he said.

We ducked down behind another boulder, I covered my ears, and Francois brought the two wires together.

The world exploded, the loudest noise I'd ever heard. Bits of rock flew in all directions, somehow missing us. When the dust settled, we looked at what we had wrought. Where the boulder had once been—a gaping hole. The road was now officially undrivable.

"I guess we'll have to hire someone to fill that," Francois said.

I nodded grimly.

Later I learned that we'd used three times as much dynamite as necessary. Next time I saw Francois, I asked him how much dynamiting experience he had before that day.

He blushed. "Never used a stick of dynamite in my life."

CHAPTER THIRTY THREE
The Trail

For months my job was to train people to service and repair telecommunications equipment for one of our largest clients, Canadian Pacific Railway (CPR). Assignments frequently took me over a thousand miles from home, and I spent many lonely nights in hotels and motels.

Whenever possible I stayed at lodgings owned by CPR. My accommodations ranged from barely adequate to majestic. One day in March 1958, I was sent to Calgary to assist CPR in the installation of equipment that STC had sold to them.

Calgary was not far from Banff, home to an exquisite national park and the Rocky Mountains Resort of Banff Springs, the showplace on the CPR line. I had heard of that luxurious hotel but had never seen it. Now I planned to spend a long weekend there.

As I drove my new rental car west, I pictured the sumptuous comforts and elegant meals that awaited me. Out on the plains of central Canada, I was shaken from my reverie by the sight of a hitchhiker. As I pulled over and stopped, I had a sense that I knew the young man. Through my rearview mirror I watched him jog toward my car. It was Patrick, the Irishman I'd met on the ship to Montreal. I'd overcome his initial hostility, and we'd become friendly, if not exactly friends.

He threw his rucksack in the backseat and piled into the front. Only then did he look at me. Recognition immediately brightened his countenance. We chatted amicably. He was struck by the new car, taking it as a sign of my financial success. When I explained that it was a rental, he was struck anew. "Rent a car, eh. Never heard of that in Ireland," he said.

An hour later I dropped him at a fork in the road. I reached into my wallet, pulled out fifty dollars, and gestured for him to take it.

"Can't take your handout," he said.

"C'mon, take it."

He paused, then his face brightened. "Let's call it a loan, Don."

"It's a deal."

I wrote down my address and gave it to him, and he promised to mail the money first chance. As I pulled away, we waved goodbye. A part of me envied Patrick's bohemianism, and I wondered what adventures awaited him.

Upon arrival at the Banff Springs Hotel, I set my suitcase on the walkway that led to the hotel and stared, mouth agape, at the magnificent stone edifice that rose up before me. I'd read that it had been built in the Scottish Baronial style, and it certainly appeared fit for royalty.

As I bent to retrieve my suitcase, the frayed cuff of my shirt caught my attention. My eyes continued down the length of my old flannel pants to the tops of my worn leather shoes. Vague doubts about my attire came and went, and I walked confidently into the main lobby and toward the front desk. The clerks were busy with other guests, and I took my place in line behind a tall woman wearing a cashmere coat.

As I waited, I surveyed the lobby, a symphony of rich textures and colors. My eyes traveled from the smooth white marble floors, accented by richly colored rugs, up the roughly hewn stone walls to the gleaming wooden archways overhead. The effect was palatial and a little intimidating.

The woman in cashmere finished her business. As I approached the clerk, he looked down his aquiline nose at me, gritted his teeth, and said, "May I help you?"

I pulled myself up to my full height, looked down at the clerk, and said, "My name is Donald Green and I have a reservation."

The clerk winced and began to thumb through the large book before him. "Mmmm, here we are," he said in a tone weighted with disappointment. He turned the book around and thrust a pen in my direction. "Just sign here."

As I was doing that, the clerk added, "We require payment upon check in. You understand, I'm sure."

I stared at the clerk and said evenly, "I am an engineer, and I'm here to do some work, at the request of the owners of this establishment. They will be covering the cost of my room . . . I'm sure you understand."

The clerk turned and took a thin book from a shelf behind him. He opened it and ran his fingers down a page. When he looked up, his face was crimson, his attitude transformed. "I am so sorry for the misunderstanding, Mr. Green."

The clerk handed me my room key and motioned for the bellboy to take my bags. Serenaded by effusive apologies from the clerk, I followed the bellboy to the elevator.

My room was enormous. The windows were draped with heavy brocade curtains, the walls dotted with ornately framed paintings. The bathtub looked large enough to dive into and swim to the other side.

I took off my shoes and stretched out on the bed, feeling myself sink into its luxurious softness. I lay there for a few moments until doubt began to assail my bliss. My shabby wardrobe! I looked at my watch—three o'clock. Dinner would

be served in three hours in what I imagined would be the most elegant dining room I would ever see.

I had nothing suitable to wear. Well, I thought, I hadn't bought any new clothes in a long time, so maybe it's time to go shopping. I found my way to the hotel shops, and emerged a half hour later with a tweed sport coat, brogan shoes, shirt, tie, and grey dress slacks.

Up in my room, I put on my new outfit and looked in the mirror. Staring back at me was a smiling, confident, well-dressed young engineer. Clothes do make the man, I thought. With an hour before dinner, I went downstairs to look for something to do. Outside the hotel, I saw a sign that said "Circular Trail." Perfect—a stroll before dinner.

The trail meandered through conifers, with occasional heart-stopping views of Banff and its sentinel of craggy, snow-capped peaks. Before long I began to see patches of snow on the trail... then more patches.

Instead of dissipating, the snowy patches got larger and larger, until I was walking only on packed snow. I didn't seem to be climbing, so I assumed the snow would soon thin out. Before I knew it, I hit a patch that had melted and refrozen, forming an icy coating over snow. I stopped, but my weight was too much. I heard the ice crack, then watched as it gave way.

Knifelike edges of ice shredded my new pants and cut into my shin. With each step, more cutting and shredding, and more pain. Little rivulets of blood seeped from the cuts and dripped into my socks. Unable to feel my toes, I wondered how long hypothermia took to kill.

Then I spotted the hotel a few hundred yards away. A flood of relief ran through me. Soaked from both sweat and melting snow, I staggered into the hotel and up to my room. Passing before the mirror, I paused and stared, struck by the contrast with the confident, well-dressed man of an hour before.

I removed my ruined clothes and threw them into a pile. Shivering wildly now, I couldn't even lament their demise, could in fact think only of a hot bath and a soft bed.

As I drifted off that night, images of white sandy beaches, gently swaying palm trees, and warm breezes filled my mind.

Next morning, as I stretched in bed, I recalled the events of the day before. Bloody legs, frozen feet, and yet I suppose it could have been worse. If the trail had been longer, I might have succumbed to frostbite or hypothermia. Or maybe run into another bear.

While checking out at the front desk, I told the clerk of my experience. His face lost color. "I, I, I am very sorry, sir. Thank you for bringing the problem to our attention, and I assure you that we will act accordingly to prevent another incident like this from reoccurring."

Moments later I walked out of the hotel, glanced over at the trail sign, and was surprised and gratified to see that it had already been covered with a piece of burlap. Smiling, I continued on my way. Seconds later, hearing an odd scraping sound, I turned and saw a bellboy with a snow shovel busily clearing the trail.

I thought again of my new shoes, gouged and irreparable, and my shredded pants, both now stuffed into the trash can of my vacated room. Yes, I suppose it could have been worse. I wiggled my toes and smiled.

CHAPTER THIRTY FOUR
Iron Ring

As I drove home, after being out on a job for three days, I realized that working for STC was putting stress on my family. In the last month I'd missed both children's birthdays. I was constantly away from home, leaving Maureen to raise the children alone. My kids were growing up without me . . . I was in danger of losing emotional contact with them.

"Where is Daddy?"

It was time to look for a new job.

I began perusing newspapers and technical journals. One evening Maureen and I were sitting at the kitchen table and I told her about some of the job descriptions I'd read. Maureen listened attentively and then said, "Don, I don't care which job you choose as long as you don't have to be away from home a lot." After a long pause, she added, "I need my husband, and David and Rebecca need their father. We miss you."

I took her hand in mine. "I know. I miss you guys, too. That's the main reason I'm going to look for a new job." I stared at the floor for a moment. "When I got home the other day, the kids barely noticed I was here. It was like they didn't know me."

Maureen said, "Don, just one more thing. This is a good neighborhood, the kids like it, and I don't want to have to pack up and move. Do you think you could find something local?"

I thought about what a trooper Maureen had been. She never complained about leaving her home and family in England. Nor had she complained about moving to another country with two infant children, or having to care for them nearly single-handed. She never nags, takes good care of me and the children—and even makes her own bread. Yep, I was a lucky man.

Maureen's voice brought me out of my reverie. "Don, did you hear me?"

I looked at her, taking in her petite frame and beautiful face. "I will look for a job around here."

A look of relief washed over her face, then a smile. "Good!"

It took me a month to narrow the selection. I arranged three interviews, the first with RCA. The RCA job involved working on semiconductor research. Funded by the Canadian Defense Department, it involved detecting the plasma generated when a missile passes through the earth's atmosphere.

I was interviewed by the head of the research lab, Dr. Goldman. He was a rare breed: a scientist with an engaging personality. I was struck by his enthusiasm and knowledge.

Although I liked Dr. Goldman, I wasn't sure he liked me. I left the interview feeling that I'd performed poorly. It was only

the third time I'd ever been interviewed and my skills were rudimentary.

A week later I was offered the position by RCA and accepted.

My first day on the job I learned that the lab was divided into two groups. One group included scientists working on highly secret projects from which the rest of the lab was excluded. The second group consisted of engineers working on nonsecret programs that had commercial value.

I was in the second group, working under Dr. Goldman. My work on microwave radios didn't require much research and development; in fact, much of my time was spent waiting for drafting resources to become available. The leisurely pace of my job at RCA gave me time to observe the workings of the company, especially how the promotion process worked. I noticed that every manager wore an iron ring on his finger.

One day at lunch I asked John Baker, a coworker, what it all meant. John, an iron ring wearer himself, said, "Oh, it's no big deal. It just means the wearer belongs to an association of engineers who graduated from a Canadian university." He went on to explain that the rings were made from railroad spikes left over from building the TransCanada Railway.

I leveled my gaze at him. "If it's no big deal, why is it that every promotion since I've been here has gone to someone with a ring?"

He squirmed in his seat, shot me a sheepish look, then managed a weak smile. "Just a coincidence."

I dropped it, but vowed to keep my eyes open. Sure enough, over the next year I saw many other examples of bias in favor of the iron ring boys.

It was time to look for another job.

CHAPTER THIRTY FIVE
Leaving Canada

As I searched for new employment, in June 1960, I imposed no geographical limitations. Maureen and I had discussed it, and she agreed that if I found a job with better career opportunities in another country, we would relocate.

I conducted an extensive job search, then applied for the most promising positions while practicing my interview skills. It paid off. I interviewed for four positions—and received four offers.

The most attractive offer came from a small company in San Francisco. I knew that the Bay Area was a hotbed of new technologies, and the idea of living and working amidst it all was exciting. Another attractive feature was that my duties would be different from anything I'd done before. I would work directly with customers, assessing their needs, and helping to design a custom product to fit those needs.

San Francisco just sweetened the pot. I'd heard it described as one of the most beautiful cities in the world. Maureen and I studied a large packet of information sent to us from the tourist bureau.

Maureen looked at me and smiled. "No more Canadian

Maureen even makes her own clothes

winters?"

"Can't happen soon enough for me."

Neither of us was yet familiar with Mark Twain's line—"The coldest winter I ever spent was a summer in San Francisco." I agreed to take the job.

* * *

It was with mixed emotions that I prepared to leave Canada. On one hand, I regretted leaving this country that had been so welcoming to our family. I would miss its vast beautiful landscapes and its people, who were, for the most part, always kind and helpful. I came to appreciate and respect that Canadians were socially responsible people who believed in caring for those less fortunate.

On the other hand, I was excited about moving to the United States, and San Francisco in particular. Maureen and I were both ready for sunny California. I was confident it would provide me with many career opportunities.

Yes, it was time to follow a new path, but Canada would always hold a special place in my heart.

* * *

Our last day in Canada was chore-filled—money transfers, immigration papers, and tying off other loose ends. As I drove the old blue Plymouth around Montreal, I decided to ignore the no-parking signs. I was sure parking tickets would not get me extradited. Turns out, it didn't matter: I received no tickets. There's never a cop around when you need one.

Our friend Ron Doyle had agreed to meet us at the railway station and to take the Plymouth off our hands. (He later sold the car for $175 and sent us the money.) Maureen and the kids hugged Ron goodbye and got on the train. Ron and I shook hands, then hugged, and I realized how much I was going to miss him. "We'll get together again, either here or in the states," I said, knowing I'd probably never see him again. "Thanks for being such a good friend."

Ron smiled. "You don't have to thank me, Don. It was my pleasure." Then, looking self-conscious, he said, "Better hurry or you'll miss your train."

We shook hands one more time, then I climbed aboard. As the train clattered out of the station, I watched, with a twinge of sadness, the Montreal skyline recede into the shadows.

But that emotion was soon swallowed up by the children's contagious excitement. They had never ridden on a train before, and we had splurged and paid $60 for our own private compartment, complete with three sleeping births.

Once inside our cozy compartment, the children began to inspect the new quarters, opening drawers, peeking in the storage areas, bouncing on the beds. They were especially intrigued by the tiny bathroom.

David went into the bathroom, closed the door, then quickly came back out. With wide eyes, he said, "Mommy, what if I'm in there and you and Daddy forget about me and leave without me?"

Maureen and I smiled at each other. Maureen knelt down in front of David, took his hands in hers, looked into his eyes, and said, "Don't worry, luv, we would never forget you. And we would never, ever, leave you behind."

David smiled, seemed to forget about bathroom needs, and said, "I'm hungry. Do you think they have peanut butter and jelly sandwiches on the train?"

* * *

 *Leaving Canada*

As we sat in the dining car, enjoying our sandwiches, we watched the Canadian landscape slip past and wondered aloud about what awaited us in San Francisco.

We crossed into the United States near Buffalo, New York. I'd been told that this was when we'd show our immigration documents and officially become U.S. residents. But when the immigration officer returned with our passports, he said, "You'll receive your identity cards in the mail."

I said, "Well, that's a little inconvenient considering we don't have a U.S. mailing address yet."

The officer was unmoved. "Let us know when you do, and we'll get the cards to you right away."

I told the officer that we wanted to cross the border once more, in Winnipeg, to visit friends. He had me fill out a "special form" that would allow us to do just that. "You should have no problem now," he said.

As we walked out of the immigration office, I thought, No problem . . . famous last words.

PART III

CALIFORNIA
(1 9 6 0 - 2 0 1 6)

CHAPTER THIRTY SIX
——— Westward Ho ———

We were excited to be in the U.S., but we still had a long way to drive. According to the map, it was 2,655 road miles from Buffalo to San Francisco.

We stepped outside the immigration office, intent on finding a pay phone and calling for a taxi. No need. A dozen yellow cabs were lined up. We went to the first one, then spent the next few moments trying to squeeze our luggage into the vehicle.

After watching me struggle, the driver got out of the car, held up his hand, and said, "Hold on, Mister. Let Sammy work his magic."

Then, as though putting together a jigsaw puzzle only he understood, he packed the car in about two minutes. I told him we were headed for the car dealership, and we were soon on our way.

At the car dealer, Maureen tried to keep the children occupied while I slogged through an endless stack of paperwork. Once that was done, the salesman handed me the keys to my new car, and I felt a tingle of excitement.

When I saw the mint-green 1960 Chevrolet station wagon, its polished chrome glinting in the sun, a wide grin spread across my face. The salesman said, "I hope you will be just as pleased with your future purchases from us, Mr. Green."

I cocked my head. "Future purchases? We're headed to California and taking only one car."

A look of disappointment washed across the salesman's face.

Turned out, he had confused us with someone else, a customer interested in buying a fleet of cars. Because of that confusion, he'd given us his best price. We drove off the lot having paid only $2,600.

Preparing for one of our many national park trips

As I drove down the road, I inhaled deeply and let out a sigh of contentment, relishing the new-car smell and a heady sense of excitement. We hadn't gone ten miles, however, when the engine sputtered, then died. I pulled to the side of the road with a sense of dread. Maureen said nothing as I turned the key and pumped the gas pedal. The engine cranked but wouldn't turn over.

Though the symptoms suggested an empty gas tank, the gauge said otherwise. "We seem to have plenty of gas," I said glumly.

"Then what could be wrong?" Maureen asked.

I thought about it. "I still wonder if we might be out of gas—"

"But you said—"

"I know, but maybe the gauge is broken. Either way, I have to go for help."

"And leave us here?"

"You and the kids stay in the car and lock the doors. I'll go to the nearest gas station for help."

Maureen, frown lines creasing her face, said, "Be careful, Don, the traffic is heavy and now it's raining."

Just then Rebecca started crying and David declared he was bored and wanted to get out of the car. Maureen, taking control, soothed them with her words and manner. She pulled a small storybook from her purse and began to read. The children sat listening with rapt attention.

We had passed a gas station a mile back, and it took me fifteen minutes to walk there. I was soaked when I arrived. The mechanic on duty, Chuck, was a large black man with a ready laugh. After hearing my story, he smiled and said, "Come with me." Then he picked up a gas can, walked over to an ancient pickup truck, and gestured for me to get in.

When we got back to the car, Maureen and the kids were fine. Chuck poured the gas into the tank, then lifted the hood and poked about, muttering occasionally. He slid into the driver's seat, pumped the gas pedal a few times, turned the key—and the car started.

He put the hood down, then looked at me and chuckled. "Don't you pay that gauge no never mind."

I nodded. "I'm grateful for your kindness. How much do I owe you?"

The words had barely left my mouth when he waved them away. "Don't you worry none 'bout that. Y'all have a good trip."

As he drove away, I shouted, "Thanks again," and Maureen waved.

We stopped at the next gas station and filled the tank, which was indeed empty. The gas gauge showed no change.

In Buffalo, we got caught in heavy commuter traffic. The Chevy seemed twice as big as the Plymouth, and I drove cautiously, nervous about getting my first dent or scratch. Soon we decided we'd had enough excitement for one day and checked into a motel.

The next day I took the car in for an inspection. The mechanic put it on a lift and immediately noticed an oil leak. He traced it to a bad valve cover gasket. "I'll phone around for a replacement," he said.

While the mechanic made his calls, I stood there thinking: maybe there was another reason the dealer gave us "a deal."

The mechanic returned and said, "I found the part. Take two days to get here." I told him I needed to get to San Francisco and start my new job. The mechanic nodded sympathetically and shrugged.

As I considered our options, I heard a popping sound and looked over to see David chewing gum and blowing bubbles. "Hmmm," I muttered.

I found a vending machine and bought three packs of bubblegum. I gave Maureen and the kids a pack each. "I have a job for you. Keep chewing this gum until I tell you to stop. Whoever gets it soft first is the winner."

In mystified silence, Maureen and the children chewed away. David was the most diligent chewer and so I declared him victorious and took his gum. After consulting the mechanic, he lifted the car and I packed the gum into the hole. The mechanic and I shared grins. "Might work," he said.

I started the car and we let it run for ten minutes. When we checked my repair job—no leak!

I pumped the mechanic's hand and thanked him repeatedly. Then we all piled in the car, and I drove away. As I glanced in the rearview mirror, I could see Rebecca still chewing her gum.

* * *

Maureen kept a journal. Here she describes traveling through Iowa:

The English must have their cup of tea, wind or not

We cross miles and miles of rolling prairie. In Des Moines, Iowa, we bought a propane stove. We amused ourselves trying to make tea in the fierce prairie wind. The water never quite boils as the strong wind cools it as fast as the flame heats.

The tea is lousy, can't really call it tea at all, but I am so thirsty I manage two cups of the stuff. Don threw most of his away.

We roll on and on, up and down. The road stretches ahead like a narrow wire, long and straight. As we top a rise, expecting to see something different, each time our view is the same old straight road passing over small swells until it reaches the next main rise, three or four miles ahead. We drive onto that rise, and the whole thing is repeated. Will it ever end? The few trees we see were mostly planted by settlers, as windbreaks. I am hypnotized by the endless road, the heat, and the sound of the roaring wind.

Now we are in Colorado. I tell Don, "It seems we don't like spending more than one night in any one state."

* * *

Once over the Rocky Mountains, I pictured a flat gentle slope to the Pacific Ocean. And so it was, for a while. We crossed hundreds of miles of desert, then reached the Coast Range. Crossing those mountains, navigating twisting roads and hairpin turns, I learned that my mint-green Chevy station wagon was no sports car. It handled turns poorly.

A few minutes into this roller coaster ride, David cried out, "I don't feel good. I'm gonna be sick!"

I quickly pulled over, turned off the engine, and glanced at Maureen. Her face had a greenish hue. I turned and looked at the children, who appeared off-color as well.

Maureen said, "Don, I know it will take more time, but we have to go slower."

David was pawing at the door handle. I got out, opened his door, and carried him out of the car. Before I could put him down, he vomited. Still holding him, I pointed his mouth away from my body, and my shoes took the brunt of it.

Maureen had found a large rock nearby, and there she sat with Rebecca on her lap. I found some tissues in the car and wiped David's mouth and my shoes. "Feeling better, son? I'm sorry . . . I'll drive slower now."

* * *

By the time we reached our motel in Fort Bragg, on the craggy California coast, we were all exhausted. We found a nearby restaurant, ate quickly, and then headed back to our room. That night, the children didn't even ask for bedtime stories; we were all asleep by nine o'clock.

Early next morning, we were on the road again. Despite the risks of car sickness, we opted for the coastal route, the famed Highway 1, with its twisting hairpin turns. But I took it slow, often at the head of a line of cars whose drivers no doubt wished we had stayed in Canada. Anyway, what was the rush? The sky and ocean were blue, the views spectacular at every turn.

Midafternoon, we reached the tony suburban county known as Marin. We went through the Waldo tunnel, then emerged from the darkness into bright sunlight—and whoa! —we were confronted by one of the most glorious sights ever.

"Look, kids," Maureen said. "The Golden Gate Bridge."

Oohs and ahhs.

"And San Francisco," I added, "our new home."

The day was sunny and fog free, and the city skyline shimmered in the afternoon light as if its outline had been etched by a magic marker. Only later did I learn how rare that was.

I pulled off and parked at a lookout. We got out and just stared— at the bridge, the city, the ocean. I wondered why they called it the Golden Gate Bridge; it was more rust-red. Turns out that in 1846, long before the bridge was built, explorer/mapmaker John

C. Fremont had named the gap linking the bay and ocean "the Golden Gate." Golden referred to the color of the grasses on either side of the bay entrance.

"I like it here," David said.

Maureen and I looked at each other and smiled.

"By the way, the bubblegum held all the way," I told Maureen. "We didn't leak a drop of oil. Maybe I could patent it."

CHAPTER THIRTY SEVEN
Recognition and Promotion

My first day on the job, I got up early and drove to 5th and Bryant Street, site of Lynch Communications. I parked and walked two blocks to the front door. My new workplace was a two-story concrete structure with no architectural merit, though it did look as if it would withstand a strong earthquake.

As I stepped inside, a pudgy receptionist looked up and smiled. "May I help you?"

Struggling to keep a calm composure, I introduced myself, adding, "I believe Mr. Ostriker is expecting me."

The smile never leaving her face, she gestured toward a small sitting area. "Have a seat. I'll let Mr. Ostriker know you're here."

A few moments later, a tall lanky man with unruly red hair emerged. He held out his hand and I shook it. "Welcome to Lynch, Mr. Green. My name is Don Ostriker and I'll be your supervisor. You can call me Don."

"That makes two of us." We exchanged smiles.

Ostriker led me into a conference room and we both sat down. He got right to the point. "I'm sorry I was not able to attend your hiring interview, but now, if you wouldn't mind, I would like to hear about your background and work experience."

As I launched into tales of past jobs and family life, I found myself distracted. My boss wasn't what I'd expected, in looks or manner. His untamed red hair gave him the look of a mad scientist. But it was his manner that I found disconcerting. It was somewhat . . . effeminate. His speech, his hand movements—

something reminded me of my mother. How well would I get along with my new boss? I wondered.

As we talked, I began to relax. Don seemed open, friendly, and knowledgeable. By the time he walked me down to the engineering lab and showed me my desk and workbench, I was feeling more at home.

At that time, 1960, the company was working on two main systems, both then essential to telephone networks. They were called the L-carrier for long-distance connections and the N-carrier for interoffice connections. I was assigned to the L team.

The product was called the L-carrier Line Unit. It consisted of three parts: an amplifier, a set of filters, and a power supply. The amplifiers were to have a new type of transistor, and the filters would utilize a revolutionary design, which used crystals to set the poles. It was well within my capabilities and should have been a straightforward task.

The filters were being designed by a consultant team: Dr. Slikever, a Dutch man with a florid face who reputedly spent most afternoons in a bar across the street from Lynch; and an aloof Arab engineer named, of all things, Kaka. He was a tall, thin man with distrustful eyes and a suspicious nature. He objected to others looking through his designs, keeping them locked up in his desk drawer by day and taking them home every evening.

I later learned that Slikever and Kaka were being paid $250,000 plus royalty payments to design the set of filters for the L-carrier.

The third member of the team, Don Eng Woo, was a Chinese-Canadian engineer with a slight stature and a nervous laugh. Having disappointed his previous supervisors, he was slated for termination, but I convinced his bosses to let me mentor him for a while.

One afternoon I had a talk with Woo. Obviously uncomfortable, he licked his lips, smiled weakly, and waited for me to speak. "I thought it would be a good idea to meet with each member of our team, to get better acquainted and learn a little of your background," I said.

He sat silent for a moment. When his eyes met mine, I saw fear in them. He managed to say, "I understand, Mr. Green. What would you like to know?"

I was taken aback. His accent was so strong, his pronunciation so odd, that it took me a moment to decipher what he'd said. My delayed response just made him more nervous. "Is anything wrong, Mr. Green?"

"Oh no, Mr. Woo. Please tell me about yourself and your work history."

I talked with him for an hour. Mr. Woo was a recent engineering graduate, with no practical experience; he'd been hired by Lynch shortly after graduation. To make matters worse, his previous supervisors had assigned Woo tasks far beyond his capabilities, and offered him no assistance or guidance.

I concluded that Woo's knowledge of design was adequate; he simply lacked experience and confidence. Determined to rectify both problems, I began assigning him tasks within the scope of his abilities. He responded well to my management style, and within two weeks was excelling at circuit design.

Though encouraged by Woo's progress, I still had a devil of a time understanding what he was saying. But one problem at a time, I thought.

After two weeks of working with this diverse team of

engineers, I'd not been given any drawings or information about the design progress. My requests had been met with excuses. I decided only one course of action remained: I'd have to break into Kaka's desk and have a look at the plans. After all, I thought, I'm in charge of this project, responsible for its success or failure. Besides, I was growing increasingly suspicious of all the secrecy.

When Kaka had a doctor's appointment, I snuck into his office and picked the lock on his desk. I retrieved the design plans, then hurried to a meeting room and shut the door. As I sat down, I felt a little like James Bond. After studying the plans, I concluded that their crystal filters were unreliable. They would resonate at different frequencies than the design node. This made the filters unsuitable for the task at hand. Rather than confronting the consultants directly, I decided to take my findings to my boss, Don Ostriker.

After a thorough explanation, I suggested to Ostriker that we give up on the crystal design and go back to standard filter design techniques. The next afternoon, Ostriker terminated the consulting services of Slikever and Kaka.

Woo approached me one day to point out a peculiarity of the new silicon transistors. When he put his hand over the circuit he was measuring, the amplifier started working. When he lifted his hand from the circuit, the amplifier stopped amplifying and the output dropped to zero. This phenomenon was the same with all of the transistors. We deduced that only one thing could cause this: light. When light was shone on a transistor, the amplifier died. The manufacturer (GE) had used translucent material, letting light fall onto the transistor.

Woo suggested a quick fix. Using a black felt pen, we painted over the translucent material. After that, the transistors—and thus the amplifiers—worked perfectly. Don Eng Woo was so pleased with himself, he walked around the rest of the day with a smile on his face.

That evening as I drove home, I thought things were shaping up nicely. It was especially gratifying to watch Woo evolve from a frightened engineer into a capable and confident one.

* * *

I'd been at Lynch about a month when one morning I slept through my alarm. I had to skip breakfast to get to work on time. When noontime rolled around, I grabbed my sack lunch and hurried to the lunchroom, stomach rumbling audibly. On the way I peeked inside to see what Maureen had packed for me. Good, my favorite: roast beef on two thick slices of Maureen's homemade bread. I quickened my pace.

The lunchroom was already crowded. I found an open seat at a two-person table in the far corner. Tony Garzoli, manager of the N-carrier design team, sat in the other seat. As I savored my roast beef sandwich, Tony stared at the wall, apparently lost in thought.

He looked down at his uneaten lunch, back at the wall, then at me. "I gotta big problem."

I probed a bit and Tony eventually opened up. First he gave me the background:

A big company, Western Electric, had long been the sole manufacturer and seller of the N-carrier systems to the telephone industry. The FCC made a ruling, designed to force an opening in this monopoly, requiring Western Electric to sell its N-carrier only to its sister company, Bell. This opened up 20 percent of the N-carrier market to manufacturing companies independent of Bell. The roughly two thousand telephone service suppliers ranged from Hat Island Telephone Company with 50 lines to General Telephone Company with 15 million lines.

Western Electric was also required to make the design/manufacturing specifications for the N-carrier available to any company upon request, and this included Lynch. A grace period gave companies like Lynch time to design their own version of the N-carriers. Thus Lynch was in a race with other companies to come up with a successful reproduction. But now the design team working on a duplicate of the N-carrier had run into a roadblock and could go no further.

"Here's the problem," Tony said. "All the parts we need to make a duplicate of the N-carrier are sold only by Western Electric. Since they're the only game in town, they can charge whatever they want. And believe me, they're taking advantage of the situation."

He paused, leaned closer, and lowered his voice. "Both Management and Sales keep telling me we need to reproduce an N-carrier that is competitively priced. And we need to do it before a competitor beats us to it." He looked back at the wall and mumbled, "Now how is that possible?"

Returning his gaze to me, he said, "So there you have it, in a nutshell. I've been racking my brain, trying to come up with an answer, but no luck."

I sat silent for a moment, searching the corners of my mind for a solution. Devoid of helpful suggestions, I said, feebly, "Boy that's a tough one. I'll let you know if I think of anything."

Looking like a man who had just bet on the wrong horse, he said, "I appreciate that, but I don't hold out much hope. Western Electric is the only supplier of the parts we need for the N-carrier, and I don't see them suddenly lowering their prices."

* * *

The solution came to me one night as I lay in bed. It began as a question: Why would the company design a product based on an old technology? What we needed was a more advanced design. As it was, we were missing out on a great opportunity. Not only would a new design free Lynch from the constraints of Western Electric, but a whole range of modern components would become available to us.

We were indeed looking at the problem all wrong. We'd been trying to produce an exact copy of the N-carrier, but that was unnecessary. It was an external device that did not demand a precise fit. We could create a product that performed the same functions as Western Electric's N-carrier, but manufactured to our specifications. And we wouldn't have to rely on Western Electric for the components.

I'd been a longtime reader of technical journals, and some of those articles came rushing up from the depths of my memory. Yes, I thought, it could be done.

That night, as I closed my eyes, various design ideas drifted through my mind, like big fluffy clouds swept along by a warm breeze.

CHAPTER THIRTY EIGHT
—— *Painted Lady* ——

We pulled up to the curb to view our third rental property of the day. "This is it, Maureen, 150 Alpine Terrace."

Our agent, Doris, was already there, standing in front of the house, holding up the keys and jingling them, as though to say, "This is the one."

Without a hello, Doris launched into her sales pitch, "Built in 1907, it's a prime example of turn-of-the-century San Francisco Victorian—"

The Painted Lady

Maureen interrupted. "Oh Don, it's enchanting. It looks like a big dollhouse."

"Was it something I said?"

Rebecca, four years old, chimed in. "Daddy, I want to live here. I want to live in the dollhouse."

Our intrepid agent picked up the scent. "Oh my, Mrs. Green, what a perfect description. It does resemble a dollhouse, with all the gingerbread trim. And inside you're going to love the detailed molding and ceiling medallion in the dining room."

We toured the house, Doris chattering the whole time: "There are three stories. On the first, the garage . . . on the second floor, the living area and kitchen . . . and on the third floor are the three bedrooms . . ."

After about ten minutes, she said, "I'm sorry but another renter is due soon to view the property."

Just her way of applying pressure, I thought. But it worked. I took Maureen aside and whispered, "What do you think? Do you want to live here?"

She smiled and whispered back, "I love it!"

Doris made a show of looking at her watch, then said, her voice tinged with fake regret, "I'm sorry, but if you are interested in this rental, I will need to know as soon as possible. There aren't many Victorians like this on the market, and they go quickly."

"We'll take it."

Alpine Terrace, San Francisco

* * *

We moved our meager belongings into our new home, and the next day our landlord, Sid Zinc, came by to welcome us. I was surprised that he was so young, only a few years older than me. I apologized for our lack of furnishings and explained that it was taking longer than expected to get our things from Montreal.

Sid was sympathetic. As I made coffee, we began to exchange life stories. A philosophy professor at USF, he was easygoing and interesting, and I liked him immediately.

We got around to sports, and I asked him if he played tennis. Sid's grey eyes lit up. "As a matter of fact, I do. I play every Saturday morning in Golden Gate Park. Would you like to play sometime?"

The courts in Golden Gate Park were only ten minutes from our houses, and we agreed to meet next Saturday. As it turned out, we were evenly matched. In fact, our games were so close and enjoyable, I sometimes forgot who had won.

Saturday tennis with Sid Zink became a ritual, both of us avoiding other commitments on those mornings. Tennis followed by a chat over coffee was a highlight of my week, and I knew Sid felt the same.

Maureen, who is not as social as I am, was pleasantly surprised to find Sid's wife, Helen, a petite but plump woman, such good company. Like us, the Zinks had two children, and many Sunday afternoons the two families got together for a meal.

Over time I shared with Sid the challenges I faced joining a new company. He listened attentively and offered some insights about company hierarchy and personnel matters. He was a bright guy and I respected his opinions. I found myself looking forward to our discussions even more than our tennis matches.

One day Sid slid a file folder across the table. "It's a paper I've written," he said. "I'd like you to read it—aloud, if you don't mind. I'd like to hear it before it's published. And I'd value your opinion."

The deeply philosophical content of the paper was well beyond my area of expertise, but I was touched that he respected me enough to ask for my comments.

About six months after our first meeting, as Sid and I were having our after-tennis coffee, he suddenly asked, "Any chance you'd be interested in buying the Victorian?"

"What? Are you kidding?"

He stared at his coffee. "Not kidding."

"Why do you want to sell the house? I thought you loved it."

He sat staring at his shoes, then slowly spoke. "Few months ago I developed a sore throat and swollen glands. The doctor said mumps and prescribed some medication. 'You'll be good as new within two weeks,' he promised."

He paused, sipped his now-tepid coffee. His gaze shifted to a bank of trees in the distance. He sighed and continued, "After the third week, when I wasn't feeling better, I went back to my doctor. They ran tests—I have cancer of the larynx."

My jaw dropped. Before I could say anything, he added, almost in a whisper, "I'm dying, Don. That's why I want sell the house."

"Sid . . . I'm so sorry . . ." Never had those words sounded so hollow.

He swallowed hard, cleared his throat, and continued in a normal voice. "I want to make things easy for Helen, leave her with as much money as possible."

"Of course." As sadness and disbelief welled up inside me, I looked at my friend, unable to grasp that this fit-looking man in front of me was dying. He's only a few years older than I am, I thought. How can this be happening?

My eyes stung with the threat of tears. I fought to keep my voice steady. "Sid . . . I don't know what to say . . . We love the house. I'll talk to Maureen about it . . ."

When we parted, Sid seemed his usual jovial self. Although I pasted a smile on my face, I felt as though a bomb had exploded inside of me.

When I got home, I found Maureen in the kitchen, pulling two loaves of bread from the oven. Gratitude nearly overwhelmed me. I went straight to her and wrapped her in a bear hug.

She smiled up at me. "What's that for? Did you beat Sid at tennis?"

"I have news, but not about tennis."

I told her about Sid's condition and about his offer to sell us the house.

Over tea we shared our sadness. Then our talk turned to the house. We agreed we wanted to buy it, but final decision would depend on the appraisal. I wasn't sure we had enough savings for the down payment.

A week later the appraisal came in at $25,000, and Sid and I settled on $24,500. We had just enough in the bank to cover the down payment. Maureen and I were going to be homeowners! I was excited and scared at the same time.

* * *

For the next two months Sid and I continued to play tennis every week. Little by little, I noticed, he tired more quickly. We took more rest breaks. During one of those breaks, as we sat on the bench drinking water, I asked, "Want to call it a day?"

He toweled the sweat from his brow. "I'm just tired. I'll be all right in a minute."

But a few minutes later he said, "I'm sorry, Don, but I think I'm done for the day. Do you mind?"

"Don't give it another thought. I can use the time to do some things around the house."

That was the last time Sid and I ever played together.

Over the next two months, I regularly visited him at his home, watching this once vital man wither and deteriorate before my eyes. And then die.

    * * *

A few hours after the funeral, I stopped by to check on Helen. The house was filled with family, friends, flowers, and food.

When Helen saw me, she came over and we embraced. We stood there hugging and crying for what seemed like fifteen minutes, both of us remembering him and sharing our grief.

CHAPTER THIRTY NINE

Secretive Innovation

Once I realized that an N-carrier could be made with different parts and still perform the same functions, I began the painstaking task of creating a Market Requirement Document (MRD). The MRD described the necessary technology, as well as the feasibility and marketability of the product. Whether or not Lynch went with my design would largely depend on my ability to produce a credible and persuasive MRD.

At home, in the evenings and on weekends for the next month, I worked on the design. At first I didn't tell Maureen about my project, hoping to show her how clever her husband was once Lynch accepted my design.

But my heightened distraction did not go unnoticed by my family. One evening, after I declined to read bedtime stories to the kids for the third time in a row, Maureen, exploded. "That's it! You've been preoccupied for weeks, Don. What are you working on? What is so bloody important?"

Looking sheepish, I said, "I'm sorry. I should have told you sooner, but I wanted to surprise you. I'm working on a new design that, if Lynch uses it, could mean a financial boost for the company and a promotion for me."

"Oh," she said in a barely audible voice.

"I didn't want to say anything until I knew if Lynch would accept my idea or not. I guess I just wanted to impress my beautiful wife."

Elegance plus

Maureen's face softened. She came to me and we embraced. She kissed my cheek and whispered, "You are a love. And I'm always impressed."

As she turned to leave, she said over her shoulder, "I'll explain to the children that Daddy is working on something very important and we must all give him lots of quiet time."

As I made myself a cup of tea, I silently patted myself on the back for marrying Maureen, then said aloud, "Thanks, dear, for your understanding and support."

* * *

As the weeks flew by and I continued to labor over my design, my confidence grew. According to my plans, Lynch's N-carrier would be manufactured using the latest technologies available, while Western Electric's model would rely on technology at least ten years old. This should give Lynch a decided advantage over Western Electric and other suppliers.

It was midday on a Saturday when I completed my design plan, ten pages of text and sketches. It had taken two months, and I felt exhilarated. I believed my basic plan could result in an N-carrier system that was faster, smaller, cheaper to manufacture, and consumed less power than Western Electric's product. I could hardly wait until Monday to show Ostriker. He, like everyone else at Lynch, had no idea I'd been working on the N-carrier problem on my own.

Monday morning, before speaking to Don, I went to see Tony Garzoli. When I promised to think about the problem, I told Tony he'd be the first to know if I came up with anything. He was sitting at his desk, peering intently at a design laid out before him.

"Hey Tony, how are you?"

"Okay, I guess. What brings you to my neck of the woods?"

Feeling oddly nervous, I jumped right in. "I've been working on a design for a new N-carrier."

Tony looked perplexed. "When did you do that?"

"At home in my spare time. Mostly evenings and weekends. Anyway, I think it may be a viable design."

I watched his face closely, looking for signs of an injured ego. Instead, he took on the look of a man just saved from the gallows. He smiled and the tension seemed to drain from his body, maybe for the first time since I'd known him.

I explained my strategy and a bit about the design. As I spoke, he nodded approvingly. "I can't tell you how relieved I am. This whole thing has been a nightmare."

Then I came to the part that made me nervous. "I planned on showing Ostriker my MRD today. How do you feel about that?"

I was thankful he didn't keep me waiting for an answer. "That's fine with me. I'd just as soon be rid of this headache of a project." He paused, then added, "Obviously, I'd be happier if I'd come up with the solution myself, but I didn't. Don't worry, Don. I don't hold it against you. Anyway, if your plan gets approved, it's an opportunity for the company to grow, and that could mean more money for all of us."

I thanked Tony and headed off to see my boss. He wasn't in his office, so I went looking for him. I found him in the lunchroom, standing next to the coffee pot, spooning copious amounts of sugar into his mug.

We chatted for a moment, then I said, "I'd like to talk to you, when you have the time."

He said, "I have a meeting in thirty minutes, but I am free until then."

I followed him to his office. Once he was seated, I dropped the MRD on his desk.

I sat down and said, "I think I have a viable design for the N-carrier, and it doesn't require any parts from Western Electric."

His face brightened. "Well, that is good news. Let's have a look."

As he pored over the plan, I could see he was intrigued. Finally he looked up and said, "I want to take this to my meeting with Don Campbell."

Campbell was the CEO. Smiling, I said, "I was hoping you would."

"I have to warn you, though. He may not commit to anything

right away. It may take time. And, of course he will want the opinions of Del Larson (vice president of marketing) and Johnny Johnson (vice president of sales) on the marketability of your design."

Still smiling, I said, "I understand, these things take time. I'm just glad you're showing it to him."

A few weeks later Ostriker told me that Don Campbell liked my design. But neither he nor Del Larson understood the new technology, and it was my job to explain it to them.

As I walked into the conference room prior to my talk, I was afraid my shaking was visible. I'd met Campbell only once and was unsure about his technical capabilities. But my talk and the discussion afterward went fine, mostly because Campbell asked the right questions and made me feel comfortable with his level of understanding.

Over the following weeks, several meetings were held without my presence. I knew there was much discussion about my proposal and the level of risk involved. Were they willing to bet on the capabilities of a twenty-nine-year-old new guy?

One evening Don Campbell invited me to dinner in a fancy restaurant. I figured he wanted one last opportunity to assess my personality and capabilities. Over dessert he announced, "We're going to make the leap. Bet the company on your design. We're taking most of the resources—staff and funding—from the engineering group and putting them into this project."

I gulped, took a sip of water, and stammered, "Thank you for your confidence."

"What confidence? I may be the least confident person in the company."

Caught off guard by that remark, I said, "Well, sir, perhaps it would increase your confidence and sense of control if I set a series of milestones and reported to you every week on our progress."

He smiled. "Sounds good." We shook on it.

* * *

Soon after Lynch made the decision to proceed with the new N-carrier, we heard about a significant and relevant legal ruling. Telephone companies could no longer charge for services between adjacent central offices. Until this ruling, telephone companies—mainly Bell—were charging for local calls on a time and distance basis.

This seemingly minor ruling was destined to dramatically increase the number of circuits and N systems needed. Because local calls were now free, we would see more calls.

A good omen, I thought.

CHAPTER FORTY
Team Assessment

Three weeks after Don Campbell accepted my design proposal for the new N-carrier, he appointed me manager of the project. Although I was only twenty-nine, I felt confident I could meet the challenge. I had just enough experience to believe that I could manage the project—and too little experience to foresee any possible snags.

Me, 29, in San Francisco

The day after my appointment, I assembled the N-carrier design team—now my team!—and introduced myself. "As you know, I've been appointed manager of the N-carrier project. I'm sure you're concerned about what that means to you. Well, I can tell you I believe in a cooperative—rather than an authoritarian—style of management. You might call it a 'walkabout' style. Rather than sitting in my office, I'll be out, talking with you individually about problems and progress. Once a month we'll meet as a full team . . ."

The team consisted of two Americans, three Italians, two Chinese, two Germans, and two Brits, including me. As we talked, I studied each member. I quickly concluded that some had leadership potential. As I listened, I grew more confident in their ability to work cohesively as a team—with one exception.

Kraus, a German, sat stiffly in his chair, arms folded tightly across his chest, lips clamped shut. His body language and lack of participation in the discussion told me he was angry about something. As we ended, I announced that I would meet with each team member individually, starting tomorrow morning.

* * *

Meeting individually with my engineers allayed another of my worries. I knew that good communication would be key to our success, and I wondered how the English-as-a-second-language people would do. As it turned out, I was impressed with both their engineering knowledge and their command of English. There appeared to be no communication barriers.

Kraus was my last appointment. When he showed up at my door, it was obvious his mood had not improved. I smiled and said, "Please come in and have a seat. Can I get you some coffee?"

He sat stiffly in the offered chair. Again he folded his arms across his chest. "No coffee, thank you."

Trying to lighten the mood, I asked him brightly, "So how long have you been with Lynch, Mr. Kraus?"

His steel grey eyes narrowed. He spat out the words like a nail gun. "I have been here four years. I was one of the first engineers to begin working on the N-carrier project . . ." As he spoke, his body seemed to tighten even more, like a bowstring drawn back.

I was silent for a moment as I considered the best strategy. "I have read your file, Mr. Kraus, and I'm pleased to have such an experienced engineer on our team." I let those words sink in, then added, "But the bigger question on my mind is this: are you pleased to be part of our team?"

A look of surprise flashed across his face. For a moment he sat very still; he opened his mouth and then closed it again.

The silence wore on for a moment more. Then he abruptly leaned forward, gave me an icy glare, and said, "No, I am not happy! A grave injustice has been committed. I should have been named manager of this project. I have been here longer than you, I have more experience, and I have been working on the N-carrier project from the beginning."

I looked at him, noting for the first time that his dark hair was shot through with grey.

Face flushed, he went on. "Then what does our genius president Don Campbell do! He chooses some kid, with his mind full of a lot of fantasies about new technology, and makes him the project manager!"

Spent for the moment, he leaned back in his chair and repositioned his arms across his chest. Pouting like a fifty-year-old child, I thought.

Despite my managerial inexperience, I knew this man would never be a cooperative member of the team. Still, I would offer him one last chance. "I can appreciate how you must feel, but perhaps, given a little time, your feelings may change. What do you say, Mr. Kraus, do you think that's possible?"

He sat there, unmoving, silent. I assumed he was forming his answer, so I let him. But when a minute or two had ticked by, I said, "Mr. Kraus, I'm sure you're aware that our company's future is riding on the success of this project. Therefore, it's imperative that everyone on the design team is one hundred percent committed to it, and the company."

Still he said nothing.

My patience was wearing thin, but I asked in a calm voice, "Would you like a few days to think about it? We can talk then."

He stood, leaned over my desk, his nose inches from mine, and shouted, "I don't need a few days—that won't change anything! I will not have you, some snotty-nosed kid, as my boss. I have been betrayed and I don't owe this company or its idiot president anything. I quit!"

Then he turned and headed for the door, slamming it on his way out.

As I sat there, two emotions bubbled to the surface—sympathy and relief. I could sympathize with this aging man who felt victimized by injustice, but I was also relieved that he was off the team. I'd gotten a break.

Of course, now I had to find a replacement for Kraus. Seconds later I knew that I wanted Sam Huey, an old friend and colleague from my Montreal days. "Sam Huey," I said, "the perfect man for the job."

I picked up the phone and began dialing.

Sam Huey

CHAPTER FORTY ONE
—————— *Invaluable Experience* ——————

During my first six weeks as project manager, I kept a low profile. I spent my time learning the limitations the company placed on design engineers and estimating the degree of freedom I would enjoy. The most important interaction was with Don Ostriker, and our relationship was going well, I thought. He was positive that he had a good ally in me, someone who would help him reach his goal—that is, to become president of the company.

People in the other departments, after some quizzical looks at me, adopted a wait-and-see attitude.

I thought it critical to implement tracking and planning tools so that we could measure our progress with ease and accuracy. I employed a fairly new evaluation tool called the Project Evaluation Review Technique (PERT). It enabled us to create a clear timeline for each phase of the design process, allowing anyone at Lynch to monitor our progress.

As the weeks ticked by, I saw more clearly how Don Campbell created unhealthy competition between employees by pitting one against another. For example, he'd give two employees the same task, make each aware of the other, and then wait to see who finished first.

I believed this type of manipulation was counterproductive. It fostered an atmosphere of mistrust while providing no incentive for cohesive teamwork. Though I didn't share those thoughts with my group, I did emphasize the importance of teamwork and open communication. I strongly encouraged all the designers to share their ideas and any concerns they had. I was gratified by how quickly my team blossomed under those conditions. This despite their collective experiences with Don Campbell's management style.

Six weeks after I took over the project, many of my fellow employees at Lynch had seen enough to have confidence in me. My visibility within the company increased dramatically, allowing me to have conversations with all levels of management. This provided me with connections that were not only helpful at the time, but would be in the future as well.

* * *

For the next six months my work on the project was so consuming that I thought of little else. My dedication and hard work were paying off in the form of an invaluable learning experience, if not in actual dollars. In fact, I'd not given my salary much thought—until one day my attention was drawn to it during the simple act of writing a note.

I found a scratchpad and began scribbling a note to vice president of sales. When I'd filled the page, I tore off the sheet and flipped it over. To my surprise, the other side already had writing on it. Apparently, in Campbell's zeal to save money, he had recycled old memos into scratchpads.

I soon deciphered the writing. It was a list of managers and their salaries. I found my name and then one by one compared my salary to the other managers. As the evidence mounted, my face fell. I looked at the numbers again in disbelief. My salary was strikingly lower than any other manager's.

Feeling heat rising in my body, I pulled on my collar to loosen my tie. I rose from my chair and headed for the door. Once outside, feeling less explosive, I decided to take a walk around the block. I needed time to let the anger recede, time to think clearly. I didn't want to do or say anything I might regret later.

Before I had completed one lap, I knew what I had to do. Walking briskly, I headed back to the Lynch building and straight for Campbell's office. I greeted his secretary and asked when he might be free.

After checking his calendar, she said, "You know, he might be free right now." She rose and disappeared into his office, closing the door behind her.

Not expecting immediate attention, I felt my heart thundering in my chest. "It's now or never," I murmured.

The secretary was back in a moment. "You can go right in."

As I opened the door and entered, I took a deep breath, then another. Campbell rose and gestured to the chair opposite his. "Have a seat . . . what can I help you with, Don?"

I pulled the incriminating paper from my breast pocket and handed it to him. "I stumbled on this about an hour ago. As you can see, my salary is nowhere near that of the other managers."

He glanced at the pad, then at the wall. His neck grew red.

I continued, "What would you do if you were in my shoes, sir?"

Then, in a voice silky smooth, he said, "I'm grateful you brought this to my attention. I'm sure it's just an oversight. I'll have a word with Personnel and make sure the situation is rectified as soon as possible."

I wasn't sure what that meant, or if I believed him. But I didn't want to push it further, not then. I said only, "Thank you, I appreciate that."

As he saw me to the door and shook my hand, he said, "Any time I can be of assistance, Don, don't hesitate to ask." A real snake-oil salesman, I thought.

Back at my desk, I felt a mix of emotions churning inside me. Gratitude was one. I was still grateful to Campbell for giving me and my idea a chance. But another was suspicion. I found it hard to believe he hadn't known that I wasn't receiving a manager's salary.

I took a few deep breaths and said to myself, "You've done what you can. Now we have to see if Mr. Campbell follows through with his promise."

Next payday, I held my breath as I opened the envelope. Sure enough, Campbell had kept his word. Not only had my salary increased, but according to the enclosed letter, I was to receive stock in the company.

I couldn't wait to get home and tell Maureen.

* * *

A few months later I was promoted to Chief Engineer.

CHAPTER FORTY TWO
Adoption

One rainy evening, after David and Rebecca had gone to bed, Maureen and I sat in the family room and sipped our tea. We shared a companionable silence for some minutes before Maureen asked, "What do you think about adding to our family, Don?"

Taken aback, I was silent for a moment. "I hadn't thought about it, because David and Rebecca were such a physical challenge for you. I still remember what you said after Rebecca was born. You said, 'I will never go through that again!'"

"Yes, but—"

"Are you telling me you've changed your mind?"

Maureen laughed. "No, I have not changed my mind."

Was this a joke? I searched her face for a clue; finding none, I said, "Okay, I'm officially confused. Do you want to have more children or don't you?"

Swallowing the last of her tea, Maureen set her cup down, pulled a folded newspaper clipping from her pocket, and handed it to me.

Before I could unfold it, Maureen added, "With David and Rebecca in school all day, I'm feeling a void in my life. Even when they're home, they don't need me as much as they used to. Oh Don, I can't tell you how much I miss having little ones to cuddle and care for."

"Yes, but—"

"Then last week I saw this article in the paper about the

benefits of adoption, and I thought, here is the perfect solution."

The light finally went on. "Ah, adoption."

Under Maureen's watchful gaze, I read the article. When I looked up, our eyes met and she said, "Don't you see, Don? There are so many children who need a family, and we want more children. It's a perfect fit."

I was stuck on words I'd never heard before: we want more children. In a soft, imploring voice Maureen said again, "It's a perfect fit, don't you think?"

Part of me felt blindsided. But, not for the first time, my wife's enthusiasm was contagious, and as we talked I began to warm to the idea. Before long I heard myself say, "Perhaps having a larger family would be good. The article says to contact the Human Services Department for more information. We could call tomorrow . . ."

Before I'd finished speaking, Maureen's arms were around my neck and she was kissing my cheek.

* * *

Ten months later, we were told we could pick up the newest member of our family, Duncan Green. A tow-headed toddler, he had a ready smile and a happy disposition.

A new member joins

Expanding family

Duncan appreciating my lullaby

Months later we had a call from Human Services asking if we would be interested in helping to form a nonprofit charitable organization called The Carriage Trade, whose main goal would be the promotion of adoption. We enthusiastically agreed to participate.

David and Duncan enjoying the beach

Duncan trying to escape Mo

Preparing for a trip to Zion National Park

I was appointed president, and my duties included promoting adoption through meetings and events, mostly in San Francisco. The organization was successful in helping to demystify and destigmatize the adoption process.

Maureen and me at the San Francisco adoption bureau, picking up Victoria

Two years after adopting Duncan, we repeated the process and brought home our beautiful baby girl, Victoria.

"I'd be glad if this house was built so I can have a proper bath"

Mother's little darling Victoria

Victoria, 10 months old, and Maureen at Stinson Beach

My personal experience with adoption and what I learned through my association with The Carriage Trade has enriched me as a man, a father, and a member of society. I've never regretted any of it.

Maureen and me in the Sierra

CHAPTER FORTY THREE
Plugging a Leak

Early in the N-carrier development phase, Arthur Fritz, one of the designers, came to me, a weary look on his face. "We are having trouble taking accurate readings," he said. "I believe it is because this building does not have sufficient ground to allow us to use our test equipment. I've tried a number of workarounds, but without success."

I pushed aside the budget documents I was working on, stood up, and said, "Let's go have a look."

I followed Fritz down to the basement lab. After assessing the situation, I told Fritz, "I think the solution is to have some holes drilled through the floor, insert some copper rods, and then connect the rods to form a mesh. That should give us the proper ground."

Fritz agreed and said he'd call a contractor immediately.

Next morning I was again at my desk, immersed in budget papers, when Fritz appeared in my doorway. He looked worried. "The contractors started drilling, but had to stop. You better come see."

I rose, sighed, and followed Fritz to the basement. There, one of the contractors stood over a newly drilled hole. His back was to me, so I did not see the problem until I walked around him and looked down the hole, which was rapidly filling with water.

I bent down, stuck my finger in the water and brought it to my lips. "It's salty," I said.

I stood for a few seconds in shock, trying to make sense of it. Then I remembered how the building shook every time an 18-wheeler passed by. Of course! We were sitting on unstable bay fill. Right below us was San Francisco Bay.

Seconds later the water bubbled up out of the hole and began to cover the floor. "Needless to say," I told the contractor, "don't drill any more holes. Meanwhile, we have some sealing compound that we can use to plug this one."

An hour later, disaster averted, I headed to Don Campbell's office to update him and to ask that our lab be moved to a new building. "We need to be somewhere that isn't built on fill," I said, "one that doesn't shake every time a truck goes by, and has sufficient ground to let us do our work."

My request was granted, not because Campbell had any great sympathy or vision, but because it was obvious we could not produce our version of the N-carrier under present circumstances.

For years I passed that building and remembered how we used a chunk of sealing compound to keep the Bay at bay. That in turn would trigger memories of our family trip across the United States when I used bubblegum to plug a transmission leak.

Sometimes the low-tech solution is best.

CHAPTER FORTY FOUR
DTS, Leap of Faith

One morning, groggy with jetlag, I sat at my desk going over the design notes I'd created on my flight from Zurich. I felt I was onto a major development, but I knew many more hours would be needed to complete even preliminary documents, including market research.

Yawning, I stood up, stretched, and said to myself, "Better run the idea by Don Campbell before I put in any more time." I picked up the phone, called Campbell's secretary, and got an appointment for one o'clock that afternoon.

As I ate lunch, I remembered how beneficial my last product idea had been for Lynch, and my confidence rose.

At the appointed time, I headed to Campbell's office, an enthusiastic smile on my face. I was immediately ushered into his office. He wasn't alone; sitting across from Campbell was Del Lawson, vice president of marketing. I barely knew Del, had never worked with him, and didn't know what to expect from him. With slicked-back hair, wearing a bow tie, he reminded me of Dagwood Bumstead.

When Campbell asked what was on my mind, I launched into my presentation. "Gentlemen, I have been working on an outline for a new product. This product will convert voice information into digital information, using a T1 multiplexer. It will allow you to use two pairs of copper wires and service ninety-six lines. It will serve subscribers at longer distances with greater voice quality, reduce the amount of power consumption, and lower installation costs. It would be installed on the tops of telephone poles—"

Del interrupted me. "So, let me get this straight . . . this new product would be physically installed on telephone poles?"

"Yes that's right. It—"

But Del wasn't listening. He turned to Campbell and complained, "There's no way Ma Bell is going to let us put a box of electronics on their poles. Plus there's the hostile environmental conditions."

I stared at Del. It's not unreasonable for you to be nervous, I thought, but you're ignorant, not even considering the merits of the product or the potential growth it could mean for the company. You're thinking only that you'd have to sell it, and you don't want to deal with that responsibility.

I reminded them that this product would increase telephone service capacity tenfold and decrease the amount of copper wire needed, thereby cutting costs.

Once I'd finished speaking, I looked into Don Campbell's eyes, hoping to see a glimmer of excitement. Instead, he shifted his gaze from mine to the floor, seemingly studying his shoelaces, and said, "You know, Don, it does sound like a good idea, but I'm afraid Del may be right about the telephone poles."

I felt disappointment flood through my veins like a toxic drug. Knowing there was no point in saying more, I thanked them for their time, headed for the door, and silently closed it behind me.

Walking back to my office, I thought of how my redesign of the N-carrier had impacted Lynch. In the last nine years, the company's net sales revenue had increased from $5 million to $40 million, largely due to the success of the N-carrier. Yet my new product idea had been dismissed peremptorily, with extreme prejudice.

Well, I thought, Lynch may lack faith in me and my product,

but I don't. I vowed to pursue it, with or without the company's support. In the years I'd been in charge of the N-carrier project, I'd made valuable connections with a number of high-level analysts who had intimate knowledge of the telecommunications market. Over the next few weeks, I presented my ideas to several of them. To a man, they were supportive, asserting their belief that money could be raised for the project.

Meanwhile, I continued to fine-tune my product concept and technical details. More and more, my thoughts turned to starting my own company. I figured I'd need at least two other engineers to partner with. I had two such in mind: Sam Huey, whom I'd worked with in Montreal and later hired to work on the N-carrier project at Lynch; and Bob Gibbens, formerly an engineer at Bell Labs who now worked for Lynch. Though confident in their engineering capabilities, I was less certain of their willingness to invest time and money. It was, after all, a gamble.

"We will find that pot of gold."

Sam, who had no family to support, was more likely to take a flyer on a risky new idea. For Bob, who had a wife and four children, the risk would be much greater. Still, I decided, I would present my plan to both of them, offer each a partnership. I'd also make clear my personal commitment, that I was prepared to take out a second mortgage on my Tiburon house.

Over dinner at an Italian restaurant in North Beach, I laid it all out to Sam and Bob. I detailed what the Line Concentrator could do. Then I showed them my business plan and spoke of the risks. "We will be in direct competition with Bell Labs and Western Electric," I said. "It's a new concept, and we will have to overcome the usual resistance to innovative technologies. We are dealing with the real world, and the real world is risk-averse. However, our willingness to invest our own money in this project will demonstrate to potential investors our belief in the product."

Sam spoke first. Excitement twinkling in his eyes, he said simply, "I'm interested."

We both turned to Bob. Obviously deep in thought, he didn't respond right away. Then: "I'm definitely intrigued by it . . . sure, count me in."

We decided the next move was to complete a Market Requirements Document (MRD) before we approached investors. Over the next several months we met frequently and eventually completed the MRD and the different phases of the business plan. We prepared ourselves to answer any questions that might be thrown at us by the venture capital community.

I began contacting the analysts I'd initially spoken to about my idea. One of them was working for a world-renowned venture capitalist named Arthur Rock, who agreed to see me. Five minutes into my presentation, Mr. Rock, a slight man with small, shrewd eyes, interrupted me. "Did I get this right? You're designing a product that will compete with Bell Labs and Western Electric?" I nodded. "No thanks!" he said.

At my next meeting with Bob and Sam, we all agreed it was time to sever our relations with Lynch Communications. Although we had no investors, I remained confident and knew that we had to devote our full attention to the new company. Sam and I provided the seed money needed to launch our business venture, humble though it was. We rented a 1,500-square-foot office, sharing the building with a plumbing shop.

We needed a name. I favored Digital Transmissions Systems, but a search revealed that it was already taken. We settled on Digital Telephone Systems (DTS).

I offered Lynn Woolsey, my secretary at Lynch, the position of office manager. While Lynn handled the details of running the office, I finalized our ownership agreement and oversaw product development. I estimated it would take eighteen months to produce a viable prototype. I left the final design to Sam and Bob.

While locking up late one evening, I felt the pride of ownership sweep over me. As I drove home, I thought about Lynch, but this time not what I had done for them; rather what the company had done for me. Although Campbell and cronies had failed to give my idea thoughtful consideration, I had two reasons to be grateful to them: One was the management skills I'd learned and developed while in charge of the N-carrier project; second was Don Campbell's refusal to develop my product idea. It was that rejection that provided the impetus for me to leave the nest and start my own company.

I knew I faced significant risks, but I felt up to the challenge.

Mutiny on the Bounty

CHAPTER FORTY FIVE
—Joining the Choir—

One Sunday I was in church singing the hymns with gusto when the woman in front of me half-turned and said, "You have a nice voice. You should join the choir."

I looked over my shoulder, certain she must be talking to somebody else. "Who, me?" More than once, Maureen had accused me of "bellowing the hymns."

"Well, you just might find you enjoy it."

For the next week, I gave the idea some thought. When I saw the woman the following Sunday, I asked, "Who do I talk to about joining the choir?"

She smiled, introduced herself as Sylvia Bowen, and took me to meet Florence White, the church organist and choir director. Florence, a silver-haired woman in her sixties, wore orthopedic shoes and a no-nonsense look on her face.

Sylvia said, "Florence, I've recruited a new choir member."

Florence's eyes swept over me, her lips tightened, and as the seconds ticked by, she continued to stare, saying nothing. I was beginning to wonder if she had a hearing problem or was just plain batty, when she suddenly barked, "Well, what are you?"

Her eyes widened slightly, as if assessing my mental acuity. Speaking slowly she asked, "Are you a bass or a tenor?"

"Tenor, I think."

"You think? Well, never mind. We'll find out soon enough. Follow me."

She headed for the church organ, sat down on the bench, hit a key, and demanded, "Sing this note."

It was a high note and I tried to match the pitch. Florence grimaced, as if she'd swallowed a bitter pill. She hit a lower key and gestured for me to sing it. This exercise went on for several minutes, with the notes becoming successively lower.

At last she turned to me and announced, "You're a bass, not a tenor." Then, with little enthusiasm, she added, "Come to choir practice a half hour early, and we'll work on next Sunday's music." Then, without another word, she turned and walked away.

Had I been a tenor, I wondered, would she have been more welcoming? Undaunted, I turned up regularly at rehearsals and made an effort to familiarize myself with the music for the coming Sunday. After six months, I was relatively competent at reading simple music. Practicing at home, Maureen would accompany me on our piano while singing along. Her piano playing was of the two-finger, hunt-and-peck variety, but her voice was solo quality.

I found myself once again impressed by her many talents. Not only could Maureen raise children, cook, knit, sew, and run a household, she could have been a professional singer.

"Maureen, you have a great voice. Why don't you join the choir, too?"

She blushed. "Oh, I'm not sure I could sing in front of other people."

I was about to respond when I noticed her eyes had taken on a dreamy quality, as if trying to imagine performing on stage in front of an audience. Reluctant to tear her away from her vision, I remained silent. A moment later she brightened and announced, "I'll do it!"

The following Sunday, Maureen joined the choir.

* * *

Singing in the choir gave Maureen and me a greater appreciation of music and an eagerness to learn more about it. One evening after dinner, while we were having our tea and the kids were busy with their crayons, I said, "I went past the Drinking Gourd today. You know that little place we stopped at a few weeks ago? A classical guitarist is playing there tonight. Why don't we call the sitter and go listen to him play."

An hour later we were sitting in the Drinking Gourd, drinks in hand, mesmerized by the elegance and emotional power of the music. Through the haze of cigarette smoke and dim lighting, I tried in vain to watch the guitarist's hands, with the irrational hope that I could somehow learn to play like him.

After his set, I went up to the stage, introduced myself, and said, "That was great. If you have time, my wife and I would like to buy you a drink."

"I'm sorry. I have another show to do across town, but thanks for the offer."

"I understand. By any chance, do you give guitar lessons?"

Smiling, he reached into his pocket, pulled out a business card, and handed it to me. "Call me and we'll set something up."

The following week I began guitar lessons. From the beginning I struggled with memorizing simple musical pieces. I also lacked the manual dexterity that classical guitar playing required. Hating failure, I persevered for a year before giving up the lessons.

"Wasted time"

Though disappointed, I found solace in the fact that I'd learned to play well enough to be asked to accompany a group from the church choir that sang folk songs and madrigals. Florence didn't seem to mind that my guitar playing was far from perfect; she was just grateful to have two additional voices in the choir. A particular pleasure was learning to sing madrigals, music written in the Renaissance period, performed by a small group, usually four people, without accompaniment.

After rehearsal one day, Florence suggested Maureen and I try out for the San Francisco Municipal Chorus. Florence was the rehearsal pianist for the group. "I'll put in a good word for you," she said.

Maureen and I tried out and made the team.

The San Francisco Municipal Chorus was directed by Waldemar Jacobson. For thirty-six years he had dedicated his life to the choir, and he alone made all key decisions, rarely delegating responsibility to anyone. So I was surprised, about a year after we joined, when he asked me to become choir president.

The past president had recently resigned, and we all assumed that Waldemar would leave the post vacant and assume the responsibilities himself. I hesitated, pondering the proposition. Face to face with Waldemar, I noticed for the first time that his tall, elegant frame didn't seem quite as erect as usual.

"Well, if you think I'm up to the task, then sure. I'll do it."

About a month later, the phone rang in the middle of the night. It was Mrs. Jacobson, Waldemar's wife. With no preamble she said, "Waldemar died earlier this evening. A heart attack."

I squeezed the phone, as though trying to crush it. Sadness and disbelief washed over me.

I had just seen him two days earlier. He seemed a little tired, but otherwise fine.

When I returned to bed, Maureen was awake. "Who on earth was that? Anything wrong?"

I sighed and told her the news. After a few moments of silence, Maureen said in a weary voice, "I don't think I can get back to sleep. I'm going to make a cup of tea. Would you like some?"

Sitting at the kitchen table, cradling my mug of hot tea, I was struck by the fact that at that moment I was not feeling sad. I would miss the man I called a friend, a man I admired and respected. But at that moment the loss only served to make me more grateful for what I had, my life and my family.

I called a special meeting of the choir. Members were all aware of Waldemar's passing, and some assumed the choir would disband, given that Waldemar had run the whole operation for thirty-six years. I told the group I was in favor of staying in business and was willing to lead the search for a new director.

Support for that plan appeared to be unanimous.

I decided to approach it as if I were recruiting a senior executive at a large corporation. I wrote a job description and placed ads in various music media. I raised sponsorship money to attract and pay for the best potential candidate, all the while keeping choir members informed of our progress.

The effort paid off. The interviews went smoothly, and the candidates were all high-caliber professionals. In the end, we selected David Babbet, an outstanding musician and director, who ably continued the life work of Waldemar Jacobson until the day he died.

CHAPTER FORTY SIX
Courting Vanguard

As Maureen ushered David and Rebecca out the front door, she called out, "Don, will you still be here when I get back from taking the kids to school?"

Soft light beauty

I glanced at the kitchen clock. "I don't think so. I have to make a call, and then I'm heading to the office. I'm not sure what time I'll be home tonight. Call you later."

Maureen's question sounded odd to my ears. It was 7:45 on a Monday, and for the last nine years at that time, I'd been picking my way through city traffic, on my way to Lynch. I smiled to myself and picked up the phone.

I called Allen Grieve, an analyst for Vanguard. I'd gotten to know Allen while managing the design of the N-carrier. Under normal business practices, the president of the company, Don Campbell, would have been the one to meet with the telecommunications analyst; but Campbell lacked the patience for such meetings and he delegated the responsibility to me. I enjoyed the meetings and consequently had formed an invaluable network of industry contacts, including Allen Grieve.

I spoke briefly with Allen's secretary, and then Allen came on the line. After brief chitchat, I told him I'd left Lynch and was starting my own company. After I described our new product and its capabilities, he became silent.

"Allen, you still there?"

"I'm still here . . . just thinking." Then abruptly: "Listen, Don, could you possibly come to Toronto next Tuesday and make a presentation to our full partnership?"

Now it was my turn to be silent. How on earth could we refine our business plan and develop a convincing presentation in only six days?

As if reading my mind, Allen said, "I know it's short notice, but the next partnership meeting is next Tuesday. After that it's another month, and I'm assuming you need financial backing sooner rather than later."

I found my voice and heard myself say, "You're right, of course. I'll be there."

I thanked Allen, hung up, and sat back in my chair. My excitement was tempered by the realization that a daunting task lay before me and my partners. I called the office to tell Sam and Bob the news and of the urgent need to polish the business plan and the PowerPoint® presentation.

There was no answer at the office. I looked at the clock and saw that it was not yet eight o'clock. I grabbed my jacket and headed for the door.

Twenty minutes later when I reached the office, Lynn was at her desk typing away, and Sam and Bob were huddled together, tinkering with our design plan. Once I'd gathered everyone together, I said, "I've got good news and bad news. The good news is, I spoke with Allen at Vanguard and he wants us to make a presentation. The bad news is that we have to polish the MRD and the presentation before next Monday."

They were all staring at me, eyes wide and mouths agape, their expressions saying loud and clear, "Are you nuts?"

Sam was first to snap out of it. "That's great news, Don, but do you have any thoughts on how we're going to accomplish those Herculean tasks in six days?"

I smiled. "As a matter of fact, I do. We will divide the business plan into segments and work on them in order of importance. It goes without saying that whatever personal plans any of us might have had for this coming weekend—reschedule them! We will need every minute of our time to meet this deadline."

Bob finally spoke. "This will certainly be a good test of how well we can all work under pressure."

Lynn rose and said, "I'll make a fresh pot of coffee. I have a feeling we're going to need it."

By eight that evening, we'd hammered out an outline of the PowerPoint® presentation and another draft of the MRD. We decided to call it a day, and as I was getting into my car, I realized how tight my back felt. I was exhausted.

* * *

Fred and Zack enjoying TV news

On Sunday, our last day of work on the presentation, Maureen asked me to take Zack, our black lab, to the office. She had a medical appointment and didn't want to leave him home alone. Zack, a young dog, did not always do what he was told, and I sometimes took him to the office as part of his training.

By that evening, fueled by six days of caffeine and adrenaline, we had our plan nearly complete. As I stared at the computer monitor for a last review, a feeling of accomplishment and relief settled over me. It lasted for all of five minutes, right up until the time Lynn announced, "The printer's not working. Our computer guy will be here in an hour to fix it."

In the meantime, I called my partners over to look at the plan. We were halfway through our review when suddenly the monitor went blank. While mumbling, "What now," I fumbled for the switch, flicking it on and off. Nothing. Feeling beads of sweat forming on my forehead, I wondered aloud how long since I'd backed up our draft.

Sam stood and began to follow the cord to its outlet. At the far wall, he said, "Aha, I found the problem." Bob and I turned to see Sam pointing down at my dog. Under his big, black paw lay the switch to the computer. Once Zack noticed everyone staring at him, he wagged his tail, unaware that praise would not be forthcoming.

Sam reached down to plug in the computer, and we all held our breath, hopeful that our work had not been lost. As the computer whirred to life, I felt dizzy, our fate hanging in the balance. In an instant our plan materialized on the screen before us, nary a comma missing.

A collective sigh of relief went up, and I silently vowed that from now on Zack would stay at home . . . and we would be more diligent about backing up our work.

On Tuesday evening I called Sam and Bob from Toronto. "This time it's just good news," I said. "Vanguard is going to invest in our company. Our hard work paid off."

CHAPTER FORTY SEVEN
Field Trial

I closed the front door and cautiously picked my way through the darkness. The frosty morning air penetrated my jacket and an involuntary shiver ran through my body. I nearly stepped on David's bike sprawled in the pathway. I shook my head, picked up his bike, parked it next to the garage, and made a mental note to talk with him that evening.

As I drove to the office, I smiled and said, "Today is the day!"

It was October 1971, and after eighteen months of hard work, our prototype of the Line Concentrator—renamed the D960—was ready for its field test. Our version performed the same functions as the Line Concentrator, but it was smaller, less expensive, and used digital technology instead of analog, producing better sound quality.

After considering several sites and companies for our field test, we chose the Roseville Telephone Company. It was relatively nearby, and the company was willing to put up with the disruption of a field trial. The company had even offered some of its technicians to help with the installation.

When I pulled into our parking lot, I noticed an unusual number of cars already there. I glanced at my watch—only 6:25—and yet at least half of our staff of twenty-five must already be inside. On most days Lynn arrived to open the office at about 7:45, followed by the rest of the staff by 8:00. But today was no ordinary day.

Although Sam, Bob, and I had the most riding on the field trial, the rest of the staff had a vested interest as well, mainly their jobs. If our product didn't perform well in the field, then its sales, and thus any revenue stream, would be postponed, forcing us to continue to pay salaries out of our small company's startup capital.

Opening the door to the office, I was hit with the aroma of coffee and the sound of overlapping voices. A large box of still-warm jelly doughnuts sat on Lynn's desk, and four engineers were gathered around the box, munching doughnuts and talking about the field trial.

As I entered, chatter ceased and all eyes fixed on me. One design engineer, Fred Nordling, asked, "Do you foresee any problems with our trial today, Don?"

With more confidence than I felt, I smiled and said, "We've run the D960 through rigorous testing in the lab and it came through with flying colors . . . no, I don't anticipate any problems."

Of course, they knew what I knew: testing a product in the controlled environment of the lab was very different from testing its performance in the field.

I found Lynn at the copy machine. "Good morning, have you seen Arthur or Joseph yet? I want to talk to them before they head out to the field."

As she collected her copies, she said, "Oh, they're already on their way to Roseville. Left about twenty minutes ago."

Lynn Woolsey, from secretary to Congresswoman

"Okay, I'll catch up with them at the site."

The sky was blue, the air was crisp, and as I drove, I tried to appreciate the beauty of the day. But invariably my thoughts returned to business. "You've started your own company at age forty . . . not bad for a poor boy from Liverpool. Let's hope we're still in business when you turn forty-one."

My thoughts spun back to my childhood . . . I was eating breakfast in our tiny kitchen in Liverpool, eavesdropping on my mother chatting outside with a neighbor . . . hearing the only words I'd ever recall from that conversation: "Thomas is the clever one."

Even then I sensed the unfairness of that statement. I wanted to say, "Mum, I'm just as clever as Thomas, probably even more!"

Instead I pretended I hadn't heard, silently swallowing my words along with my porridge. But I felt a hard resolve forming in the pit of my stomach: I'd prove to my mum and everyone else that I was clever. I'd show them! I wasn't sure how, but the seed of determination had been planted.

As my thoughts glided back to the present, I realized that incident, painful as it was at the time, had spurred me to do better. It was a constant reminder to keep my eye on the goal, remain focused, and work hard. I smiled and said aloud, "Thanks, Mum."

When I arrived at the site, I was dismayed to find nothing had happened. Our equipment was still in its shipping boxes, and Arthur and Joseph were nowhere to be seen. Two men, Roseville technicians, were standing idly by our equipment, which lay on the ground next to a telephone pole. They were discussing last night's football game.

Exasperated, I interrupted, "Have you guys seen our engineers?"

The older of the two men, whose leathery skin spoke of too many hours working in the sun, pointed up the street. "They're at the coffee shop."

I found Arthur and Joseph sitting in a booth near the door. I took a deep breath, summoned what little patience I had left, and sat down. "Why haven't you guys started installing the D960 on the telephone pole? Is there a problem?"

They exchanged looks before Arthur explained, "We're not sure of the best way to attach it to the pole. That question hadn't occurred to us until we got here."

With a hangdog look, Joseph said, "I guess I should have told you before, Don, but I'm not crazy about heights. I don't think I can climb that pole."

My impatience drained away, as I realized where the blame lay. "It's not your fault," I said. "I should have thought this through beforehand. But that can't be helped now. Our priority is to find a solution, and fast."

Then suddenly, in my mind's eye, a picture of a wooden scaffold floated into view. "Let's go. I have an idea."

We headed back to the technicians, still embroiled in football talk. I explained our dilemma, then asked hopefully, "Is there a lumberyard close by? I want to build a scaffold for my engineers to stand on while they install the D960."

The younger technician pointed to his right. "There's one a mile up the road."

It was a slow day at the lumberyard, and the manager, fascinated by our project, lent me everything I needed. I borrowed his tape measure, a pencil and paper, and a saw. I cut the 2 by 4s into suitable lengths, drilled holes in the appropriate places, and completed in an hour a crude but effective scaffold, complete with safety rail. We were ready to install the D960.

Eyeing the safety rail, Joseph smiled and said, "C'mon, Arthur. Let's get this thing installed." Thirty minutes later, the D960 was in place. When we turned it on, all the lines connected to it received a dial tone. By the time we left that afternoon, everything was working without a glitch.

A week later, when the testing was complete, we had a new problem. Or rather Roseville Telephone Company did. When I met with the general manager, he said, "The ninety-six subscribers used in the test have been flooding our offices with complaints." He looked sheepish. "They don't want to go back to the old service and its . . . inferior sound quality."

With that, the Roseville Telephone Company placed an order: one unit for $50,000. Our manufacturing cost: $30,000.

We promised them the first D960 to come off the production line.

Groundbreaking in Novato for DTS building

CHAPTER FORTY EIGHT
Searching for New Technology

The Hawaiian afternoon was warm, even in the shade. Allen Grieve and I had just finished a hard and sweaty tennis match, and now we sat under awnings, sipping beers. Feeling satisfyingly tired and relaxed, I savored the cold liquid gliding down the back of my throat. Although I had no desire to talk business, Allen, a partner at Vanguard Venture Capital, brought up recently passed legislation designed to break up the Bell system monopoly.

"It's all a farce!" Allen erupted. "The Bell system may have been broken into pieces, but it's still business as usual. The little Bells are not acting as independent entities. Bell Labs continue to produce their design work, and Western Electric continues to manufacture products for Bell. The legislation has scarcely made a difference . . . it's as unfair as ever!"

I felt relaxation slip away. "I know what you mean about unfair," I said. "I was at a Bell Lab office in New Jersey several months ago, checking on some network system specifications. On my way out, I happened to glance in one of the lab windows. Something caught my eye, and I peered closer. I couldn't believe what I was seeing. There, sitting in a rack, surrounded by testing equipment, was one of our D960s. The label on it said, "Our Competition."

Allen leaned forward and in a conspiratorial tone asked, "What did you do?"

"I just stood there, shocked and confused. Then I became aware of footsteps behind me and hurried out to the parking lot. By the time I reached my car, disbelief had given way to anger. Bell was planning to steal our designs and become our competition!"

I paused, took a long swallow of my beer, and shook my head in amazement. "Even now I can't believe how unethical Bell was."

Allen drained his beer. "Wow, that's a shock. But you were fortunate in one regard. Better to be surprised now rather than one day seeing their version of your D960 on the market. At least you have some lead time to plan your next move."

"Oh, that ship has sailed," I said, ordering another beer. "Northwestern Bell just cancelled their orders for our D960 because they can now get the equivalent from Western Electric. No surprise there. Bell had only bought from us because we had the technology and Western Electric didn't."

The waiter brought two Dos Equis beers. We drank, then I said, "I've been racking my brain to come up with a new product, but no luck so far. And time is running out. The D960 was our only moneymaker, and DTS won't stay afloat long if we aren't able to create a new product."

Allen was quiet for a moment, then his eyes lit up and he said brightly, "Hey, there's a guy I met recently, name is George May. He's a professor of electrical engineering at the University of British Columbia in Vancouver. He's brilliant, and he's working on some cutting-edge stuff. You should visit him. Who knows, maybe you'll see some technology that could be useful in designing a new product."

"Thanks, Allen. I'll think about it."

* * *

A week later I was sitting at my desk, fretting about the future, when I remembered my conversation with Allen. I called him and I asked him to set up a meeting with his expert, George May.

The following week I walked into George's tiny lab and workshop. Cluttered, with few windows, the effect was claustrophobic. I stood for a minute taking it all in, when seemingly out of nowhere a tall, rangy man with a rather feverish look in his eyes appeared and held out his hand. "You must be Don. I'm George, and welcome to my lab."

Before I could answer, George launched into an extended monologue about a design he was working on—for a spaceship! "The design part is nearly finished," he said proudly. Then in an almost childlike voice: "What do you think?"

What I thought: I've wasted my time coming here. What I said: "I'm sorry, I don't know anything about spaceships." Clinging to a last scrap of hope, I added, "Maybe you could show me some of the other projects you're working on."

For the next hour George did just that. The most intriguing was a device called a time-slot interchanger. I thought it might be useful as a router in a telephone switching system, but I wasn't certain. I made a few notes and told George I'd call if I was interested in anything.

Over the next few days I thought about George's inventions. I kept coming back to the time-slot interchanger. I grew more confident that it could be utilized to create a new product for DTS. I sent David Malloy and Martin Stevenson, two of our most creative circuit designers, to see George. When they returned, they told me the interchanger could be used as the heart of a small Private Branch Xchange (PBX). A PBX is a telephone switching system that provides connections between offices.

Next we had to find out if a market existed for such a product. I put Lee Gendo from our marketing department on the job. He looked at the PBX systems available through telephone companies and concluded they were using old technology. He argued persuasively that indeed there was a market if we upgraded from analog to digital.

A few days later, at a meeting of the DTS management team, we decided we would develop a digital PBX system. We also decided we wanted George May aboard. He'd designed the interchange and was most familiar with its capabilities and function.

I called George and asked if Lee and I could meet with him. George invited us to dinner and we accepted.

George's house was as unusual as he was. The walls were made of compacted earth. His electricity came from solar power, his water from the ocean. It was piped through a reverse-osmosis, desalinization system. I was impressed. Whenever the man could put technology to work, he did.

I also noticed an alarmingly large number of unfinished projects in George's house and all around his property. My image of him as a bit of a mad scientist was supported when he told us he often flew his plane to work, adding, "Once I ran out of gas and was forced to land on a stretch of highway." He laughed. "No, that happened twice."

When Lee and I were headed home, we shared thoughts on George and his ability to fit into the DTS design group. We agreed that George's free-spirited nature, delightful as it was, would not be compatible with the disciplined design team at DTS.

Next day I told George that although we wouldn't be using him as a designer, we'd like to license his time-slot interchanger. I assured him he would receive royalties, and he agreed in principle.

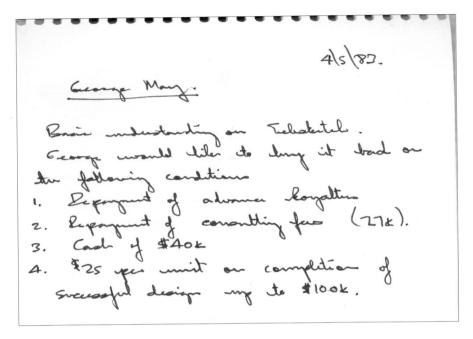

Art of the deal

When we sat down with the attorneys, Mike Halloran, our lawyer, had trouble relating to George. Mike, a no-nonsense kind of guy, wasn't convinced that George understood the contract. "Let's go over each clause, one by one," he said with forced patience.

George brightened, slipped into his spaceship-inventor mode, and said, "There is no need to do that. I have converted all the clauses into Boolean algebra symbols and solved it all mathematically."

Mike's jaw dropped, and he turned to me. "What the hell does that mean?"

I shrugged and asked to see George's notes. I quickly saw that George's math had reduced his percentage of gross product sales from 10 percent to 3 percent.

I took George aside and explained the error of his ways. "That could cost you millions," I said. His attitude was instantly transformed. He realized I'd declined an opportunity to cheat him, and now was oozing with gratitude.

Once the contract was signed, we rose to leave. At the door George took my hand and thanked me again. I thought he'd never let it go.

* * *

Fifteen months later, I sat at my desk and recalled those events. "That was a close one," I thought. "A race against time. With the loss of our D960, DTS desperately needed another product, a big moneymaker. Our survival was at stake, and the PBX was our answer."

And a good one, the first digital PBX in the world. With no competition, sales and profits were growing daily.

I stood, stretched, and said aloud, "I could use another vacation."

CHAPTER FORTY NINE
—————— *Touring with the PBX* ——————

By September 1973, at the end of the PBX design stage, we decided to take our first working system on a European tour. We wanted to introduce DTS, and our new digital, technologically advanced PBX system, to the world. Holding demonstrations of our product was a key part of our marketing strategy. Our PBX had features that no other manufacturer currently offered, and we intended to show the world.

We were able to pack the essential electronics into a case, a cube that measured 26 inches to a side and weighed 62 pounds. This portable packaging, we believed, would allow us to transport our PBX with relative ease.

To accompany me, I chose our vice president of finance, Patrick Hayes. I chose Patrick because he was the youngest and strongest member of the management team. Though we called our cube portable, I knew I'd need help hauling it around.

First stop: Munich, Germany, where Seimens, a large electronics manufacturer, offered its design lab for our demonstration. I politely declined, preferring the relative privacy of a hotel conference room.

The conference room, as it turned out, was located on the third floor. The elevator was a tiny, old-fashioned, open-cage affair. I stared in disbelief at the tiny space, wondering how a four-star hotel could have such an inadequate elevator.

We asked for help, and the hotel sent two bellboys to assist us. One weighed about 250 pounds, and when he stepped into the elevator there was room for nothing else. The other, a little old man, looked wobbly just standing on his own.

We dismissed the larger man and moved to plan B. We would put the PBX in the elevator with the old man sitting on top of it; from there he could reach the buttons. Then Patrick and I would take the stairs and meet the elevator on the third floor.

When the old man was told of the plan, he glared at me, shook his head, and loudly repeated, "Nein, nein!"

I reached into my pocket, withdrew my wallet, and peeled off a twenty-dollar bill. The old man smiled, removed the bill from my hand, and went and sat down on the cube.

* * *

Installing our PBX was much simpler than other available systems. We plugged it into the wall socket and connected four telephones. When we lifted one hand set and dialed the right number, one of the other telephones rang.

The demonstration went well. The twenty or so German engineers we'd invited seemed impressed, but mystified. After my presentation ended, I removed the cloth covering our PBX. How could such a small box of equipment provide such capabilities?

There was a collective gasp of surprise when the engineers saw how few equipment cards it required. They applauded, then asked for another demonstration.

Two hours later, three stretch limos arrived, pouring out curious Seimens engineers who'd come to see our revolutionary system. After the show, we told them we might be interested in licensing the technology, and then left them to consider what they'd seen.

Next stop: Zurich. Upon arrival at the airport, I went to the freight area to wait for our PBX to be unloaded. Suddenly a door opened and four large bags of coffee beans were pushed out, thudding onto the tarmac. "Boy, I hope they don't do that with my—"

And there it flew! Propelled by some unseen force, it sailed through the doorway and landed on the coffee bags, eight feet below. "No-o-o-!" I screamed ineffectually, the sound swallowed by the noise of jet engines.

Nervously, we gathered up the PBX, and Patrick and I headed for our hotel to see what damage had been done. When we unpacked it, we were delighted to see that it had sustained no damage. I smiled and said to Patrick, "Well, at least we know our PBX can pass a crash test."

"Demonstrating its robust mechanical design," he said with some pride.

As a result of our international efforts, we secured licensing agreements in France, Switzerland, Italy, South Africa, Australia, Germany, Mexico, Peru, Chile and the UK.

CHAPTER FIFTY
—— *Independence Lost* ——

By October 1976, DTS employed nearly a thousand people, and its annual sales revenue had grown to $60 million. By everyone's estimation, including my own, DTS was a great success.

These thoughts played in my head as I pulled out of the DTS parking lot and headed for home. As rain drops pelted my windshield, I shivered. I turned on the heater and fantasized about warm climes, silky-sand beaches, swaying palm trees . . .

My lips curved into a smile. "That's it," I thought, "I'll surprise the family with a tropical vacation." Being part of a startup did not lend itself to family vacations; it had been almost two years since our last one.

As soon as I walked in the front door, I was embraced by the alluring aroma of baking bread. Following my nose, I headed for the kitchen. Maureen wasn't at the stove, as I expected, but rather at the phone. She held it out for me, saying only, "It's Allen Grieve."

I kissed Maureen and took the phone. As soon as Allen heard my voice, he launched. "Hey Don, I tried to reach you at work, but you'd already left. I want to give you a heads up."

I could feel my shoulders tighten. "What's going on?"

He hesitated a beat, then said, "I just came from a meeting... Vanguard has decided to dissolve its partnership. All our DTS stock will be sold to the highest bidder, which most likely will be Farinon Electric. Farinon has two divisions, Farinon Electric and Dracon."

I stood in stunned silence, letting the words sink in. Absently, I thanked Allen for calling and hung up the phone. I quickly connected the dots: controlling interest in DTS would soon be in the hands of another company. I could feel my control slipping away.

Vanguard's sale of its DTS stock was certainly a surprise, but the identity of the buyer was not. The previous year, Farinon had purchased some stock in DTS, so its purchase of the newly available shares seemed logical. I was acquainted with the CEO, Bill Farinon, and aware of his idiosyncratic, top-down business philosophy, which rejected managerial input.

I disagreed with that philosophy, but until now I hadn't had to worry about it affecting DTS and its employees. As these thoughts swirled around in my brain, I reminded myself that DTS was prosperous and thus, I reasoned, it was unlikely that Bill Farinon would impose any changes.

Only then did I become aware of Maureen staring at me. "Are you all right? You had a strange look on your face . . ."

Determined not to alarm Maureen, I calmly repeated what Allen had said.

Maureen continued to stare at me. "You would tell me if you were worried about this, wouldn't you?"

"The sale of the stock came as a surprise, that's all. I'm fine. No need for you to worry."

As she opened her mouth to respond, I changed the subject. "As soon as I walked in the door, the smell of your bread baking made my mouth water. When will it be ready? I wanted to steal a warm slice before dinner."

She smiled. "It's almost done. In the meantime I'll make you a cup of tea."

* * *

First thing next morning, I scheduled an all-hands meeting for that afternoon. Once roughly 750 people were settled, I made the announcement.

"The controlling shares of DTS, once owned by Vanguard, will soon be sold to Farinon Electric." I hurried on: "I don't anticipate any management changes and expect business will carry on as usual."

When no one spoke, I broke the silence. "Are there any questions?"

A woman in the front row asked, "How will this sale affect employee-owned company stock?"

I smiled faintly. "Your DTS stock will be exchanged for Farinon stock. And since Farinon stock has been registered and approved by the SEC for sale to the public, you could immediately sell those shares on the NASDAQ exchange."

For the next half hour, I fielded questions as best I could, taking care to keep my tone neutral and my answers positive, whenever possible. Although I privately fretted about Farinon's management style, I felt responsible for employee wellbeing and didn't want to burden them with worries about changes that might never materialize.

Throughout the meeting, I tried to read their faces, looking for signs of stress. No one appeared upset, and I sighed with relief when the meeting ended.

Later that evening, after the other employees had gone home, I met with my management team. Less upbeat now, I shared with them some of my concerns, especially regarding Farinon's management style and company culture.

After an hour of discussion, we concluded that it was pointless to speculate. Try as we might, we couldn't predict the future. We would just have to wait and see.

Driving home that evening, I recalled that a mere twenty-four hours earlier I'd been contemplating a vacation. "Wow," I said, "What a difference a day makes."

CHAPTER FIFTY ONE
—————Looking for a White Knight —————

Three weeks later, standing at the sink, I gulped down the rest of my coffee and stared out the window. I was still rocked by how quickly we—the DTS management team—had lost control of DTS.

Before Vanguard sold its DTS stock to Farinon, DTS management and employees held 40 percent of the company; Vanguard had 40 percent and Farinon 20 percent. We had planned to attract other venture capitalists and eventually raise enough capital to take DTS public—that is, make its shares available to the public on the NASDAQ market. Moreover, we expected that Farinon would use its relatively small percentage of DTS stock purely as a way of diversifying revenue.

Smiling in spite of myself, I thought, Boy, did we get that wrong. It hadn't occurred to us that Farinon would take over.

Now just three weeks later, Farinon owned 60 percent of DTS shares and had no plans to sell. Taking DTS through an Initial Public Offering (IPO) was a goal that I and the other members of the management team would have to abandon.

DTS had become a subsidiary of Farinon Electric.

Looking out the window but seeing nothing, I said, "Well, at least I'd been right in my initial assumption that Bill Farinon wouldn't interfere with the management of an already-profitable company." Once the acquisition of DTS was final, he had named me president of the DTS division of Farinon Electric, and left us to carry on as usual.

Sensing a presence, I turned from the sink and saw Zack, our black lab, leash in mouth, his pleading eyes boring holes in me. When I took the leash from his mouth, I noticed for the first time how grey his muzzle had become. As I clipped the leash to Zack's collar, his body shook with excitement. Then, with the zeal of a puppy, he dashed toward the front door, pulling me with him.

As Zack took me for a walk, I continued to dwell on the Farinon debacle. Shortly after the purchase of DTS, Bill Farinon had retired from daily management. He set off to fly around the world with his wife and another couple in his remodeled seaplane. When he left, Farinon Electric was profitable, and its publicly traded shares were considered a solid investment.

The Board of Directors chose Mike Fridenbach as Bill Farinon's replacement. Previously chief financial officer, he was now CEO and president of the full company. Unfortunately, Mike had limited experience in general management and even less in engineering. When things began to fall apart shortly after Bill Farinon's departure, Mike was ill equipped to pinpoint the problem, let alone deal with it effectively.

To be fair to Mike, the problem—Bill Farinon's business philosophy—had been there all along; it became apparent only after senior staff members began to retire.

Bill Farinon was a believer in a management philosophy espoused by Robert Anderson in a book entitled *Up the Organization*. Anderson asserted that everybody in management was doing it wrong. Following Anderson's advice, Bill happily removed all job descriptions and titles, increasing the chances of miscommunication. He also eliminated all private offices, eliminated executive parking spots, slashed the purchasing department, and granted more freedom to salespeople to set prices, which was like putting the fox in the chicken coop.

Although everyone, including Bill, believed they were following this new philosophy, it was only partially true. Despite the absence of formal job descriptions and titles, employees who had worked together for years continued to communicate well with each other. On the other hand, new employees, who lacked this experience, struggled with communication problems and murky job descriptions. This resulted in loss of control and departments exceeding budgets.

When the Farinon founding members began to retire, they took their hidden management with them. When new people came aboard, they were lost. The result was a breakdown in communication, uncertainty about job duties, ill-defined responsibilities, and increased costs. Significant errors were made in foreign exchange rates and the granting of discounts, leading to a loss of accountability.

The Farinon stock price took a dive, then continued to drop. The board members came to believe that predator companies were sniffing around and that the weakened financial state of Farinon made the company vulnerable to a hostile takeover.

Bill Farinon cut short his global travels, returned, and took back the reins. He called an emergency meeting of managers from Farinon's three divisions: Farinon Electric, DTS, and Dracon, the latter a small but profitable plastic-molding company.

I arrived early for the meeting, but when I entered the conference room, twenty men were already seated around a large walnut table. Immediately engulfed in cigar smoke, I wondered how long I'd be stuck there.

As soon as I was seated, Bill Farinon stood and began pacing, his small, wiry frame vibrating with energy. As he spoke, his sallow complexion turned red. He spent ten minutes restating his business philosophy. I couldn't believe what I was hearing.

This egotist didn't have a clue that those exact policies were what had landed his company in trouble in the first place.

After fifteen more minutes of exalting the virtues of his business philosophy, he went on to heap blame for Farinon's recent difficulties on its current managers. I sensed panic in the air. He raised his nasal voice and said, "You guys gotta stop pissing in the soup and start working harder!"

An uncomfortable silence enveloped the room. I shot glances at the others. Most, including Mike Fridenbach, had lowered their eyes and were earnestly studying the table.

Disgusted by Farinon's off-target rant, I mustered an even tone and said, "Bill, sorry to interrupt, but perhaps a careful analysis of the problem should be done so that we can find the right solution."

Bill stopped moving and stared at me, an incredulous look on his face. At first he said nothing, his face turning a new, darker shade of red. Then a thin smile creased his enraged face and he replied, "Don, we've been a successful company for fifteen years, with a management structure in place that produced outstanding results and profits, making many people very wealthy. So I don't agree. A careful analysis is a waste of valuable time!"

That was too much. I said, "The company is currently held together by Scotch tape and bailing wire. It's being supported financially by DTS and Dracon, both of which are performing significantly better than the mother ship." I stood up and headed for the door. "It doesn't sound like we're on a path that will allow me to contribute much, so I'll be going."

As soon as I stepped outside, a sense of relief came over me. It felt good to speak my piece without losing my temper.

The following weeks other management meetings were held; I did not attend any of those meetings. Bill Farinon announced that since management could not agree on how to solve the company's problems, the hunt was on for a "white knight," someone to buy Farinon before profits eroded further.

A white knight company buys other companies with the intention of keeping them intact. This is in contrast to predator types who buy companies in a weakened financial state, then sell them off piece by piece, like dismantling a car and selling its parts.

Once the decision had been made, I did my part, earnestly looking for the most appealing white knight company. After all, the future of DTS depended on the quality of that company.

One being considered was Harris Company. Harris, a Fortune 500 company, had a good reputation. It included five major business divisions and owned about thirty smaller companies in various markets.

During subsequent meetings I quietly but enthusiastically endorsed Harris as our white knight savior—and it worked. Farinon and its subsidiaries, DTS and Dracon, became part of the Harris Corporation.

CHAPTER FIFTY TWO
—— *Goodbye Harris, Hello Optilink* ——

For seven years, my life as a Harris executive was relatively smooth. Unlike Farinon Electric, with its odd management style, Harris/DTS, as we were now called, fitted well into the Harris corporate culture.

"Who are these people?"

Then things began to change. Meetings were held for managers in all the divisions under Harris. Reviews were conducted, and a strategy for all the companies under the Harris umbrella was developed. This included long-term and short-term goals.

It was explained that the performance of all the companies under Harris would be measured by a quarterly review of the balance sheet, and essentially nothing else. That made me squirm. Experience told me that it didn't make sense to compare a small-scale business entity such as DTS, whose sales contracts and revenue may fluctuate month to month, with a company holding steady long-term contracts with the military. Such a company's monthly balance sheet saw little fluctuation.

While walking to my car after the meeting, I concluded, "This method of evaluation is a potential problem for all the divisions under Harris lacking long-term military contracts."

As the months passed, I saw my assumption confirmed. The result: heavy management turnover in the nondefense divisions.

A few months later, at another meeting, they announced a reorganization of the DTS division. This reorganization would likely redirect responsibility for our international sales to a newly formed international division. My job was about to change.

Sitting there, I wanted to shout, "Much of the success that DTS has enjoyed over the years is not only due to the superior products we produce, but to the relationships we've forged with our customers over the years!" I knew, of course, that nothing I said would change a thing; however, I still wrote Jack Davis, division manager, one last memo.

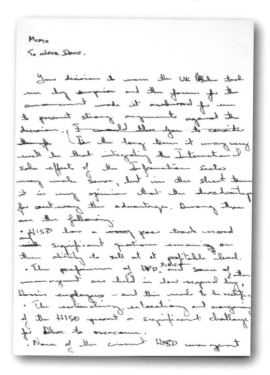

An attempt to influence organization changes

Driving home that evening, I felt an unprecedented weariness. Sure, I'd been physically and mentally exhausted before, working doggedly on a project, but this felt different, mental as well as physical.

I knew the proposed change would make it more difficult, maybe impossible, for DTS to meet Harris's objectives. I also knew that nothing I did would change the situation, and that was the source of the weariness I was feeling . . . lack of hope.

Sitting at a red light, I made a decision: I would retire. For the first time in my professional career, I didn't feel compelled to set my sights on a new goal. After all, I was 55 years old, old enough to retire.

The sound of a blaring car horn brought me back; the light had turned green. As I accelerated through the intersection, I smiled and thought, "Now I'll have plenty of time for choir, tennis, and bird watching.

Tom, Duncan and Don enjoying the sporty life

* * *

I soon discovered that my tennis partners were at work during the week, and choir and bird watching weren't enough to keep me occupied. I spent a lot of time wondering what I was going to do with myself.

Then one day, while sitting on my Tiburon deck, I received a phone call from Dave Shelly, a venture capitalist I knew. "I just heard you retired from Harris, and I called to see if you had time to check out a new startup telecommunications company. My venture capital partnership is considering investing in it, but none of the partners is technologically savvy enough to evaluate the market or the company."

I laughed. "Well, since my biggest task for the day is taking my dog Zack for a walk, I guess I could find the time to look into it "

In a relieved voice, he said, "That's great, Don. We really need your expertise."

A week later I met with the founders of the company, four engineers. After talking with them for two hours, I concluded that although they knew their technology very well, they lacked the management experience to make the company a success.

In my report, I stated that unless they acquired someone with management experience, I would not advise investing in the company.

Within a month, word had gotten around that I was available for consulting work, and I quickly had a pile of business proposals on my desk for review. After consulting on half a dozen venture opportunities, I asked myself if this was what I wanted to do, and the answer was NO.

It occurred to me that the missing ingredient in most of the business plans I'd reviewed was the same: business and management experience. "What those companies need," I decided, "is someone experienced, like me."

I went back through the pile of business plans, this time from a different perspective. I led with a question: "If I added myself to the management team, would it make success more likely?"

One business plan that caught my interest was from two engineers named Pinsky and Brown. They produced a multipurpose data switch that I believed could be refined and utilized in the telecom industry. Before contacting them, I wanted to have the technology checked by experts. I called two design engineers, David Malloy and Tom Eames, and asked them to review the technology and its limitations.

Several weeks later Tom and David called with their analysis. They believed the switch needed some modest changes to its architecture in order to serve the purpose I envisioned, as a large-capacity voice-data switch.

During my research, I learned that the line concentrator market had grown dramatically. In fact, one out of three telephone lines in the world was connected to a central office using a line concentrator with an architecture identical to the twenty-year-old D960.

I made a proposition to Pinsky and Brown: "I'm interested in procuring your technology and forming a company to develop a product that would be based on some of your system ideas. I haven't raised any capital yet. I plan to pay for the technology using shares in the new company I'm forming."

For a moment neither spoke, and I found I was holding my breath.

Pinsky and Brown eventually agreed to the arrangement, and I felt a tingle of excitement travel up my spine. Here I go again, I thought.

I recruited several engineers. One was Al Negrin, my associate at Harris, who helped me write the business plan for our new company, which we decided to call Optilink. Soon we would have a new product, the Litespan2000.

I was back in the saddle again.

Dave Loby, me, Bob Law, John Kurn, Al Negrin, and a consultant

Elegance in motion

CHAPTER FIFTY THREE
Doing Time

While attending church one Sunday—All Saints Episcopal—I sat listening to our guest speaker with great interest. He was a small, graceful man with piercing eyes and a pleasant voice.

"The primary mission of our program is to lower the recidivism rate in our country's prisons," he said. "After interviewing hundreds of prisoners, I've concluded the primary reason prisoners return is that they have not been prepared for life in a free society. While incarcerated their focus is on one thing and one thing only: their day-to-day survival!"

He paused, looked out into the congregation, and his eyes met mine. I looked away. I was doing my best to see myself in the shoes of a prisoner, and contemplating such a primal level of existence made me feel uncomfortable.

He went on to talk about prison life, focusing on our local prison, San Quentin. He explained that his organization had a program that allowed a select group of prisoners to meet with people on the outside. "It achieves two purposes," he said. "First, it helps socialize the prisoners, making the transition to mainstream society easier. Second, the volunteer becomes more aware of what prison life is like and the types of changes needed within our prison system."

His eyes again met mine. "Here's your chance to make a contribution to your local community, to your fellow man, and to society as a whole."

Before our speaker left that morning, I told him I'd like to participate.

Two weeks later I received a letter stating that I'd been assigned a prisoner and could start as soon as my schedule permitted. Visiting hours were from 10:00 to 1:00.

I made arrangements to meet my prisoner. On the appointed day I pulled into the prison parking lot at 10:00 am, anxious to get started. As I got out of the car I noticed a small booth in front of the entrance. I headed in that direction and showed the guard there my letter and identification.

He studied my driver's license and letter, and then me. His mouth was set in a permanent scowl, and his eyes looked cold and threatening as he stared at me. Then he pointed and growled, "Go through that gate and get in line."

Happy to leave his presence, I walked quickly toward the gate. Once through the gate, I found the end of the line. I felt like a cow heading for the slaughterhouse. We were enclosed by ten-foot-tall chain link fences topped by razor wire. In the back of my mind I could hear a faint voice saying, "Are you sure you want to do this?"

To distract myself, I scrutinized the others in line: about twenty adults and a few children, a mix of races, mostly black and white. The grownups tended to be women in their twenties and thirties. No one was making eye contact; not wanting to offend anyone, I followed suit.

The line moved slowly because everyone had to be frisked, and nearly an hour later I was led into the visitors' room. The room suggested a large cage, stark and bare, with maybe fifteen tables and fifty chairs scattered about. Most of the seats were already taken by the visitors ahead of me in line. I was instructed to sit at the only remaining empty table and wait for my prisoner.

After many more minutes of waiting, I became aware of my

rising anger. I took a deep breath and considered why. Then it hit me: being in this prison was like entering another dimension, where one's normal relationship with time and the expected rules of civilized social conduct did not apply. Here, time was not an asset or a resource, but rather a powerful weapon the authorities used against the inmates, a constant reminder of who was in control.

Finally, a few prisoners in blue denim shuffled in. They quickly found their family or friends and sat down at other tables. At a nearby table a short, heavily muscled white man with a shaved head greeted a young woman and a small boy. The boy, maybe three years old, smiled and clutched the man's leg and shouted, "Daddy, Daddy, Daddy!"

Seeing that the man was not going to respond, the boy's mother reached down and gently pulled the boy's grasping fingers from his father's pants and sat him down in one of the three chairs that surrounded the table. The man sat down in the remaining chair, his eyes staring off into the distance, his expression blank.

I covertly looked around to see how the others were interacting. Most inmates were at least talking to their visitors, but few made eye contact; the expression on their faces could best be described as guarded.

The room grew heavy with the weight of repressed emotion, and I had to fight the urge to get up and leave. At last a guard and a large black man arrived at my table. The guard silently retreated to his place by the door; the black man held out his hand and in a voice incongruously high for such a large man, said, "Hi, my name is John Adams, but everyone just calls me Sweetpea."

Until now I'd forced myself to follow the unspoken rule of no direct eye contact, but it seemed rude not to look at a man when shaking his hand. I was surprised to see that Sweetpea was returning my gaze, and smiling. I introduced myself, and as we sat down I looked directly over Sweetpea's shoulder at the oversized clock on the far wall. We had an hour left for our visit.

We chatted about the program, and then I asked Sweetpea if he'd mind telling me a little about himself. He offered sparse details, so I asked why he was in San Quentin. He said, "Oh you know, man, you do stupid stuff. And that's what I did, somethin' stupid . . . I stole a car."

It didn't add up. I doubted that a single car theft would land someone in a high-level security prison like San Quentin. Besides, I knew that Sweetpea was not housed with the general population, but instead was in protective custody, something else a car theft wouldn't normally warrant.

I resisted the urge to say, "Do you think I'm completely gullible?!" Instead I smiled and asked, "Why do they call you Sweetpea?"

"It's because of my voice, and, you know, they's always wantin' me to sing to them. I do when I'm in the mood."

Then he smiled, his large white teeth gleaming, and said, "I know that through this program visitors are allowed to bring prisoners stuff . . . like cigarettes and gum. Me and my friends sure could use some of those things."

Again I smiled and tried to change the subject. But Sweetpea kept up his campaign to get me to agree to bring him "stuff."

I began to doubt the effectiveness of this program. Clearly Sweetpea saw me only as his personal Santa. Just then a buzzer sounded, indicating that our visiting time was up. As Sweetpea rose to leave, I heard myself promising that I would be back to visit in two weeks.

My next visit went slightly better than the first, mostly because I knew what to expect. The wasted time was undiminished, however: two hours of waiting, one hour of visiting.

Sweetpea again pressed me to bring him some things. I tried to change the subject, but he was relentless. Finally I said in a firm voice, "I am not a personal Santa for you and your friends, so can we please talk about something else?"

Showing no sign of resentment, he said, "Sure, man, what do you wanna talk about?"

Feeling relieved, I asked, "Do you like sports—say, baseball or football?"

He did, and we discussed the 49ers and Giants for a while. I thought we had made some progress, but at the end of our visit, he renewed his request, upping the ante. "Man, I could really use some sunglasses. Ray Bans would be nice."

As he headed toward the door, I told him that would not be possible.

Despite my irritation, I kept participating, visited Sweetpea maybe ten times. Although I wasn't sure how much benefit Sweetpea was deriving from it, I'm not easily deterred once I commit to something. I wanted to make a difference, though I wasn't sure what that meant.

Then one day I got a call at home from Sweetpea. As he spoke, I stood there in the kitchen, shaking my head in disbelief, wondering: how did he get my number?

I was pulled from my reverie when he said, "Now next visit, don't forget to bring those Ray Bans I want."

Striving to sound nonchalant, I asked, "How did you get my number, Sweetpea? It's unlisted."

He chuckled. "If you got money, or if people owe you favors, you can get just about anything you want in here. You dig, man?"

Deciding not to push it, I promised to visit, said nothing about the sunglasses, and hung up. My mind racing, I calculated that since I lived in Tiburon, Sweetpea was only five miles away, way too close for comfort. I decided then and there that I would no longer participate in the program. I couldn't expose myself or my family to the risk.

Tiburon house after renovation

Before I could follow through, one of the program's administrators called me the next day. "I have bad news," he said. "Sweetpea has been transferred to Folsom prison, 150 miles away. We've assigned you a new inmate, if you want to continue to participate in the program."

I managed a laugh, and then explained about the call I'd gotten from Sweetpea the day before. "No, I do not wish to continue."

The program administrator was shocked to hear about the call. He said he would pass on the information to his supervisor, then he thanked me for my participation and hung up.

I made a cup of tea and sat thinking about my time at the prison. Despite the unnerving phone call from Sweetpea, I was glad I'd participated. Although nothing about the experience had been especially pleasant, it had provided me with a broader perspective on our society, on humanity, and a greater appreciation for my own freedom.

CHAPTER FIFTY FOUR
Optilink

We recruited a team of design engineers and raised enough capital to begin development of our new product, the Litespan2000. It was a complex switching system that allowed larger amounts of information to be sent and received more efficiently and with greater flexibility.

It was 1986, and the telephone industry was just beginning to employ similar systems in its infrastructure. My partners and I concluded that in light of this technological evolution, the development and release of our product was well timed.

Unfortunately, when we went looking for the second round of investors, conditions in the financial markets were not as favorable. The VC market had become more conservative, and investors were reluctant to take a chance on us and our new product. This forced us to try to find alternative sources of capital.

We asked engineers from Bell Systems to give us an informal analysis of our product, in the hopes that they might be interested in buying it. They concluded that they liked the product, but couldn't take the risk of deploying a product of such strategic importance from a company with such an immature balance sheet.

We had in-depth discussions with Seimens, Alcatel, and several other large companies, but none was willing to move at the pace we needed, leaving us financially strapped.

I was growing increasingly worried about Optilink's survival.

Then one day we were approached by a midsized company called DSC. DSC made an offer to buy Optilink.

I discussed the merits of the offer with my partners and Optilink cofounder Al Negrin.

We agreed that the offer, which involved a complex stock swap, was generous. We also liked that all our employees would retain their jobs. In fact, I'd been asked to stay on and continue to manage the day-to-day operations of Optilink for two years.

I argued that the offer was the answer to Optilink's financial problems. Al agreed, and three days later the sale was completed.

That evening as I was driving home, I found myself smiling, humming along with the radio music, and feeling more relaxed than I had in weeks. Then a disturbing question skipped across the placid surface of my mind, causing a ripple of uneasiness.

What if the company culture of DSC and Optilink were vastly different? I realized that I should have done more research. Given our desperation to save the company and DSC's tight time frame, we felt compelled to act in haste. Well, no use worrying about it now, I thought. Tomorrow was my first day on the new job, and I would soon know the truth.

     * * *

My first duty was to have lunch with the CEO of DSC, Jim Donald, in his private dining room. I can do that, I thought. Anxious to meet with my new boss, I arrived fifteen minutes early and presented myself to his secretary.

As I approached her desk, she glanced up from her paperwork and with a puzzled look on her face asked, "May I help you?"

I smiled and said, "Hi, my name is Don Green. I have a noon meeting with Jim Donald."

Her face relaxed. "Oh, yes. You need to see Miss Ross, Mr. Donald's secretary. I'm Miss Bonner, Miss Ross's secretary." She gestured toward the large oak doors directly behind her desk. "Please go in. She's expecting you."

It was my turn to look puzzled—his secretary had a secretary! —but I said nothing. Smiling once more at Miss Bonner, I went through the double doors.

The office was large and elegantly furnished, with an oversized mahogany desk and subdued, recessed lighting. Along the left wall sat a long leather couch and an antique coffee table decorated with inlaid wood. I had the strangest sensation that I'd just stepped into Boodle's, or some other English men's club. I half expected to be offered a brandy and cigar.

Miss Ross quickly dispelled that fantasy when she rose from her desk and said in a no-nonsense voice, "You must be Mr. Green. You're early, and Mr. Donald never sees anyone before the appointed time. Please be seated."

Then she returned to her work, sifting through a file that lay before her. Pools of light cascaded down from the two banker's lamps that sat on opposite sides of her desk. As I sat and waited, I stole glances at her. In her late-fifties, I estimated. Her white hair was pulled back into a tight bun.

Just as I glanced at my watch and saw that it was noon, Miss Ross said, "It's time now, Mr. Green. You may go in."

She stood up and motioned for me to follow her. She led me into the next room, which held a pair of chairs and appeared to be a waiting room of sorts. In front of us were three doors. Miss Ross approached the door on the far right, opened it, stood to one side, and said, "This is Mr. Donald's private dining room. Go in, have a seat, and he will join you in a moment."

I did as I was told. Without another word, she closed the door, leaving me alone. Where to sit? Five large round tables were scattered about, each covered in snowy white linen and set with elegant china, crystal stemware, and gleaming silver.

Suddenly I felt the presence of someone else in the room. I turned and there before me stood Jim Donald. He was about my height, just over six feet tall, but his build was less substantial. His dark, close-set eyes were slightly hooded, his sharp nose somewhat beaky.

As I reached out my hand to shake his, I couldn't decide who he reminded me of more: Jack Nicholson in *The Shining*, or a large bird of prey. In either case, he appeared to be a man under pressure, with fists slightly clenched and a smile that suggested a grimace.

We shook hands and he said, "Let's get started with lunch, and while we eat I'll fill you in on my company."

In contrast to the elegant setting, our meal was a homage to Jim Donald's home state of Texas. It featured barbecued brisket, beans, slaw, and a basket of Wonder Bread.

As we ate, he did his best to present a glowing history of DSC, highlighting successes and minimizing any failures. For over an hour he went on about how DSC had flourished under his masterful management. He ended his tribute by saying, "And that is why DSC's revenue growth is so strong, and why we are a major supplier for the telephone industry."

Jim asked me no questions and did nothing to include me in the conversation. I left thinking that my new boss had the biggest ego, I'd ever encountered. Dealing with him on any level would be a challenge.

The following day, when I stopped by Jim's office to drop off some paperwork, my impressions were confirmed. As I entered his secretary's office, the frosty Miss Ross narrowed her eyes and said, "I see you are wearing a blue shirt. Mr. Donald doesn't like blue shirts."

Stunned, I handed her my paperwork and started to leave. Then, impulsively, I turned back and said, "Then I hope he doesn't buy any."

By the end of the day, seemingly every DSC employee had heard about the exchange. Jim was not pleased, I was told. That's lesson number one, I thought: Jim Donald has no sense of humor.

* * *

Family group, 1985

The following week I was to attend my first management meeting. I figured it would give me a chance to gain a better understanding of Jim Donald's management style. The first item on the agenda was an announcement outlining company objectives. It included a large-scale purchasing plan that Jim Donald and his staff had prepared for the following year.

I couldn't believe what I was hearing. If the company implemented the purchasing plan, the obvious result would be a surge of inventory. And these objectives had been created without input from the line management team. Clearly, Jim Donald favored a top-down process.

Unable to contain myself, I stood and said, "I haven't had enough time to look at the impact, but if we come up short on the revenues side it will put great pressure on our cash reserves."

An uncomfortable silence enveloped us. I scanned the room and saw lowered eyes. No one was looking at me except Jim Donald.

The crimson flush in his face and the tightly clenched fists suggested rage, and I braced for the explosion. He said nothing. The silence stretched on, broken only by the ticking of the wall clock.

Finally he spoke through clenched teeth, his manner suggesting someone struggling to keep control of himself. "I expect you..." He paused, pointing his finger at me like a gun. "... to perform your duties as you're told and not concern yourself with any other portion of the business plan!"

Before I could respond, he said, "Let's move on to the next item on the agenda."

I took my seat, thinking, Lesson number two: Never disagree with Jim Donald unless prepared to pay the price.

I had to keep that lesson uppermost in my mind because one of my mandatory duties as a consultant was to attend those meetings every week. I found them supremely annoying—no exchange of ideas, just listening to other managers reporting to Jim—and they took a big bite out of my workweek.

Since the DSC corporate office was in Texas, a four-hour flight from my home in California, I'd spend Mondays flying to Texas, attend the meeting, and then fly home on Tuesdays. That meant I didn't even step foot in the Optilink office until Wednesday morning.

Flying home after the third meeting, I found myself gnashing my teeth. "Well, there goes another meeting in which none of the information disseminated had any relevance to Optilink.

That evening as I drifted off to sleep, I told myself, "Just be patient."

* * *

As I hung up the phone a week later, I had to remind myself of the virtues of patience. I'd just spoken with Miss Ross, Jim Donald's secretary, and my mind was still whirling as I replayed the conversation in my head.

She had informed me that "Mr. Donald will be visiting your facility next Wednesday. He will need two limousines, which must be driven on the tarmac to meet the company plane. One of the limousines will be for Mr. Donald's exclusive use—he prefers to ride alone—and the second will be for his entourage. The temperature of the car must be set to 68 degrees. His hotel room must have a king-size bed and—"

"Why are you telling me these things?" I interrupted. "You should be talking to my secretary. I'll transfer you."

Lesson number three: Jim Donald is inflexible.

* * *

My employment contract with DSC was for two years. During that time, I could be fired only for cause and I was restricted from working for any other tech company. I avoided dealing with Jim Donald as much as possible, looking forward to the date when I would be free.

One afternoon, eighteen months into my contract, two security guards and a man in a black suit entered my office at Optilink. I looked up from an engineering blueprint and said, "Yes, what can I do for you?"

The man in the black suit was vice president of human resources. He did the talking but refused to meet my eyes. While looking at the floor, he said, "I'm sorry, Don, but I'm here to relieve you of your DSC duties. I have been sent to inform you that Mr. Donald no longer requires your services. We are here to escort you off the premises. You will be allowed to return after five, to retrieve your personal items from this office."

I reached for my jacket that hung over the back of my chair and followed the men out. Numb at first, I soon felt a mix of anger and relief. I was angered by the lack of integrity, the absence of professionalism, the personal insult—but also relieved to be away from this madman.

I opened the front door, stepped outside, took a deep breath, felt the sun shining on my face, and smiled. Just as I was about to get in my car, I saw John Webley and Jim Hoeck, two old friends and employees of mine. They were now contract engineers for DSC.

John saw me, waved me over, and said, "We just heard about your termination. I'm sorry, Don."

I smiled. "News certainly does travel fast. Well, don't feel bad. I don't. I'm not going to miss Jim Donald, his ego, or the endless flights to Texas."

Jim asked, "What are you going to do now?"

"I'm sure I'll find plenty to do. Something always seems to appear to keep me occupied."

John smiled. "As a matter of fact, we've been working on

something we think you might find interesting."

"I'm intrigued already."

We arranged to meet a few days later. Driving home, I thought, "This has been quite an eventful day."

* * *

Before long John, Jim, and I had formed a fruitful partnership. We called our new company Advanced Fibre Communications (AFC) and our new product the UMC1000. It was a switching system; in tech-speak, a digital loop carrier. Using newer technology, it was an improved version of the D960. We seemed to have a winner.

CHAPTER FIFTY FIVE
AFC Fitted for a Lawsuit

I'll never forget the date: August 31, 1993. I was in the middle of a staff meeting when my secretary, Dolores Woodburn, entered and handed me an envelope. "I'm sorry to interrupt, Mr. Green, but this was just delivered by a process server. I thought it might be important."

I nodded. Mrs. Woodburn was known to me as a woman of sound judgment. I glanced up at her, trying to read her expression. She just stared down at the official-looking document. I read the sender's address: "The United States District Court for the Eastern District of Texas." I felt a ripple of foreboding pass through me.

I sighed and said to my staff, "Let's take a break, and I'll see what this document is about."

The document was four pages of legalese, but with effort I was able to grasp its meaning. I sat there for a moment staring at the pages in my hand. Disbelief and shock were soon replaced by anger.

I called the staff back in. As they found their seats, I could hear the murmured question: "Is it good news or bad news?"

Once I had their attention, I held up the letter and announced, "DSC is suing us. They claim AFC has stolen their trade secrets and intellectual property." The room erupted in snorts of disbelief that soon turned to fear.

As I drove home that evening, I chewed on the problem. The news could not have come at a worse time: we were close to finalizing the third round of investments from our VC group. The likelihood of venture capitalists ignoring the lawsuit was close to zero; they were not inclined to fund lawsuits. It seemed our careful financial planning was about to blow up in our face.

I called our lawyers and gave them the news. Besides AFC, four individuals were named in the suit: John Webley, cofounder; Al Negrin, Vice President of Operations; Henri Sulzer, International Sales Manager and cofounder of AFC; and me.

I faxed a copy of the summons to our attorneys, waited thirty minutes, then phoned them to get their assessment of the strengths and weaknesses of DSC's case. Although a thorough analysis would take a day or two, they said suits like this are common. Large companies often sue employees who start "new product" companies. I was told, "DSC may be using the law to remove competition."

After hanging up, I sat for a moment, building my nerve for what lay ahead. I took a deep breath and called our lead VC investor, BJ Cassin, to deliver the bad news. No sooner had I summarized the case when BJ responded, his voice crackling with anger. "DSC is trying to put us out of business! Well, they're not going to get away with it!"

"I'm happy to hear you say that, BJ."

BJ was still vehement. "You know, they recently did this same thing with another rival company. They eliminated the competition by using a legal battle to drain the company of its assets."

I couldn't help but smile. I pictured BJ, his wiry frame all wound up, his already florid complexion turning from red to purple.

He continued, "Keep working hard, Don. Don't let this distract you. Work with the lawyers on a counterattack! In my time, I've experienced just about every imaginable problem. So help me, we're not going to let them ruin our business with their baseless claims!"

Though relieved by BJ's passion and optimism, I knew not all of the investors would be so supportive, and I was right.

What followed was a series of meetings between me and the VC investors. I had four weeks to convince them they should continue with their plans to invest in AFC. I decided to go with full disclosure, total honesty—and to remind them, repeatedly, of the great progress we'd made. It took time and effort, but I finally persuaded them all to continue with the funding.

There was one caveat. None of the VC funding could be used to pay legal bills. That meant we had to squeeze more out of the fund earmarked for product development. It all translated into tight budgets and long working days. Fortunately, our employees were a loyal and dedicated group; they would rise to the challenge. Of course, they had an added incentive: keeping the company afloat. They liked their jobs, and what's more they were shareholders. This lawsuit could be the kiss of death for AFC, but we were all united and not giving up without a fight.

* * *

The first phase of our battle plan was to file a countersuit claiming DSC violated antitrust laws with its frivolous and baseless lawsuit. Its true objective, we argued, was to destroy our business by draining our company of assets and discouraging investors.

Next we filed a motion for change of venue. The suit had been filed in Marshall, Texas, which just happened to be the hometown of Jim Donald, CEO of DSC. Donald was obviously counting on a home-court advantage, including a biased jury. Additionally, they named three "non-Americans," presumably hoping that a Marshall jury would be biased against foreigners. John Webley was from South Africa, Henri Sulzer from France, and I was from the UK.

We filed a motion for change of venue to move the trial to Sonoma County, where both AFC and DSC were located. Saddling AFC with travel and hotel expenses would help DSC achieve its goal of forcing us to spend all of our money on legal fees before completing our product development.

After waiting months for a ruling, we learned our motion to move the case to California had been granted. We barely had time to celebrate. DSC filed an appeal, and two weeks later the change-of-venue decision was overturned. We would have to defend our company on Jim Donald's turf.

I was grateful not to have to take the time and effort to search for a law firm to defend our interests in the upcoming suit. AFC already employed a prestigious law firm, Brobeck, Phleger & Harrison. Our usual lawyers, specialists in commercial law, were replaced by a team of litigators specializing in trial law.

AFC's lawyers hailed from both California and Texas. In all, at least a dozen people contributed to our defense. The lead attorneys were Brock Gowdy, team leader and chief strategist; Rollin Chippey, second in command; Ron Wynn, litigator strategist; and Hopkins Guy, trial attorney and technical expert. Advising us was a retired Chief Justice of the Texas Supreme Court. He was especially helpful with Texas's interpretation of antitrust laws.

The image we would present was of a small startup company struggling for commercial life, marshalling every resource available to us to defend ourselves and the integrity of our name. I believed we had right on our side, as well as experienced, capable lawyers. What's more, I liked that our two lead lawyers,

Brock Gowdy and Rollin Chippey, were exceptionally tall. Former college basketball stars both, Brock was six-foot-eight, Rollin six-foot-nine. They would be an imposing presence in the courtroom.

* * *

The rules of discovery allowed each side virtually unlimited access to the files of the opponent. Ron Wynn was the first of our lawyers to pore over DSC documents. To his surprise, he found photocopies of AFC's documents. The trove included letters and memos regarding AFC's finances, capital-raising plans, and product details. They had provided DSC with the information it needed to inflict maximum damage on the financial stability of AFC.

Some of the AFC documents had what appeared to be garbage stains. We soon learned why. In the eighteen months AFC had been in business, our trash had been systematically gone through. A retired San Francisco police chief turned private investigator had been hired by DSC. Once a week, in the middle of the night, he climbed into our fenced garbage area and collected every piece of paper in the AFC dumpster. He took the garbage bags to his client's office, photocopied anything of interest, and then carefully returned the bags to the dumpster.

When Ron told me this, I was silent for a moment. Finally I sputtered, "This is . . . almost unbelievable. Can they really be this unethical . . . not to mention illegal?" I felt new resolve steel my spine. "If DSC thinks we're just going to roll over, they better think again. We'll fight them with all we've got!"

* * *

We took an aggressive and proactive approach, trying to anticipate every issue. We hired a jury consultant. We conducted a mock trial in Longview, Texas, a town twenty-five miles from Marshall. In this way, we tested our case before a mock jury that was typical of the community. We received feedback on the strengths and weaknesses of the case, allowing the lawyers to modify their strategy before the actual trial.

When I returned home after the mock trial, Maureen greeted me with a kiss, a scotch, and a question. "Well, what did you learn?"

"I found out I'm less likeable than I thought."

* * *

In response to DSC's dumpster-diving operations, Brock filed antitrust, trade-secret theft, and other counterclaims against DSC. That put DSC on the defensive. Then we learned that, besides dumpster-diving, DSC had tried another type of espionage. They sent a private investigator to our office, masquerading as a VC investor, in order to glean information about AFC's product development. Lucky for us, Dolores had a keen eye and turned him away.

Before the trial opened, the attorneys prepared the witnesses, asking us questions likely to be asked in court. They advised us on appearance, mannerisms, anything that might influence the jury's response to a witness and thus to our case.

Henri Sulzer was a sophisticated international sales executive, fluent in seven languages, had a PhD in chemical engineering and a degree in accounting. Henri raised red flags when first questioned by Rollin, as he came across as a condescending Frenchman. After Henri was coached for two days, however, he was magically transformed into a charming, elderly French peasant worried about his pension.

* * *

When we arrived in Marshall in late June, waves of heat could be seen shimmering up off the asphalt. The largest hotel in town was closed, its windows boarded up, and many of the businesses that lined the main street looked in similar disrepair. With a population of 25,000, Marshall was a comatose east-Texas town that had seen better economic days. I glanced around for signs of life, but tumbleweeds provided the only movement. It reminded me of a ghost town in a Western movie.

We were relieved to find a large Victorian Bed & Breakfast that could accommodate our group. With Maureen along, we numbered seven.

Marshall boarding house, defense headquarters

* * *

It was already muggy-hot next morning as Maureen and I walked up the courthouse steps. I thought, here we go, AFC's fate will be decided inside those doors. Just then Dan Boyd, lead counsel for DSC, dashed past me. He sidled up to a man a few feet ahead of us, clasped his shoulder, and said in a loud voice, "So nice to see you again, Judge Folsom." Then, stealing a glance back at me, he smiled.

I smiled back—or was it a grimace? —and thought, you can't intimidate me. I've done nothing wrong and we're about to prove it.

* * *

In his opening statement, Brock reviewed the evidence and concluded, eloquently and persuasively, that DSC's complaint was a sham. AFC, he said, would show major differences between the UMC1000 and the Litespan2000.

David Ereth, the first witness called by DSC counsel, was well known to me. I had mentored him through a number of promotions at Optilink, and I considered him a loyal manager and friend. So it came as a surprise to see him sitting on the prosecutor's side.

Ereth had been involved with the creation of DSC's product, Litespan2000. He testified about the history and context of the technology, and about "the negative impact" AFC had created on DSC. "Everything about the Litespan2000 is a trade secret," he asserted.

Hopkins Guy was the AFC lawyer responsible for cross-examining Ereth. Hopkins went through the model of the UMC1000, component by component. Standing seven feet high, it contained nearly a hundred circuit boards. As Hopkins removed the circuit boards, one by one, he asked after each one, "Mr. Ereth, does this circuit board have anything to do with this case? Does it contain any of DSC's secrets or intellectual property that you accuse AFC of taking?"

With each circuit board, Mr. Ereth's head dipped slightly lower, as did his voice when he answered, "No."

Hopkins Guy turned, smiled at the jury, and said, "Just so we are clear, Mr. Ereth . . . you're saying that you could not identify one circuit board, or a single item on those circuit boards, that used any of DSC's trade secrets, is that right?"

Ereth hung his head even lower and almost whispered, "Yes."

Hopkins cupped his hand to his ear, "Could you speak a little louder, Mr. Ereth. I couldn't hear you."

Ereth glared at Hopkins. "No!" he announced loudly. "I didn't see any of DSC's trade secrets being used in the circuit boards!"

Hopkins then pulled a single circuit board from the bottom of the Litespan; I recognized it as something we call a line card. He pointed it at Ereth like a pistol. "Isn't it true that all the trade secrets involved in this case are on this circuit board alone?"

"Yes."

"And that this board is available at any telephone-equipment supply house?"

"Yes."

Hopkins smiled again. He turned and headed for his chair, saying, "I'm through with this witness, Your Honor."

DSC lawyers called to the stand their technical expert, Dr. Maglebe. He was in his fifties, with wild grey hair and thick glasses. He wore a Harris tweed sports coat that was stretched taut across his ample belly, a bad choice in the 90-plus degree heat. His speech was somewhat hesitant, and his manner did not inspire confidence. He was clearly nervous.

On direct exam, he simply described AFC's "misappropriation" of DSC's trade secrets. Claiming to be the only person to have analyzed both systems, he testified that AFC'S product derived from the Litespan2000.

On cross, Hopkins was intent on penetrating the basis of Dr. Maglebe's opinion. As he was also the only witness claiming AFC stole anything, attacking his testimony and opinion was crucial. Through a series of probing questions, Hopkins established exactly what the alleged trade secrets were. As it turned out, they were a combination of six or seven well-known techniques.

Several times, in one way or another, Hopkins asked, "Doctor, are you certain all of these techniques are in the AFC product? Then the follow-up question: "And if any one of these techniques is missing in the AFC product, there's no misappropriation, correct?"

Maglabe agreed it was so.

Hopkins then asked about one of the critical techniques—the data rate: "Doctor, what is the maximum data rate on the AFC back plane from one section of the mother board to another?"

Dr. Maglebe smiled at the jury and tried to avoid the question. "Well, I'm sure I could easily determine the number if I had a calculator."

At which point Hopkins pulled a Hewlett Packard 12C calculator from his coat pocket and handed it to Dr. Maglebe, whose smile faded. "We're in luck," Hopkins said with a wry smile.

Maglabe fumbled with the calculator for several minutes before confessing, "I haven't used this particular model before . . . it's in Reverse Polish." Reverse Polish was the nickname for the unique way all HP calculators worked in the 70s and 80s.

Hopkins turned to the jury and said, "I'm surprised that you are unfamiliar with this HP calculator, Doctor . . . since you have worked for Hewlett Packard for over ten years!"

Big rosy splotches began to form on Maglebe's cheeks. As Hopkins retrieved the calculator from Maglebe, he asked another question. "Could you describe the allocation of the bandwidth provided by the AFC system?"

Dr. Maglebe asked for and received the judge's approval to move to the chalkboard to help him answer the question. Beads of sweat dotted his forehead, and large wet patches could be seen around his armpits, soaking the heavy Harris tweed sport coat.

The doctor, it turned out, even lacked command of the chalkboard. His drawing was supposed to represent the wiring of the back plane; I thought it resembled a drunken spider's web.

Hopkins couldn't resist. "So, Doctor, this diagram shows your understanding of AFC's system?"

"Yes."

Titters of laughter rippled through the courtroom.

Maglabe eventually produced a number for the data rate and bandwidth.

Hopkins then handed the witness a parts catalogue and asked him to identify the exact part in the AFC product that controlled the back plane and determined the data rate. Once Maglabe had done so, he was surprised to learn that the part's data rate was twice the rate he had just testified to.

Later I explained the significance to Maureen: "Hopkins got Maglabe to say that the only trade secret at issue is a very precise one, relying on a specific data rate. Yet he showed surprise when told that the part's data rate was twice that of DSC's. His testimony showed that AFC could not have copied DSC's design."

* * *

The prosecution called Henri to the stand. He had worked for both companies, and for a time was selling both products; he knew both products' technical specifications. We all crossed our fingers, hoping that "good Henri" was sitting in the witness box.

The first question posed by Dan Boyd, lead DSC lawyer, was "Mr. Sulzer, did you sell equipment to your former DSC customers?"

"But of course!" Henri said, irritably. "My responsibility as international sales manager is to make sure customer needs are served. AFC sells components that allow the customer to start out small and then add on, if needed. For customers with larger needs, I sold them the product produced by DSC. In fact, I could be serving my customers right now instead of spending precious time participating in this wasteful trial."

Dan Boyd peppered Henri with questions, trying to show conflict of interest. He had no success, and Henri kept his cool. His confident, placid side came across. Hopkins, who frequently scrutinized jurors' reactions, decided the jury loved him.

* * *

Our most important trial exhibit consisted of steel models of the competing technologies: our UMC1000 and the DSC product we allegedly copied, the Litespan2000. The models allowed us to show the jury that, although both serviced the same number of lines, the AFC product was one-tenth the size of the DSC product, relied on more modern components, was technologically superior, and used less power. In short, our product was not just different; it used newer technology and was smaller and more powerful.

By day three of the trial, DSC's lead counsel Dan Boyd was showing signs of deflation: slumping body language, lack of eye contact. On the other hand, the AFC lawyers' speech and mannerisms suggested confidence.

* * *

Next morning Judge Folsom announced that he would like to meet with a representative of each party, separately. Since no one on our team wanted the assignment, I volunteered.

Inside his chambers, the judge greeted me and gestured to a chair. Without his robes, he looked younger, maybe fifty, and reasonably fit. Once he was seated, he loosened his tie, and said, "I'll get right to the point, Mr. Green. I think you will win the lawsuit, but you need to consider some things. As you know, DSC is ten times larger than AFC. The company can file appeal after appeal and tie you up in court for the next ten years. And even if you survived a lengthy court battle, it's possible that DSC could go after your suppliers and continue to disrupt your business that way. In other words, you could win the battle but lose the war."

I knew the judge was right. DSC had done this before; in one case, they'd been awarded damages of $360 million. Flushed with success, they'd then created a separate division devoted to pursuing legal matters. So I knew that an ongoing and expensive legal battle with DSC was a near certainty.

* * *

We couldn't know exactly what went on at Judge Folsom's meeting with DSC, but our lawyers surmised that the judge would warn their lawyers they were headed into dangerous financial waters, and putting their company at great risk. After all, lose an antitrust case and you could be on the hook for triple damages.

Our team met to discuss a possible settlement. Jim Hoeck, one of AFC's cofounders, was adamant. "We shouldn't pay a dime! This is blackmail! Those bastards!"

I sighed and said, "I agree, Jim. But think about it: if we don't make a deal and they appeal, they can bleed us dry. And it's unlikely the VCs will continue to support us."

John Webley said, "I am annoyed by the whole situation, but I'm open to finding out what DSC has in mind."

"I have to go back in and negotiate the best possible deal," I said. "I suggest I do it one on one, and that I have the authority to close the deal. I also suggest we offer company stock instead of cash."

BJ concurred, and soon we had an agreement. We would low-ball the cash and offer no more than 5 percent of AFC stock. I went into the meeting ready to negotiate.

My counterpart was a guy named Keneson, a DSC vice president. I knew him as a man of limited intelligence. As I soon learned, he also had limited knowledge of the details of the suit. Even before everyone was seated, he demanded, "We want 50 percent of the company as compensation for dropping the lawsuit."

I burst out laughing. Sputtering through my laughter, I abandoned any pretense of courtesy. "Have you lost your mind? Your demand is outrageous."

My reaction unnerved Keneson and he settled down. We negotiated for the next hour in relative calm and reached a tentative agreement. In the final settlement, DSC received 3 percent ownership of AFC, and AFC paid all legal fees, which totaled $10 million.

Some interpreted it as a DSC victory. But we had achieved our major objective: removing the lawsuit and opening the door to an Initial Public Offering.

When Judge Folsom pounded his gavel for the last time, I felt a rush of relief. For three years we'd battled an enemy with ten times our resources—and fought it to a standstill. I was sure we would have won in the end. But given our judicial system, we could have won the suit and had no resources left to operate the business. Now AFC was free and unfettered.

Most of the AFC employees posing

CHAPTER FIFTY SIX
IPO

An unexpected benefit of the DCS lawsuit was that it delayed the timing of our public offering for a little over a year. By then AFC had a proven track record of steady sales, market growth, and rising quarterly profits. Investment bankers, especially Jim Chamberlin at Morgan Stanley (one of our investors), were taking notice.

Ten days before our IPO, Chamberlin and others from Morgan Stanley met with AFC's management team: Dan Stiemley, Carl Grivner, and me.

Jim Hoeck, Dan Steimle, Greg Steele, Larry Marshall, John Webley, Karen Godfrey, Rick Johnston, Glenn Llilich, Henri Sulzer, Mike Hatfield, me

Carl had recently been hired as my replacement as CEO of AFC. His current job title was Chief Operating Officer; a position that allowed him to learn all about the day-to-day operations of AFC.

According to AFC's bylaws, which ironically I helped craft, the mandatory retirement age was 65. I'd turned 65 some months earlier, but it was agreed that I would remain in my position until after the IPO, giving Carl time to learn more about AFC.

Chamberlin stood, took a moment to straighten his navy-blue tie, surveyed the table, and said, "I'll get straight to the point, gentlemen. You've asked my advice regarding the opening price for AFC shares . . . and my suggestion is that we begin with an asking price of between $15 and $17 per share."

Jim looked around the room; no one spoke. He cleared his throat and continued, "As you all know, the price we ask for the shares and what the public is willing to pay for them may be two very different things. Therefore, in order to help ensure that we get our asking price, I have devised a marketing plan. Time is of the essence, and so I've taken the liberty of chartering a small jet and scheduling an eight-day marketing blitz . . . "

Jim's eyes traveled around the room and came to rest on me. "Don, if you agree to the plan, you and your management team will make five or six presentations a day to our Morgan Stanley sales staff in Toronto, Edinburgh, New York, Chicago, and Miami." He paused, his eyes still fixed on me. "Well, Don, are you up for it?"

Although taken aback by the daunting schedule that lay before me, I smiled and said, "Of course."

* * *

A week later, I stepped out onto the balcony of my hotel room and collapsed into a teak chair. Exhausted, I felt as though I might never get up again. A warm tropical breeze ruffled my hair. No wonder people love Miami, I thought . . . middle of September, after eight o'clock, and still warm.

Deciding to celebrate the fact that I had only one more day of presentations left, I had raided the mini-bar for a beer. No sooner had I gotten the bottle to my lips when the phone rang.

I lumbered back into my room and picked up the phone. Stifling a yawn, I managed, "Hello."

"Don, this is Jim Chamberlin. You sound tired . . . how ya holding up, big guy?"

I laughed mirthlessly. "I feel like I could sleep for a week. If your plan was to kill off the AFC management, you have nearly succeeded."

Jim chuckled. "Well, from what I've been hearing, your hard work is paying off. I've gotten very positive feedback regarding your presentations."

I yawned and said, "Thanks for the encouragement, Jim."

"Of course, the real proof will be when AFC's stock opens on the NASDAQ."

After we hung up, I sat on the bed and took off my shoes. I was going to return to my beer on the balcony . . .

Next thing I knew, the phone was ringing and it was getting light outside. Disoriented, I picked up the phone. "Hello?"

No answer. I hung up and looked at my watch: 6:15. In the morning? Then it hit me: that was my wakeup call. I stretched, stumbled to the shower, and began the last day of my marathon.

* * *

Two days later I was on the trading room floor of the NASDAQ, with Carl, Dan, Jim, and other interested parties. As the clock ticked toward 9:30, I held my breath. The bell sounded, and I was reminded of an announcer at a horse track: "And they're off!"

Soon AFC shares were trading at $20 . . . $22 . . . $25, each rise punctuated by loud cheers from our group.

I felt a pleasant flutter in the pit of my stomach. Surveying the room, I saw nothing but smiles. Still, tension was in the air, for we all knew that what goes up can come down. But our fortunes held. At the four o'clock close, AFC stock was selling for $38 a share.

That evening I boarded a redeye flight for San Francisco. Once seated in first class, I put my seat back, closed my eyes, and smiled. As exhaustion and elation vied for control, I realized I was feeling a greater sense of accomplishment than maybe ever before. My first IPO—what a kick!

By the end of the second week, our stock had soared to $60 a share. AFC was now a well-financed company, positioned to take on the competition.

Christmas family shot, 2004

The brains of the outfit

A revolutionary's introduction

CHAPTER FIFTY SEVEN
Buyout

In AFC's first quarter as a public company, we enjoyed a continuation of smooth growth and rising profits. One day a former employee of AFC, Ajaib Bhadare, came to see me. He and two other engineers were developing a network-switching product and were looking for investors. The name of the new company would be Fiberlane.

I listened to his presentation and thought it would be a great complementary product to the UMC1000. After careful consideration I recommended to AFC's Board of Directors that AFC invest in Fiberlane. AFC had a good deal of cash on its balance sheet, thanks to the IPO, and we thought Fiberlane's product would fit well into the national telephone network.

Product development was well along, but would require millions to get it to the field-trial stage. AFC purchased 20 percent of Fiberlane for $5 million, and in the summer of 1997 I agreed to serve on the Board of Directors.

The company's name was changed from Fiberlane to Cerent and was split into three design centers, located in Vancouver, Washington; Mountain View, California; and Petaluma, California.

Other venture capitalists invested, providing funds necessary to complete the development phase. Two of the investors were added to the board, Vinod Khosla and Promog Hague, and soon the board was bitterly divided. After a number of heated discussions, it was decided to divide the company into two separate entities, Cerent and Syrah. Cerent would be based in

Petaluma; Syrah in Mountain View. This restructuring allowed each company to pursue its market without compromise. AFC's interest was in Cerent only.

* * *

One morning a telephone call awoke me from a deep sleep. I glanced at the bedside clock: 6:02.

It was Carl Russo, CEO of Cerent. "Good Morning, Don. Sorry to wake you, but you're going to want to hear this."

"I'm awake," I lied.

"Well, I hope you're lying down, or at least sitting. I just received an offer from Cisco to purchase Cerent."

"How much?"

"The offer is 6.8 billion dollars."

After a long silence he asked, "Don, you still there?"

"I'm not sure if I'm here. Sounded like you said $6.8 billion. That's Billion with a capital B?"

Carl confirmed the amount.

Another silence followed as I tried to make sense of the numbers. Finally I said, "We might be able to accept that bid. Meanwhile, I'm getting dressed and heading out to buy a yellow Lamborghini."

Once I hung up, Maureen rolled over and said, "What was that about?"

"Oh, just Carl Russo saying that Cisco offered to buy Cerent for $6.8 billion."

Maureen yawned and said, "That's nice. Tell me more in the morning." And fell asleep.

* * *

AFC owned 500,000 shares of Cerent, which translated into $680 million. The transaction instantly created thirty new millionaires.

Shiloh house, Santa Rosa

Shiloh house

Santa Rosa house under construction

CHAPTER FIFTY EIGHT
Accidental Winemaker

One hot summer evening in 1995, I pulled into my driveway and let out an audible sigh. It had been a long week, and I was ready for two fingers of scotch and some relaxing silence.

When I walked into the kitchen, Maureen was bent over four dog dishes, carefully adding bits of hard-boiled egg to each. She looked up, smiled, and said, "Michael called today."

Envisioning my grandson's face, I smiled and asked, "What's new with Michael?"

Michael, my first grandson.

"I'll tell you over dinner. Right now you just sit down, relax, and have a drink."

Finding no fault with this plan, I poured my scotch and spent the next half hour enjoying my drink and reading the paper.

Halfway through our meal, Maureen said, "Don, remember Bob Bagnal, Michael's maternal grandfather? We haven't seen him in a while, but—"

"I remember him. Is he all right?"

Maureen paused, sipped her wine, and said, "He feels he's too old to take care of his property any longer and has put it up for sale."

I recalled Michael's stories of his grandfather Bob's property on the banks of the Navarro River, complete with a vineyard, redwood grove, and tree house.

Michael and dog Zack

The sound of Maureen's voice brought me back to the present. "Don, you know how much that property means to Michael. He suggested we buy it and keep it in the family, and I quite agree."

I was silent, letting the idea wash over me. Before I could respond, Maureen continued, "Why don't we take a ride out there tomorrow and have a look at the place."

Warming to the idea, I smiled. "Well, I guess there's no harm in having a look."

As soon as the words left my mouth, Maureen was out of her chair. She sat down in my lap and wrapped her arms around me. "I'll call Bob and make the arrangements."

* * *

As soon as I set foot on the property, I knew why Michael loved the place. It was forty acres of some of the most prime grape-growing land in Anderson Valley, nestled amidst the redwoods on the banks of the Navarro River.

After walking the property for only a few minutes, we decided it would be a good long-term investment. We agreed to pay the asking price: $450,000.

And so we became the owners of a tiny vineyard. Only four of the forty acres were planted, all in Gewürztraminer grapes. Obviously I couldn't maintain the vineyard myself; I needed a caretaker, preferably a family member. Michael's parents, David and Ann, were divorced, and Michael's mother, Ann (daughter of Grandfather Bob), had remarried a man named John Connelly.

Since Ann and John enjoyed spending time at the property, I asked if they'd be interested in staying there on weekends to help maintain the vineyard. They agreed.

Things ran smoothly for a few years. Then in 1998 John and Ann proposed expanding the vineyard from four to twelve acres and replacing the Gewürztraminer with Pinot Noir grape vines. After reviewing their business plan and making some changes, we agreed to put in the additional money required to expand the vineyard. It appeared to be a good plan.

My next visit to the property was to mediate a dispute. John and Ann were battling the hired viticulturist, Jim Barber, who was responsible for the vineyard's expansion. John and Ann were unhappy with the growth of the vines. To my inexperienced eye they looked fine. The real problem, I decided, was a clash of personalities. John and Ann felt Barber was not respecting their opinions. In the end, we were able to resolve their differences well enough so they could complete the planting of the grapes.

Working in the vineyard

Four months later John called me. "I've been hearing around town that we're likely to lose our riparian rights to take irrigation water from the Navarro River," he said. "I think we should be proactive and drill a well now."

"All right," I said with a sigh, "I'll pay for a well, but you make all the arrangements."

The first hole came up dry, so I agreed to fund another try. Although we dug deeper, over 100 feet, we again came up dry. Finally, the third hole, 120 feet deep, hit a gusher that produced a strong flow of 125 gallons per minute.

With an irrigation system in place, we were confident the young vines were receiving an appropriate amount of water. But soon a third of the 5,000 vines appeared wilted and stressed.

A nearby vineyard manager suggested we test the well. The test revealed too much boron in the water. This meant extensive replanting. I didn't have time for such a distraction. I was fighting a ridiculous lawsuit, trying to stabilize and grow a company, dealing with venture capitalists—and now Mother Nature!

One day I asked John where he'd gotten the information about us losing the riparian rights to Navarro River water.

He hesitated, then said, "I'm not sure."

My first thought was that I had failed as a manager; I had allowed John and Ann to wonder off into unfamiliar territory. John was silent. After a prolonged pause, I said, "What's done is done. We can't go back and change any of it so let's just move on. We'll talk again next week."

Deciding to do my own research, I learned that vineyards all along the river were still using the river for irrigation and frost protection. Moreover, everyone seemed to think a ban unlikely.

The vineyard was replanted. The grapes were flourishing with the help of the Navarro River water. I had a meeting with John and Ann to discuss their plan when twenty tons of grapes ripened. It soon became clear that, despite their best intentions, they lacked sales and marketing experience. There was insufficient time for them to learn enough to rescue the grape harvest.

I discussed the vineyard project with my daughter, Rebecca. She had an MBA from Dartmouth and twelve years experience as a marketing executive at Hewlett Packard. We decided the solution was new management. I was able to persuade Rebecca to take over as manager of the project.

I phoned and made arrangements to meet with John and Ann. At that meeting, I got right to the point. I told them I was relieving them of any responsibilities in the grape-growing operation. "You can still use the property for vacations and weekends," I added.

They were greatly disappointed. Their dream of making wine had been dashed. As I drove away, I reconsidered my decision. Did I really have to be the dasher of dreams? Yes, I did.

In the end, I turned over the whole operation to Rebecca, and later her husband Tom Birdsall came on board. Thus began the story of Black Kite Cellars.

Black Kite label

Rebecca hired Paul Ardzrooni, a viticulturist with a reputation for delivering the highest-quality grapes the land could produce. Then she hired Jeff Gaffner, an experienced winemaker.

President and proprietor of Black Kite

In 2005, we offered our first official release, a Pinot Noir called Redwoods Edge. The investment in time and money had paid off. We scored a 93 in the *Wine Spectator*, and Black Kite was named one of the hot new Pinot Noir producers of 2007. The accolades continue today. In 2013 and 2014, we won the Critic's Choice award for producing one of the world's great wines.

Great wine

The winery has flourished beyond my expectations. We now produce 3,000 cases a year. Though the industry considers us a small boutique winery, our distribution has spread across the United States. Black Kite can be found in prestigious restaurants from coast to coast.

What we began with modest intentions has become a source of great pride.

Sunrise over Black Kite vineyard

CHAPTER FIFTY NINE
Retirement Revisited

In 2001 I decided, for the second time in my career, to retire. Fifteen years earlier, my first attempt at retirement had been unsuccessful. Within a few months I was bored and missing the excitement of the business world. Now, at age 70, I was ready to relax and let go of the reins.

Dogs under control

In honor of the occasion, AFC employees presented me with two first-class roundtrip airline tickets to Paris and two seats at a World Cup soccer match. After the match Maureen and I would be driven to dinner at La Tour d'Argent, a Michelin four-star restaurant.

As I drove home following the ceremony, my mind drifted back to 1947 and the beginning of my career. At sixteen, I'd been a GPO apprentice riding a bicycle from house to house, filling up batteries with distilled water. And now . . .

Too tired to reminisce, I yawned and said aloud, "And now, more than half a century later, I am truly ready for retirement." I imagined filling my days with gardening, woodworking, singing . . . and who knows what else.

Another retirement party

* * *

The day before our plane was to leave for Paris, I stopped by my "old" office to tie up some final loose ends. On my desk lay an envelope with my name on it. With a vague sense of foreboding, I tore open the envelope and extracted the single sheet inside. A rush of nausea overcame me as I read the two sentences of text. I read them again, then blindly pulled out my desk chair and fell into it.

The letter was the resignation of Carl Grivner, my replacement as AFC's CEO.

After a few deep breaths, I felt my dismay turn to anger. Still fuming, I picked up the phone and called BJ Cassin, a friend, an investor in AFC, and a board member.

As soon as he answered, I skipped the niceties and blurted out, "BJ, I just found Carl Grivner's letter of resignation on my desk!"

"You got to be kidding! Damn! What does he say in the letter?"

"Nothing, no explanation . . . and he wasn't even professional enough to tell me face to face . . ."

"Don, are you sure Carl never said anything that might indicate he was thinking of quitting?"

"Well, I knew he was upset over the loss of two important accounts. But we had devised a plan to rectify the problem, and Carl seemed fine with it. No, he gave me no indication he was contemplating resigning as CEO."

BJ's tone became tentative. "I know you're retired, Don, but—"

"My retirement can wait. First, we need to find a way to fix this hole in the bottom of the boat. AFC cannot be left without a CEO. I was going to leave for Paris tomorrow, but I'll cancel.

Maureen won't mind, she's tired of traveling . . ."

* * *

Next morning, board members were called into emergency session.

In the office, AFC employees were surprised and unhappy to learn of Carl's resignation; he'd been a popular choice as replacement CEO. In the boardroom, everybody agreed that we had to move quickly to find Carl's replacement. The board officially asked me to stay on as CEO until a suitable replacement could be found.

My first task was damage control. I needed to reassure shareholders and employees alike that it would be business as usual at AFC, that everything would be fine. I also started the process of looking for a CEO, beginning with the list of qualified candidates collected during the Grivner recruitment.

* * *

Six months later AFC was back on track. We had recovered the revenues lost while Carl had been at the helm. Our stock price, which had dipped when he resigned, was now back up to its former value. And at last we had a CEO.

John Schofield, an Aussie, had enjoyed a successful career in the telecommunications business and had excellent references. He passed our rigorous interview process with flying colors. Physically he wasn't imposing, but his strong and professional demeanor inspired confidence.

Thanks to John, I was able to withdraw from AFC with a clear conscience. As I left the office for the last time, I said to no one, "Retirement here I come."

Happy family bunch

Cirque du Soleil? North Carolina

CHAPTER SIXTY
— A Special Birthday Gift —

The phone rang early one morning as I was pouring my first cup of coffee. I scurried to answer it before the noise could wake anyone else.

"Hi, Dad. Happy seventy-first birthday!"

"Same to you." David and I shared the same birthday.

"Get your hiking boots on, because I've got a surprise for you!"

"My hiking boots?"

"Yeah. Here's what I need you to do: Drive to the Occidental Hotel parking lot and meet me there in one hour. I have something to show you."

Though bewildered, I followed his instructions and met him at the appointed time. We got into his rusty pickup and set off, destination still unknown to me. We soon turned on to a logging road, which we followed for several miles, until it became too narrow for the truck.

I looked at David and smiled. "I guess this is where the hiking boots come in."

"Yep."

We got out of the truck and began walking along a narrow trail. The path was level, the walking easy, and I was enjoying the serene quiet of the forest when I heard what I thought was the hoot of an owl. Ahead of me, David hadn't slowed his pace. "Hey," I said, "did you hear that?"

Without even glancing my way, he continued walking and

said, "Hear what? I didn't hear anything."

Moments later we reached a clearing in the forest. Mostly tall conifers, they formed a canopy over our heads. We stopped and I relished the silence until—there it was again! The hoot of an owl, accompanied this time by a fluttering of wings.

Then we saw it. A mature spotted owl landed on a branch about six feet over our heads. David reached into his knapsack and pulled out . . . a live mouse! Holding it by the tail, he lifted it into the air. The mouse wiggled to get free. The owl swooped down from its perch, grabbed the mouse with his talon from David's hand, then flew back to his tree branch, where he devoured its prey.

An endangered species taking a mouse from David's hand; no wonder they are endangered.

A second fluttering announced the arrival of another owl. David pulled out another mouse and placed it on top of his camera tripod. To my surprise, the mouse did not jump off the tripod, but instead sat up on its hind legs and sniffed the air. The second owl swooped down, grabbed the mouse, landed on the ground nearby and began eating.

While I stared in amazement, David snapped a few photos. Two more owls appeared, fledglings recently out of the nest and not yet fully plumed. Following their parents' example, they snatched the last two mice David set on the ground, then disappeared into the forest, hooting all the way.

My birthday gift

When the show was over, David finally spoke, his voice tinged with sadness. "The tragedy is, though the spotted owl is listed as endangered and is protected, its habitat continues to shrink. It shows you how bad it is when they can be lured out of a tree in broad daylight by a man holding a mouse."

Shifting moods, he smiled and said, "Dad, I had two reasons for this birthday gift. To give you the chance to see these majestic birds in their natural habitat. And to remind us of the importance of protecting their habitats."

A longtime birdwatcher, I had a life list of almost 300 birds. But until today, no spotted owl. I gave David a hug. "Thanks. It was both enlightening and entertaining. I'll never forget it."

David and Michelle Green

CHAPTER SIXTY ONE
World Travels

From the time I started my first company in 1969 to the present, I have traveled for business and pleasure to at least thirty countries. I certainly enjoyed meeting new people and experiencing other cultures first hand. Occasionally, though, things did not go according to plan . . .

Me with the family and Rebecca's friend in the Sierra Nevada

Maureen in the Sierra Nevada

Flight to Argentina

It was 5:00 a.m. and I was tired, cramped, and crabby. I stood up to stretch my legs. I'd boarded the plane in San Francisco ten hours earlier; Buenos Aires, Argentina, was still two hours away.

I was anxious to get off the plane, to breathe something other than recycled air. As I reluctantly returned to my seat, I glanced at my watch—5:01—and then out the window, noting that the dark sky was growing lighter.

The man across the aisle had been drinking steadily throughout the night and was now passed out. His head rested against the window, a thin line of drool glistening at the corner of his mouth. Every few minutes, he erupted with a series of loud snorts and grunts. I tried to be grateful he wasn't snoring, but mostly I just felt annoyed. A woman I took to be his wife sat next to him, her face a mask of disgusted embarrassment.

In an attempt to ignore my surroundings and be productive, I opened my briefcase, withdrew my business notes, and began to study them. I was soon interrupted by the captain's voice over the intercom: "Due to mechanical difficulties, we will be landing in Santiago, Chile, instead of Buenos Aires. There is no need to be alarmed. We will assist all of you in finding another flight to Argentina. We apologize for the inconvenience, and thank you for your cooperation."

Sighing in resignation, I tried to calculate whether I could still make my meeting on time, but there were too many unknowns. The murmurings of the other passengers grew louder. An elderly woman's shrill voice rose above the rest: "What's wrong with the plane? Can we land? What's going on?!"

Other passengers, spooked now, joined the chorus. The stewardesses dashed about offering reassurances and free drinks. After a few minutes, the din subsided, then died away completely, leaving only an eerie silence.

Though I'm not usually a nervous flyer, my fellow passengers were making me one. Most wore the distressed look of someone whose plane was going down. I found my senses keenly tuned to the sound of the engines, alert to any sputtering or other signs of mechanical failure.

A moment later, we began our descent. Exhaling in relief, I put my papers back in my briefcase. We would be on the ground soon, and I wanted to be ready to make a quick exit. Besides, I couldn't concentrate.

As the wheels of the plane touched down, I could almost hear a collective sigh of relief echo through the cabin. The moment the plane stopped, I unbuckled my seatbelt and stood up. The man next to me had taken a sleeping pill and was still fast asleep.

I leaned over and gently shook his arm. "We've landed."

He opened his eyes and looked around, trying to orient himself. I went on, "I hate to be the bearer of bad news, but—" As I explained the change in itinerary, he looked confused, then annoyed. Then he chuckled and said, "Oh well, what can you do? Life is full of surprises." I had to admire his attitude.

Just then the captain's voice came over the intercom. "I've been informed by the control tower that we all must remain on the plane until further notice. I will update you as soon as I have more information. Thank you for your patience. The flight crew will be around shortly with refreshments."

The captain's words had been punctuated by groans that now turned to complaints. As I fell into my seat, feeling a growing hopelessness, I said aloud, to no one in particular, "I wonder what this is all about . . ."

My seatmate and I chatted a bit. His name was Tommy. "I

know there's been some tension between Chile and Argentina lately," he said. "Maybe that has something to do with it."

A moment later, Tommy, who had the window seat, pointed outside and said, "This does not look good."

On the tarmac, about fifty armed soldiers were marching toward the plane. As other passengers caught sight, the plane erupted into a multilingual cacophony of laments and demands that could be reduced to "What the hell's going on?!"

The soldiers surrounded the plane and stood at ease. The captain's voice came booming over the intercom. "Everyone please stay calm. There has been recent military action between Chile and Argentina, but the leaders are in negotiations at this very moment . . ."

"Then why the soldiers?" I mumbled.

". . . Since this flight was bound for Argentina and there are Argentineans on board, the Chilean leaders would like everyone to stay put while the two countries can come to some agreement about how to handle our situation. Try to relax and I will keep you updated. Thank you again for your patience and cooperation."

For a moment the plane grew quiet as everyone tried to make sense of what they'd just heard. As for me, I lacked both patience and options. I would not make my meeting.

The man across the aisle was awake, but I could tell by his slurred speech that he was still drunk. He was patting his young wife's hand, trying to comfort her. "It's okay, babe, they wouldn't dare harm us."

With that he got up from his seat, inched past his wife, stood in the aisle, and suddenly shouted, "They can't keep me here! I'm an American citizen! Who the hell do they think they are?"

A stewardess rushed up. "Please, sir, calm down and stop

shouting. You're upsetting the other passengers."

Looking around the cabin, he found few friends. His wife glared bullets at him. Red faced, he slithered back into his seat. His wife growled between clenched teeth, "Yes, George, do sit down and stop making a scene. You're embarrassing me."

The flight crew served drinks and snacks, trying to sooth and distract the passengers. As the minutes ticked by, outrage turned to stolid resignation. The chatter diminished.

Finally, after three hours on the tarmac, the captain's voice came over the intercom. "I am happy to report that Chilean and Argentinean leaders have been successful in their negotiations . . . a truce has been declared—"

The cabin erupted as if our side had just scored the winning goal. The captain droned on: "Once inside the terminal, please proceed to our ticket counter, where our agents will assist you in booking your flight to Buenos Aires. Thank you for flying . . ."

Though I have flown dozens of times since, the memory of that flight returns to me every time I enter an airport.

Mugging in Mexico

Our distributor in Mexico, Señor Rodriquez, invited Maureen and me to his son's wedding in Mexico City. Henri Sulzer, vice president of international sales, and wife Cornelia were also invited. We accepted gladly, figuring to combine a vacation with what we anticipated would be a lavish wedding celebration. We also looked forward to spending time with Henri and Cornelia, whom we liked.

The wedding was indeed beautiful and the reception filled with good food, music, and conversation. As we stepped outside the reception hall, I shook Senor Rodriguez's hand and thanked him for a wonderful evening.

All the eating, drinking, and dancing had caught up with me, and I stifled a yawn. "I feel like I could sleep for a week," I said to Henri.

"You and me both, pal," Henri said. He pointed to two taxis parked at the curb, both Volkswagen bugs, and said, "You and Maureen take the first cab, and Cornelia and I will grab the second."

As Maureen and I climbed into the cab, I was already picturing our bed with its big fluffy pillows.

* * *

I was awakened by Maureen's shrill voice; she was looming over me, phone in hand. "Don, wake up! It's Cornelia. She's crying, nearly incoherent . . . I can't understand her."

I glanced at the bedside clock: 1:15 a.m.. I sat up and took the receiver from Maureen. "Cornelia, what's going on?"

Amid sobs, she sputtered, "I . . . we . . . I mean, what if something had happened to Henri?" Then all sobbing, no words.

"Cornelia, where are you? . . . Try to calm down . . . what's going on?" More sobbing. With the most reassuring voice I could manage: "Cornelia, it's going to be okay . . . tell me where you are."

She exhaled and said, "In the hotel lobby."

That was a relief; at least she was safe. "Where's Henri? Is he there with you? Is he okay?"

"He's here, too. He's talking to the police."

"We'll be right down." I hung up.

As we dressed, I told Maureen what little I knew. In the lobby, Henri and Cornelia were just finishing with the police. Once the officers left, we found four chairs in the deserted hotel lobby and

350

sat down to hear the story.

Maureen, ever solicitous, asked Cornelia, "Are you sure you're up to talking about it now?"

"Oh, I'm all right. The desk clerk saw how distraught I was and brought me a little brandy."

With only a little input from Henri, Cornelia told the story. "For a few blocks our taxi was right behind yours. But then our driver made a left turn and headed down a side street. We thought he was trying to avoid traffic, that he knew a shortcut. But after a couple of minutes, with the streets dark and deserted, Henry called out to the driver, 'Hey, this isn't the way to the hotel.'

"With that, the driver pulled off the road, slammed on the brakes, and turned to us. He pointed a gun at us and demanded, 'Give me all your money and jewelry, and no one gets hurt!'"

"Oh, my!" Maureen stifled a sob.

Cornelia continued: "The driver looked away for a second, and Henri suddenly lunged forward and got the driver in a chokehold. He told me to get out of the car and run for help. But I didn't want to leave Henri."

"What did you do?" asked Maureen.

Cornelia chuckled mirthlessly. "I took off my ring, the emerald ring Henri gave me for our anniversary. This guy may get our cash, I thought, but he's not getting my ring. So I slipped it off my finger and swallowed it—"

"You what?!" I heard her, of course, but couldn't believe it.

"That is, I tried to swallow it. I could feel it getting stuck in my throat. My eyes began to water, but eventually I got it down. Then I took off my bracelet and swallowed that."

I felt my jaw drop to my knees. "And all this time Henri still has the driver in a chokehold?"

"Yep," Henri put in. "And then the guy starts pleading, 'Señor, let me go, por favor, and I will not bother you again!' So I loosened my grip, and wham! He hit me in the head with the pistol butt, and in the blink of an eye was out of the car and running down the street."

Tears in my eyes, I wrapped Henri in a big hug while Maureen embraced Cornelia.

Cornelia said, "Only later did it hit me—I could have lost my Henri. That's why I was so incoherent on the phone."

I sat there stunned, trying to digest the fact that Cornelia had eaten her jewelry. Finally I sputtered, "But how did you swallow that ring without choking to death? It's huge."

Cornelia ignored my question. She took Henri's hand in hers and cooed, "Sometimes I think we have a guardian angel looking over us."

I rejected the temptation to point out the obvious: If their guardian angel had been on duty, they never would have been mugged in the first place.

As we said goodnight, I clasped Henri on the shoulder and said, "You were some kind of hero tonight."

He smiled wearily. "I'm lucky the driver didn't shoot me."

I nodded, wondering how I would have reacted in Henri's place. One thing I knew for sure: Under no circumstances would I swallow any jewelry.

* * *

A few weeks later, back in San Francisco, Maureen called Cornelia to catch up. They had a nice chat, and before signing off Cornelia confided in Maureen that "all her jewelry had come out all right in the end."

Beauty on the beach

How Not to Do Business

My company, DTS, was approached by a company in South Africa wanting permission to license and possibly manufacture one of our products, the D960 concentrator. We needed to send someone to South Africa. The logical choice was Chet Stevens, vice president of international sales. I decided to accompany him. We hoped to negotiate the licensing terms and evaluate the company's manufacturing capabilities.

After a twenty-three-hour flight and a long drive from the airport, Chet and I arrived at the corporate offices. From behind the reception desk, a tall blonde woman, wearing a short skirt and a tight sweater, told us to take a seat. "Mr. Staulker will be with you in a moment."

It was actually fifteen minutes before a tall, lanky man appeared. Mr. Staulker, whose title was Executive Vice President, greeted us warmly and ushered us into a conference room.

Mr. Staulker and his associates were friendly, reasonable, seemingly capable people. Although the contracts and licensing terms were quite complex, communications went smoothly and the contracts appeared ready to be signed just after lunch on the third day.

Once we had all returned from lunch, I rose to say thanks for an acrimony-free negotiation. "It's been a pleasure doing business with you all, and I'm confident the terms we have negotiated will benefit both of our companies." I went on to praise their manufacturing division.

After a round of smiles and nods of approval, Mr. Staulker announced that the president/owner, Mr. Johns, would like to meet with us. Mr. Staulker left the room and returned a moment later with Mr. Johns. He was a short, heavyset man with a shaved head, close-set eyes, and thin lips that seemed to disappear into his face.

As he stood at the head of the conference table, I noted that although his suit was obviously expensive, it was made of a shiny material that only served to emphasize his short stature and protruding belly. His square-cut diamond pinky ring glinted as he reached into his breast pocket and pulled out an enormous cigar. Then, with exaggerated flair, he produced a cigar cutter and clipped the tip off. From his pocket he brought out a silver lighter, held the flame to the cigar, drew deeply, and expelled a nimbus of smoke.

As I sat there watching this theatrical display, I had the distinct feeling that Mr. Johns viewed the conference room as his personal stage and us as his captive audience. He never introduced himself, but instead began reading the contract aloud. Periodically he'd grunt or mutter terse phrases like "We don't do that" or "That's not going to work."

I sat quietly for some minutes, feeling my patience slip away with each complaint over terms we'd just spent two and a half days negotiating. Before he'd gone through half the document, I stopped him.

"I don't mean to be rude, Mr. Johns, but may I ask what you are doing?"

He looked up from the contract, and his thin lips curved into an arrogant smile. "I am just checking certain points of the contract to see if any adjustments need to be made. You're a businessman, Mr. Green, so I'm sure you understand."

I felt anger and disbelief bubbling up inside me, but I wouldn't let it show. In a calm, firm voice I said, "We've just spent two and a half days doing that. We didn't come all this way to negotiate with an executive not empowered to make the final decision."

I paused for a moment and gazed around the conference table. All eyes went from me to Mr. Johns. His face still wore a haughty smile, but now it seemed to take all his concentration to keep it there.

I continued, my voice rising slightly, "And furthermore, Mr. Johns, I find your business practices unethical and your behavior unprofessional. This farce of negotiations was a big expensive waste of time."

I looked at Mr. Staulker and asked, "Would you please call us a cab, sir?"

Looking stricken, he replied, "Of course, Mr. Green."

As Chet and I left the conference room, I could hear Mr. Johns, a pained look on his face, struggling to explain to Mr. Staulker how he had just fumbled away a profitable business opportunity.

Shot in Indonesia

Chet and I were flying to Indonesia on business. We had to change planes in Jakarta. The uniformed officer scrutinizing our passports eventually made it clear to us in fractured English that we lacked the proper immunizations to enter Indonesia.

Chet and I were ushered into separate rooms. Twenty minutes later we were reunited back in the terminal.

As we headed for our gate, I joked, "How was it?"

He chuckled mirthlessly. "What's not to like about a cholera shot?"

I stopped and stared at him. "You got a cholera shot?"

He nodded. "Yeah . . . what you'd get?"

"Yellow fever." I showed him the certificate.

After a moment of silence, we broke into simultaneous laughter, then rushed to catch our plane.

Music Recognition

In the business world, I usually feel quite confident of my memory. In the world of music, however, such is not the case. Perhaps my brain has been conditioned to regard music as a lesser priority. One time, while I was driving Maureen to the store, a piece of music came on the car radio. It seemed familiar, but I couldn't place it. "Maureen, what's this piece called?"

She stifled a laugh. "You stupid blockhead, you've performed it in concert at least eight times, not to mention dozens of rehearsals. It's Bach's B Minor Mass."

Perhaps I was an idiot savant, I thought. I recalled a flight to Australia. After eating everything in sight and watching two mediocre movies, I still had about four hours left before we landed in Sydney. So I opened a thick book I'd brought: the musical score to Verde's Requiem. As I flipped through the pages, I could hear the sound of the score in my head, not a full orchestra but enough that I could pick out the bass section and thus learn my part.

I'd been studying the score for about an hour when my seatmate, apparently unable to contain his curiosity any longer, asked, "Excuse me, do you mind if I ask what you are doing?"

"I am trying to learn the bass part for Verde's Requiem."

He shot me an incredulous look. "How is that possible without musicians or at least a piano?"

"I don't know how it's possible. All I know is that I'm able to do it."

I could see doubt in his eyes, but he didn't challenge me, and I heard nothing more from him the rest of the flight.

Trapped in a Bathroom

One summer, Maureen and I rented a car and drove from Maine to Georgia, staying mostly at B&B's. We figured it would put us in closer contact with local culture than staying in hotels.

One afternoon we arrived at the Bluebonnet B&B in Raleigh, North Carolina. We had been driving for nine hours and were stiff and road-weary. So when we discovered that our bathroom housed a large Jacuzzi tub, Maureen and I smiled at each other and began to undress.

Maureen and me on holiday

Leaving a trail of clothes behind us, we headed for the tub. Once inside the bathroom we closed the door and stood for a moment staring at the myriad of faucets. Operating more on instinct than knowledge, I turned what I thought was the tub faucet.

"Bingo," I said, as hot water poured into the tub. Steam billowed up and soon enshrouded us. Maureen found the controls for the jets and turned them on, and we both slipped into the tub with a sigh. I closed my eyes and let the water jets ease the tension from my back. I felt myself starting to drift when the phone in our room rang.

Stifling a curse, I stepped out of the bath. Standing there naked, dripping, I said, "Where the heck are the towels?!"

Maureen slowly opened her eyes and said, "Oh, they're on a wicker rack, just outside the bathroom door."

I turned the door knob, but nothing happened. I pulled harder. The door didn't budge. Apparently the wood around the doorjamb had swollen from the steam. I grabbed the knob with both hands and jerked—and the door knob came loose! I stared in disbelief at the now-useless piece of metal in my hands.

Our one small window overlooked a parking area, but I could see no one below. I tried calling and whistling, but no one came. Maureen, seemingly untroubled by our plight, was still relaxing in the Jacuzzi.

"I have an idea," I said. "You're a trained singer and your voice is much higher than mine . . . Maureen, I want you to come over by the window and belt out your best high C, at full volume."

The piercing sound of her soprano voice echoed around the parking lot. A moment later we got a response from a passerby. I explained our situation. "Please tell someone at the hotel desk that the couple in room three are locked in a bathroom. And ask them to bring towels!"

Feeling chilled, Maureen slid back into the tub. Just as I was about to do the same, I heard footsteps and then the owner's voice: "I'll have you out in a jiffy, Mr. Green. I have a screwdriver and I'm going to take the door off."

A few moments later, the owner told me to put my shoulder to the door and push. Without thinking, I did as I was told. The door quickly gave, and it, and I, went crashing to the bedroom floor.

I looked up to see the owner's wife running from the room, as if from a fire, and the owner himself trying to suppress a grin. It was then that I remembered I was naked as the day I was born.

Panic in Hawaii

In the summer of 1972, Maureen and I decided to take our two youngest children— Duncan, 9, and Victoria, 7—on vacation to Hawaii. David had long since moved out, and Rebecca was away at college. Both of our older children already had previous plans.

We checked into the Kona Village Hotel on a beautiful morning. After finding our room, Victoria and Maureen opted to explore the local shops and boutiques, but for Duncan and me white sands beckoned. The hotel's private beach was famous for its eye-popping snorkeling, and soon Duncan and I had on mask and fins and were paddling about the 80-degree water.

Lava flows had formed underwater sea caves nearby that provided habitat for schools of tropical fish and other colorful sea creatures. Duncan and I began exploring some of the closer caves, frequently coming up for air and talking excitedly about what we'd seen.

When we came ashore and removed our mask and snorkel, I could see Duncan's eyes were filled with wonder. "Did you see that big sea turtle, Dad?"

I smiled, feeling the child in me emerging. "Yes, I did. It was beautiful . . . did you see the baby octopus on the long flat rock near the opening of that large cave?"

Frowning, he said, "I must have missed it. But if we hurry back, Dad, maybe we can find it!"

We donned our gear and headed back into the water to hunt for the octopus, but it had moved on. We snorkeled for another hour, enjoying each other and our adventure together, until a rumbling in my stomach reminded me it was lunchtime. While bobbing in the gentle surf, I entertained visions of tropical fruit and large sandwiches.

I glanced over to where I'd seen Duncan just a moment before, but he wasn't there. Knowing he was a good swimmer, I was sure I'd see him soon. After another few minutes of scanning the water and seeing no sign of Duncan, I began to feel an odd sinking sensation in the pit of my stomach.

Heart pounding, I headed toward the beach thinking Duncan might be there, maybe catching his breath. No sign of him. Stifling an eruption of panic, I headed down the beach, first walking, then running. "Duncan! Duncan!" I called.

A middle-aged woman in a sun dress approached me and asked, "What's the matter? Can I help?"

I managed to say, "I can't find my son! His name is Duncan . . . he's nine."

With sympathy and concern in her eyes, she asked, "What does he look like?"

"He has . . . light blond hair."

The woman walked away, calling his name and alerting others on the beach.

As I moved along the shoreline, calling Duncan's name louder and louder, I was close to losing my composure. Could he still be in the water? How long could he last? My legs shook as I put my snorkeling gear on and headed back out.

As I dove in, I could hear others on the beach calling his name. Some had his name wrong, calling "David," which added to the confusion. Taking a deep breath, I plunged in and headed for the caves. I tried to calculate how long my son had been in the water, but in my panicked state, I couldn't think.

Finding no sign of Duncan, I surfaced and again headed for the beach. Still in shallow water, I paused, feeling dizzy and hyperventilating. Standing there, trying to catch my breath, I realized something: All my years of successfully navigating the business world, with its challenges and stresses, had not prepared me for this crisis. I felt powerless, incompetent, and more frightened than I'd ever been in my life. Tears began to form in my eyes.

I had barely set foot on dry sand when I heard a familiar voice: "Hi, Dad, do you want a towel?" I turned and saw Duncan, smiling, arm outstretched, towel in hand.

Receiving no guidance from my brain, my mouth opened and I barked, "Where have you been?! Don't you know I've been worried sick about you?!"

Duncan's smile faded, "Gee, Dad, I just went to get us fresh towels so we could dry off and go get something to eat, 'cause it's lunchtime."

I stared at him, saying nothing. Host to a roiling mix of rage and relief, I was torn between wanting to hug him and grounding him for the rest of his life. I swallowed, counted to ten, then got down on one knee and hugged him. "I'm hungry too," I said. "Let's go get some lunch. And while we eat, you and I are going to have a talk."

Victoria and the Jaguar

In the summer of 1973, we went to Europe for a family vacation. When we landed in London, I went ahead of Maureen and the kids to complete the purchase of a car. The plan was to take the cross-channel ferry to France, then drive through Holland, Germany, and Switzerland.

I was greeted at the purchasing office by a middle-aged man dressed in proper English tweeds. He led me out to the lot and said, "Mr. Green, here is your new car!"

I couldn't take my eyes off it: shiny, green, gleaming chrome, low sleek lines, and that iconic hood ornament. A Jaguar. In my mind I was already negotiating hairpin turns on narrow mountain roads, adrenaline coursing through my veins. Problem was, I hadn't told Maureen—

"Don . . . Don . . . Donald Green!"

I turned and found myself the target of my wife's disapproving gaze. She gestured toward the Jaguar and said in an exasperated tone, "I see the car you're ogling, and I'd like to remind you that you have five passengers to consider! How in the world do you think we can all fit in there?"

Feeling sheepish, but still determined, I said, "Let's take a look at the back seat. I'm sure it's larger than it looks from here."

By this time, David, Rebecca, Victoria, and Duncan had joined us. The Green family surrounded the car and peered inside. David, who was seventeen, said, "I wouldn't mind being a little squished if it means we can buy this really cool Jag."

The other children echoed that sentiment. "Let's vote," I said.

Predictably, Maureen was the only holdout. But she smiled, shook her head, and said, "It seems the Green family has spoken.

Who am I to argue with the majority?"

The children cheered; I beamed. Starting toward the sales desk, I was stopped by the sound of Maureen's voice. "Hold on a minute, Don. I want to say something before this transaction is completed."

I turned to see Maureen staring intently at the children, silently demanding their attention. She pointed at each of them and said, "You four . . . are going to be jammed in that backseat like tinned sardines for many miles, and I don't want to hear fighting or complaints! Is that clear?"

Solemn nods all around were quickly followed by hoots of triumphant laughter.

* * *

We waved goodbye to Tweed Suit and drove off the factory lot. Soon rain began to fall. I reached for the wiper switch and turned it on. The wiper on my side didn't work. I turned it off and on—nothing.

To see properly, I would have to lean right and peer through Maureen's windshield. "This won't do," I said, turning the car around.

Tweed Suit was apologetic, and downright embarrassed when the parts department guy told him that he didn't have the parts in stock. A two-hour wait followed. At last Tweed Suit informed us that the closest part was in Rotterdam, Germany. "Well," I said, flashing Maureen a hopeful smile, "at least it's on our route."

"I hope it doesn't rain," Maureen said.

We piled in and I drove slowly toward the ferry terminal at Harrich. We hadn't gone far when Maureen said, "Why are those people pointing at our car? . . . Don, there's smoke coming from the hood."

I stopped, jumped out, and lifted the hood. A cloud of smoke poured off the engine. A trucker stopped and used a fire extinguisher to douse the fire.

I thanked him, turned the car around, and headed back to Tweed Suit, driving even more slowly. Soon half a dozen mechanics and technicians surrounded the car, debating the problem. The consensus: A frayed fan belt had caused the engine to overheat. Then brake fluid had leaked onto the hot engine and caught fire.

Tweed Suit said he would put us up in a hotel and assured us that all would be well by tomorrow.

We shunned the local hotel in favor of an ancient B&B. Maureen and I had agreed to stay at small B&Bs whenever possible, all the better to expose the family to the true culture of the people. We believed large chain hotels insulated us from that experience.

* * *

The Jaguar people came through, and next day we were back on the road. Though cloudy, it did not rain, and on July 4th we rolled into Koblenz, a quaint, centuries-old town on the Rhine River. The little inn we found looked like something out of a fairytale. We were all enchanted. After checking in with Herr Schmitt, the proprietor, we walked around the town, surprised to see Fourth of July celebrations. We soon learned that the hoopla was not for American Independence Day, but rather to honor an ancient battle fought on the banks of the Rhine.

Later that afternoon, seated in an outdoor café, we fell into conversation with some other American tourists. They recommended we visit the next town over, Mainz, the real center of the celebration. So we returned to the B&B to get our car and ask Herr Schmitt for directions. When he learned of our plans, he said in broken English, "That great. I also plan to attend celebration. My daughter, Greta, and I will lead the way in my car."

Ten minutes later we set off for Mainz, following close behind Herr Schmitt and Greta.

In Mainz, a full-fledged country fair was in progress. Local vendors were hawking everything from crafts to knockwurst and beer. Lots of beer. Local breweries had erected beer tents and the lines were long.

After several hours of throwing balls at objects, eating sausages, and admiring the skills of burly waitresses in vintage German garb who could carry four one-liter steins in each hand, I thought it time to head home. Greta, who was eight, same age as Victoria, had stayed with us, and the girls had become pals.

I went looking for Herr Schmitt and found him in a beer tent, propped up against the bar. As I approached, he gave me a crooked grin and in slurred speech invited me to join him for a beer. Oh no, I thought. He's so drunk he can barely sit up, let alone drive.

I left him and went to hunt for someone in charge. When I found him, I was relieved that he spoke English. Together we walked to the entrance of the tent. Pointing at Herr Schmitt, I explained that he was in no shape to drive and somebody should see him home.

"Don't vorry," he said, nodding. "I know all about zat one. I make sure he get home."

"And please tell Herr Schmitt that we have taken his daughter back to the inn with us."

* * *

While driving home, I came to a T junction in the road. Maureen and I were busy disagreeing on which way to go when Victoria said, "It's that road," and pointed to the right.

Victoria, age 7

Maureen and I looked at each other and shrugged. "Okay, Victoria," I said, you break the tie."

Victoria guided us home that night. Twice more we came to junctions that flummoxed Maureen and me. Each time Victoria made the right choice. She had obviously memorized the route and the landmarks along the way. Her sense of direction remains excellent today.

* * *

Victoria in her teens

As promised, the children endured their confinement in the back of the Jaguar without complaint. When it came time to turn the car in for shipment to the U.S, all of us, except perhaps Maureen, were gravely disappointed that our holiday in a crowded car was over.

Singing in Mexico

In 2003, the San Francisco Bach choir, of which Maureen and I were members, were invited to perform in Mexico. We were excited at the prospect of singing in some of the most historic and beautiful cathedrals in Mexico. And we looked forward to traveling with the other choir members, many of whom had become personal friends.

Teotihuacan, outside Mexico City. We climbed the pyramid and contemplated the sun. At the top we sang a piece of music that was written by a Mexican composer.

The choir was a diverse bunch, with a variety of backgrounds, ethnicities, and ages. The common thread that bound us together: our love of the music.

Bach choir touring Mexico

The first ten days were everything we had hoped for. Then one afternoon we were all gathered around the hotel pool having drinks, when our choir director, Bob Worth, approached us, his face a mask of disappointment.

Once he had our attention, he said in a weary voice, "I have something to tell you. . ."

Silenced by those foreboding words, we looked at one another, then at Bob.

Taking a hanky from his pocket, he mopped his brow and continued, "While I was in the lobby just now, the desk clerk gave me some news.

"'Your country has just invaded Iraq,' he told me. 'You are at war, amigo.'"

The choir members, mostly political liberals, let out a collective sigh. An animated but brief discussion followed.

Worth, who was dedicated to his faith and peace in equal measure, again silenced us: "Please, everyone, I think it would be fitting at this time to sing Dona Nobis Pacem, as a prayer for peace."

Bob Worth directing the Bach choir

We quietly gathered together, and as our voices rose in harmony, I was taken aback by the near-perfect acoustics provided by the pool area. I was moved both by the beauty of the sound and the emotion of the collective prayer.

That moment will be etched in my memory forever.

Birdwatchers having fun

CHAPTER SIXTY TWO
Sea Ranch Tales

In the early days after our move from Montreal, we spent weekends exploring points of interest within a couple of hours of San Francisco. On one of those day trips to the north, we visited a coastal development called The Sea Ranch. We were quite taken with it. We loved that the houses were constructed of natural materials and gently nestled into the pristine landscape.

Out birdwatching

We stayed overnight in the Sea Ranch Lodge, and the following morning enjoyed a walk along the bluff tops. A thin layer of fog cast a pearly light as the sun broke through, adding to our enchantment. We left there with a strong desire to own property at Sea Ranch.

Maureen and Victoria, 1987

* * *

We kept a vigilant eye on properties that went up for sale at The Sea Ranch. Our patience paid off: we bought a lot there and hired a local architect, Obie Bomen. He'd built several houses at The Sea Ranch and had an excellent reputation. After months of struggling with the requirements of the Coastal Commission, we received permission to build.

Rebecca, 29, and Duncan, 22

* * *

I arranged to meet Obie at our new property site to discuss how best to proceed. On my way to the meeting, however, I saw a house for sale that had a breathtaking view of the waves breaking over the rocks. It also provided more privacy than our newly acquired property. I quickly found a pay phone, called Obie, and postponed the meeting.

I raced home, ran up the front steps, and burst into our kitchen. Maureen looked up in surprise. She was kneading a large ball of dough, and her left cheek was smudged with flour.

"What in heaven's name is wrong with you, Donald?"

Unable to control my excitement, I blurted out, "Maureen, I have just found the most perfect house with the most incredible views and loads of privacy . . ." I took a breath. "It's at Sea Ranch and I want to buy it!"

Maureen stared at me in bewilderment. Then she dropped the dough, turned to face me, and calmly said, "Have you gone barking mad? We just bought a piece of property at Sea Ranch."

Determined, I spoke with more confidence than I felt. "I know, but once you see this house, you'll agree it's the one we should have."

Then in a pleading tone: "Leave the bread, please, and come with me right now to see the house."

Maureen shook her head and smiled, and I knew I had her.

Two hours later Maureen and I were staring at the house. Seeing it up close, I realized it was more run down than it appeared from a distance. Undeterred, I said, "I know it needs a little work, but look at the location. The privacy of the woods but still a great view of the ocean."

Almost completed Woodland House at The Sea Ranch

Maureen turned to face the ocean, then turned again to face the forest. "You're right," she said, "The views, the privacy, it's impressive."

But Maureen's next words wiped the smile from my face. "The house is a mess, and it's not going to require just a little fixing up. It's going to take a complete overhaul. You do realize that, don't you?!"

"Okay, you're right about that, but don't you still think it's worth it, Maureen?"

She sighed. "You know, Donald, fixing up this house may cost as much as building a new one from scratch."

Smiling, I grabbed Maureen, hugged her tight, and whispered in her ear, "I know it's going to cost us, Mrs. Green, but let's do it anyway."

We quickly sold our lot and put an offer on the house. Our offer was accepted, we took ownership, and immediately hired Obie to make it livable.

Once that was done, we quickly realized we had a problem. Ironically, given my career past, we had terrible phone service. It took me an hour to find the source: Obie had used acid-etched sheets of copper to achieve a decorative effect around the fireplaces and bookshelves. The copper effectively shut out the radio signals used by the telephone companies.

For a time we had to hang out the window to talk on the phone.

The Sea Ranch: alongside the ocean, multistory windows, light and airy

* * *

One Saturday afternoon, coffee cup in hand, I stood gazing out at the ocean, watching small white caps roll toward the shore. I took a deep breath and felt my whole body relax.

An oceanside seat

Then my gaze wandered over to the building site, our work-in-progress home, and my body tensed. I remembered my ever-growing to-do list and pulled it from my pocket.

The next item on the list required a visit to my neighbor, Laurence Halprin, an accomplished architect. His house and ours shared access to the beach. I wanted to discuss my plan to use one of my surplus pine logs as the support for a rope bridge.

Laurence was seated in an Adirondack chair on his deck, reading a newspaper. I said hi and quickly explained my plan.

He was silent for a moment, a look of disapproval on his face.

"I gather you don't like the idea."

"That is correct. Nor would I like a mustache painted on the Mona Lisa." With that, he turned and went into the house, slamming the door behind him.

I stood there for a moment, toying with the idea of trying further persuasion. But then I remembered: He was the architect who designed the Roosevelt Memorial in Washington D.C., and I was a former telephone technician.

* * *

I had been spending a lot of time working with Ginger, our four-month-old border collie. I had her on a training regime, and she was making good progress. Ginger followed me nearly everywhere I went, and sometimes I forgot she was there.

What a backhand

One afternoon I met with Obie at Sea Ranch to talk about the building project. Afterward I decided to go down to the beach for some exercise. Access to the beach was by rope. I rappelled down the bluff face, about forty feet, and dropped onto the sand. Distracted by something Obie had said, I was wrenched back to the real world by a scraping sound above me. Looking up, I watched in horror as Ginger scrambled down the rocks, skidding to a stop at my feet.

Sea Ranch from the air overlooking the ocean

Me and Ginger at the end of a training session

Now I had a problem: one dog, one rope, and one very steep cliff.

Ginger had, I believed, mastered the basic commands: sit, stand, and stay. "Well, girl, we're about to see how effective our training has been."

Scrutinizing the cliff face, I saw some ledges that should support a forty-pound dog. I would scramble up, dog under one arm, climbing the rope with the other arm, using the ledges for rest breaks.

When we reached the first ledge, I placed Ginger on it and said, "Stay!" Breathing heavily, I grasped the rope with both arms to relieve the screaming muscles in my right shoulder. Then I climbed a little higher, grabbed Ginger, and continued to the next ledge. Ginger obeyed my commands and we soon reached the top of the bluff.

Once I caught my breath, I kneeled down, scratched Ginger's head, and said, "Good girl."

She wagged her tail in appreciation, and I could've sworn she smiled.

"You're welcome," I said.

CHAPTER SIXTY THREE
Green Music Center

Once Maureen and I joined the choir, choral music became our creative outlet, my escape from the pressure-cooker world of telecommunications.

Soon after we moved to Santa Rosa in 1987, we found a new community choir, the Sonoma State University Concert Choir. Director Bob Worth once asked me why I invested so much time and effort in the choir. "Because it's so different from what I do for a living," I said. "Here I don't have to be the leader."

Full-voiced Bach choir

Still, leadership pursued me. When some members of the group and I founded a Bach choir, I served as its president. I soon recognized that the choir needed a hall with better acoustics than Sonoma State could provide.

In 1997, Maureen and I offered $10 million toward the

construction of a world-class music venue.

A building site was chosen and purchased, a parcel at the northeast corner of campus. The project gained momentum when the Santa Rosa Symphony agreed to leave Wells Fargo Center and move to the new hall at SSU. Corrick Brown, the orchestra's former director, Ruben Armiñana, SSU president, and I launched a campaign to raise the rest of the money.

The three accents, Ruben, me and Corrick

At the ceremonial groundbreaking for the Donald and Maureen Green Music Center in 2000, Armiñana predicted the center would cost $41 million and open in 2003. But steel prices soared, as did other costs, and by 2003 the building site was still bare. SSU put construction on hold, and failure loomed.

Then, in 2004, Armiñana announced that a new private-public funding strategy was in place. The strategy included paying for the center's academic wing with state education-facility bonds.

Construction began in 2006, with no shortage of critics.

Many, including dozens of faculty members, objected to the relentlessly rising cost of the project. The faculty even voted "no-confidence" in Armiñana. I was sympathetic. The military employs the phrase *mission creep* to describe unintended growth in the scope of a mission; this was a case of mission gallop.

Yet my support for the project did not flag. One of my biggest contributions was a belief that it could happen, but at times even I had doubts. In 2010, when SSU music students presented their first performances in the hall, it was still unfinished. Where would we get the millions needed to complete it?

Green Music Center from the west

That year, Sanford Weill, former chairman of Citigroup, bought an estate in the Sonoma Valley. After touring the unfinished music center, the Weills donated $12 million. Weill then recruited world-acclaimed pianist Lang Lang to perform at the grand opening of Weill Hall, centerpiece of the Donald and Maureen Green Music Center.

A nighttime view of Weill Hall's main entrance

* * *

The Green Music Center cost $128 million to complete. The Grand Opening took place on September 29, 2012. Local glitterati were in attendance. Columnist Chris Smith, in the Santa Rosa *Press Democrat*, called it "one of the largest and most widely noticed social-cultural events ever in Sonoma County."

Full house at the Green Music Center

A champagne reception preceded the performance by Lang Lang, followed by dinner and fireworks. More than 3,000 people attended the concert, 600 the reception and dinner. I was asked to say a few words, and said more than a few.

What a wonderful thing we have created. All of us from Sonoma County and the North Bay should feel very proud of what we have accomplished.

Weill Hall, facing the stage

For me this project started fifteen years ago. I was having lunch with Bob Worth. Bob was a professor and the Director of Choral Music at SSU, and I was a member of his community choir. During lunch we agreed it was a pity that SSU did not have a suitable venue on campus to perform choral music. Without a great deal of thought, I said that one of the companies I had founded was going public in a few weeks and, if it was successful, Maureen and I would contribute to a fund to build an on-campus choral hall.

A short time later, and after my company went public in the fall of 1996, Dr. and Mrs. Armiñana invited us to dinner to discuss and refine our choral hall proposal. As it happened Ruben already had a clear idea of what he wanted, and that was a replica of the Ozawa concert hall at Tanglewood, in Massachusetts, the summer home of the Boston Symphony Orchestra. He had been there and fallen in love with it.

We concluded our dinner with Maureen and me making a donation of $5 million and also committing to visit Tanglewood the following spring, 1997.

Tanglewood lived up to its reputation; the acoustics were superb, the ambiance pleasant and elegant. The impact of Tanglewood on the local community was also very positive— hotels and restaurants were plentiful and flourishing; other performing arts venues and cultural activities, including dance, theatre and museums, were thriving; and the sound of music was all around. The cost of constructing the concert hall was relatively modest at about $10 million.

Ozawa Hall at Tanglewood

We were so impressed that we committed an additional $5 million in a matching grant towards the construction of a similar venue in Sonoma. We came home from Tanglewood energized. Architects were chosen, the site was selected, we partnered with the Santa Rosa Symphony to build their new performance home, and fundraising began in earnest.

Ruben Armiñana, Corrick Brown, and I became known as the three accents—Cuban, American, and English. We were welcomed into many homes to communicate the project's vision and to raise funds. We lost track of how many presentations we made, probably more than a hundred. Many friendships were formed, many commitments were made, and more than 1,600 donors responded. The capital campaign became the largest ever in Sonoma and Napa wine country.

While we were fundraising, the outside world did not stay constant. The cost of materials rose dramatically due to construction in China, and we rode the dotcom bubble up and down. With all of this financial turmoil, I was reminded of this quote by Rudyard Kipling: "If you can keep your head when everyone around you is losing theirs, you probably don't know what's going on."

I personally would like to congratulate Ruben and SSU for maintaining its commitment to building a world-class, acoustically marvelous concert hall with uncompromising standards.

So here we are today. Why did I support this project and work on it for more than fifteen years? From the beginning, I have cited three reasons:

First, as a choral singer, I know it's important to hear clearly the voices surrounding you, to blend and harmonize, to provide maximum pleasure from the performance for both the performers and the audiences. The acoustical perfection that our new Weill Hall has achieved will enable musical magic to take place.

Second, as an entrepreneur and employer, and having founded three companies and funded many more in the North Bay, I have always needed to recruit highly skilled and highly paid employees in a variety of technical areas. To do so I have had to compete with places like Silicon Valley for talent. The Green Music Center is a significant cultural enhancement to the North Bay, which will make it easier to recruit and retain these highly skilled people. A number of people that I recruited to Sonoma County are now leading companies that are employing hundreds of people.

Third, as a philanthropist, I wanted to help with a project that would benefit generations to come. We take for granted what our forefathers have built for us in the form of great libraries, concert halls, cathedrals, and museums. This was our turn to make such a contribution. The Green Music Center, and the now open Weill Hall, by any standards, have met the challenge of creating a transformative place. We have succeeded in creating an incredible asset for many generations to come.

As I was sitting in the hall this evening, I had two thoughts. One, we were hearing musical perfection—thank you, Lang Lang. As the beer commercial puts it, it doesn't get any better than this. And two, I felt pleased with myself for having played an instrumental role in creating such a beautiful place.

Not too bad for a kid from the Liverpool docks.

Thank you.

Taking shape

* * *

I regularly attend concerts at the center. Every time I enter the hall, I shake my head and wonder how we did it, how we got it built. And not just a building, but a world–class music venue.

Sir Clive Gillinson, artistic and executive director of Carnegie Hall, has attended several concerts at the Green Music Center and declared the acoustics at Weill Hall "definitely as good" as those at Tanglewood.

Bay Area classical music critic Robert Commanday praised the aesthetic appeal of its design and its acoustics. "When an orchestra is playing, you can put your hand on the floor and feel the vibrations. The entire hall is responding as an instrument. There is nothing in New York City of that quality."

The Santa Rosa Symphony enjoying the acoustics in Weill Hall

* * *

By 2012, the only missing piece of the Green Music Center was Schroeder Hall. As the website describes it, it was to be "a 240-seat cathedral-like recital hall, designed specifically to accentuate instruments, organ, and voice in an intimate setting." It was named after the Beethoven-loving, piano-playing character in the Peanuts comic strip, created by local resident Charles Schulz.

Schroeder Hall

Once again the Weills made a generous donation, a matching gift of $1 million, and Schroeder Hall opened in August 2014.

That left only the pipe organ to acquire. An organ committee had been formed back in 1998. Members included Maureen and Bob Worth. The committee was charged with scouring the globe for the right instrument. Over the next eighteen months, Bob Worth and others made ten trips to look at pipe organs.

One day Worth was clearing his desk of unwanted papers when a flyer caught his eye. It was a tracker organ for sale. In a tracker organ, the organist presses keys and pulls stops which control the organ's pipes through a complex matrix of levers and valves. The valve, which admits air to the pipe in order to produce the sound, is controlled by the force of the organist's finger on the key. Tracker organs date back to the 17th century, when Bach was a child.

Trackers had almost died out, but recently organ builders had rediscovered the old techniques, and tracker organs endure today.

The audience that filled Schroeder Hall on Opening Night was treated to the unique sound of a tracker pipe organ, a sound that echoes back more than 400 years.

Schroeder Hall is home for the Brombaugh tracker organ used in the Bach Era (1685-1750)

* * *

Though my appreciation of the center's acoustics and beauty remains undiminished, I sometimes worry that its reputation as a world-class facility will overshadow, perhaps subvert, what I believe is its true purpose: education.

As I told Chris Smith, "The main objective of the building is to increase educational opportunities. It's important that we maintain and increase student access."

I would like to see the Sonoma State music department play a greater role. We need more programs to fund music scholarships. And we need to remember what the center is in business for, what it aspires to be: a superb college choral hall.

Congratulations, Doctor Green

Honorary degree from
Sonoma State University

Green Music Center from the air

CHAPTER SIXTY FOUR
Parkinson's Disease

It was August 2006 and I was seated on a stage at the Red Lion Hotel in Rohnert Park, California. I had been chosen by some local businessmen to present my friend, John Webley, an award for Businessman of the Year. As I sat there waiting to be called, I began to feel dizzy.

I heard the Master of Ceremony say, "And here to present the award is Sonoma County's own, Donald Green, otherwise known as 'The Father of Telecom Valley.'"

Applause filled the room. As I staggered to the podium, I thought I might collapse. The room was swimming before my eyes, and the lights seemed to have dimmed. Somehow I found my chair, slid back into it, and slumped forward, holding my head in my hands.

A moment later I heard someone shout, "Is anyone in the audience a doctor?"

Next thing I knew, someone was taking my pulse. The dizziness and sensitivity to light had left as quickly as it had come. But after the doctor checked my vital signs, an ambulance was called "as a precaution."

At the emergency room, after an examination, the white coats decided to keep me in the hospital overnight "for observation."

Next morning a doctor stopped in to see me. "Good morning, Mr. Green. I am signing your release forms and you're free to go home. But I'd like you to see a colleague of mine for some further testing."

A week later I was examined by a neurologist. When he had completed his exam, he said in a stern voice, "Get dressed, then meet me across the hall in my office."

As I sat down across from him, I felt an uneasy fluttering in the pit of my stomach. This time the doctor spoke in a softer tone. "Tell me, Mr. Green, do you know anything about Parkinson's disease and its effects?"

I swallowed and took a deep breath. "I've heard of it, of course, but, no, not really . . . So you think I have Parkinson's, is that it?"

His pale blue eyes met mine and he nodded. "Yes, I think you are experiencing the early stages of the disease."

He removed a pamphlet from his desk and handed it to me. I glanced at the title: "Living with Parkinson's."

Before I could read more he said, "Parkinson's disease is a degenerative disorder of the central nervous system that mainly affects the motor system. The motor symptoms result from the death of dopamine-generating cells in the midbrain. Since the cause of the death of these cells is not yet understood, there currently is no cure."

Pausing only briefly to let this sink in, he added, "However, we now have drugs that are fairly effective in helping to lessen some of the early symptoms, such as problems with balance, shaking, rigidity, and walking."

I sat silent for a moment, trying to absorb this life-altering information. I could feel myself sinking into despondency, when a voice in my head said, "Donald Green, you're no quitter! Now buck up and find out what needs to be done!"

With as much confidence as I could muster, I said, "Doctor, just tell me what I need to do to stay as healthy as I can, and I'll do it."

* * *

A second opinion confirmed the diagnosis. In the ten years since, I've seen a steady degradation of my motor skills. I now have 24-hour care. Yet my ability to function and participate in everyday activities remains strong. I continue to contribute in business affairs, still regularly attend events at the Green Music Center, and enjoy many other activities as well. I am working on a yoga program that may delay the effects of the disease.

Parkinson's has slowed me down some, but it has not stopped me from continuing to lead an active and vital life.

Victoria's wedding: me, David and Michael

Declaring my love to Maureen on our 50th anniversary

CHAPTER SIXTY FIVE
—— *Maureen Develops Alzheimer's* ——

By 2010 it had become apparent that something was wrong with Maureen. She was forgetting recent conversations and events, and it was getting worse. After testing, it was confirmed that she was suffering from the early stages of Alzheimer's disease.

After hearing the diagnosis, I felt frightened. Deciding I could ease my fear with knowledge, I researched the disease. Instead of finding comfort, I became more disturbed and sad. As the literature suggested, the Maureen we all knew and the Maureen who knew her family and friends began to disappear. In the past six years we have seen her body taken over by a complete stranger.

That is, in my opinion, the cruelest aspect of the disease. Your loved one looks the same, but the brain continues to deteriorate, as does your ability to reach her.

What began as minor memory loss has progressed to include an inability to recognize her children or to feed herself. The impact on our family has been severe. Each family member has had to deal with Maureen's disease, and their loss, in his or her own way.

Maureen is now 86 and the decline continues. She has two trained, full-time caregivers and a safe, peaceful living environment. Her care plan includes daily activities that promote mental stimulation, routine massages, and frequent visits from family members.

As for me, I continue to spend time with Maureen every day. Sitting with her, I take her hand in mine and recall all those wonderful years I shared with this independent, intelligent, beautiful woman. Those cherished memories enable me to be grateful for what I had rather than sad for what I've lost.

Renewing our wedding vows

Posh dudes

Three beautiful ladies: Victoria, Maureen and Rebecca

CHAPTER SIXTY SIX
——— *Investing in the Future* ———

John Webley and I met regularly to discuss business opportunities. One day in 2014, he called to say he'd formed a company, Trevi Systems, and he wanted me to invest. "We have one product," he said, "a work in progress. If it works, and I believe it will, it offers a more economical way of separating salt from seawater . . . "

I required no convincing of the importance of such a product. California was in the midst of its third straight year of drought. The Sierra snowpack, which one-third of Californians rely on for water, was a fraction of its former self. And yet all around us, salt water. At times desalination—desal—seemed like the only solution.

I agreed to invest in Trevi.

Was it a good investment? Too early to tell. John's opinion that the product would be market-ready in one year turned out to be optimistic. It's been nearly two, and we're in the trial phase. Trevi has working systems in Saudi Arabia, United Arab Emirates, and southern California.

* * *

I believe in science (how far would I have gone in telecommunications if I hadn't?), and I believe in the science of climate change. I also believe we have an obligation to be responsible stewards of the planet, to leave life-sustaining ecosystems for our grandchildren.

Accordingly, I have continued to invest in socially responsible, environmentally conscious companies. The focus has been on solving problems important to the entire global population, such as solar and wind power, clean water, a more efficient electric grid, and bringing electricity to developing countries.

Victoria and her son Kyle

Granddaughter Danielle, Duncan's daughter

Duncan Jr. and Grandad in Lake Como, Italy

Granddaughter's husband T.J McGuire; great granddaughter Ella; granddaughter Jennel; great granddaughter Ava

The Green family invades Italy

Daughter in-law, Michelle Green; granddaughter Jennel McGuire;
granddaughter Jessica Werle

Duncan and Daisy's bundle of joy, Danielle

Peter Eustace, brother-in-law, and my eldest son David Green

Duncan Jr., Rebecca and Tom Birdsall, Julie Floyd, in Hawaii

50th wedding anniversary, 2001

The little rascals, Kyle and Nicholas

Grandparents with Victoria's children, Nicholas and Kyle

Nicholas, Duncan, and Kyle taking Grandad for a ride

Happy couple, wedding day

Grandchildren

Michael and Wendi's wedding party

Real estate developer Bill White still remembers that fateful day in 1986 when Don Green first walked into his Petaluma office. "He wanted to acquire space for a startup. We hit it off. . . many times over."

Maureen, Bill White and his wife Pat, early supporters of the Green Music Center

It was the beginning of a beautiful relationship—and numerous partnerships, most sealed, at least initially, with nothing more legally binding than a handshake. White estimates that over the next many years, "we built a million square feet in Petaluma, driven by Don's companies, and companies that flowed out of his companies."

Prior to Don's arrival on the business scene, Sonoma County was home to only a few tech companies, Hewlett Packard and maybe one or two others. In thirty years, those companies had created no spinoffs, White says. In the dozen or so years after Don founded Optilink, at least thirty spinoffs were created, including Cyan, Calix, Cerent, Turin, Noller, Telenetworks, Diamond Lane, Enphase, Next Level, Cisco, and Sierra.

In this way, Telecom Valley was born.

It began in Petaluma, with the creation of the Redwood Business Park, then migrated to Santa Rosa and points in between. This high-tech eruption didn't just create employment, it created high-quality jobs, luring skilled engineers, technicians, and programmers from Silicon Valley to the Redwood Empire.

In a speech to the Petaluma Rotary, White backed this up with a few facts:

- From 1993 to 1996, Sonoma County had the strongest job growth in the Bay Area.

- AFC grew from three employees in 1993 to 800 employees in 1998, with an average salary (in 1998 dollars) of $71,000.

- On January 16, 1999, The Santa Rosa *Press Democrat* reported that Sonoma County's jobless rate had fallen to 2.6 percent, while the state unemployment rate was 5.4 percent. In 1980 the county's unemployment rate had been 2-3 percentage points higher than the state's unemployment rate.

White concedes that many tech companies that trace their roots back to a Don Green company have left the county, but a momentum was created that persists even today. "The facilities built for those businesses are still in use," White says. "For example, Cisco came to Petaluma, bought Cerent, a company in which Don was an original investor, then took over a 300,000-square-foot facility in Petaluma. Cisco is gone, but other businesses have moved into those spaces."

White is more than comfortable assigning Don the title "Father of Telecom Valley."

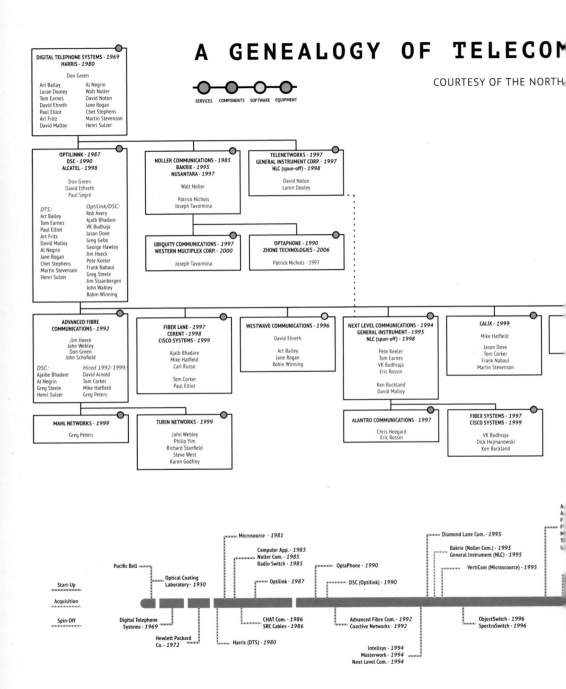

DIGITAL TELEPHONE SYSTEMS - 1969
HARRIS - 1980

Don Green

Art Ballay	Al Negrin
Loran Dooley	Walt Noller
Tom Earnes	David Noton
David Ehreth	Jane Rogan
Paul Elliot	Chet Stephens
Art Fritz	Martin Stevenson
David Malloy	Henri Sulzer

SERVICES COMPONENTS SOFTWARE EQUIPMENT

OPTILINNK - 1987
DSC - 1990
ALCATEL - 1998

Don Green
David Ethreth
Paul Segre

DTS:
Art Balley
Tom Earnes
Paul Elliot
Art Fritz
David Malloy
Al Negrin
Jane Rogan
Chet Stephens
Martin Stevenson
Henri Sulzer

Optilink/DSC:
Rob Avery
Ajalb Bhadare
VK Budhaja
Jason Dove
Greg Gebo
George Hawley
Jim Hoeck
Pete Keeler
Frank Nabaul
Greg Steele
Jim Staanbergen
John Wabley
Robin Winning

NOLLER COMMUNICATIONS - 1985
BAKRIE - 1995
NUSANTARA - 1997

Walt Noller

Patrick Nichols
Joseph Tavormina

TELENETWORKS - 1997
GENERAL INSTRUMENT CORP. - 1997
NLC (spun-off) - 1998

David Noton
Loren Dooley

UBIQUITY COMMUNICATIONS - 1997
WESTERN MULTIPLEX CORP. - 2000

Joseph Tavormina

OPTAPHONE - 1990
ZHONE TECHNOLOGIES - 2006

Patrick Nichols - 1997

ADVANCED FIBRE COMMUNICATIONS - 1992

Jim Hoeck
John Webley
Don Green
John Schofield

DSC:
Ajaibe Bhadare
Al Negrin
Greg Steele
Henri Sulzer

Hired 1992-1999:
David Arnold
Tom Corker
Mike Hatfield
Greg Peters

FIBER LANE - 1997
CERENT - 1998
CISCO SYSTEMS - 1999

Ajalb Bhadare
Mike Hatfield
Carl Russo

Tom Corker
Paul Elliot

WESTWAVE COMMUNICATIONS - 1996

David Ehreth

Art Bailey
Jane Rogan
Robin Winning

NEXT LEVEL COMMUNICATIONS - 1994
GENERAL INSTRUMENT - 1995
NLC (spun-off) - 1998

Pete Keeler
Tom Earnes
VK Budhraja
Eric Rossin

Ken Buckland
David Malloy

CALIX - 1999

Mike Hatfield

Jason Dove
Tom Corker
Frank Nabaul
Martin Stevenson

MAHL NETWORKS - 1999

Greg Peters

TURIN NETWORKS - 1999

John Webley
Philip Yim
Richard Stanfield
Steve West
Karen Godfrey

ALANTRO COMMUNICATIONS - 1997

Chris Heegard
Eric Rossin

FIBEX SYSTEMS - 1997
CISCO SYSTEMS - 1999

VK Budhraja
Dick Hejmanowski
Ken Buckland

Microsource - 1981

Diamond Lane Com. - 1995

Pacific Bell

Computer App. - 1985
Noller Com. - 1985
Radio Switch - 1985

Bakrie (Noller Com.) - 1995
General Instrument (NLC) - 1995

Optical Coating
Laboratory - 1950

OptaPhone - 1990

VertiCom (Microscource) - 1995

Start-Up

Optilink - 1987

DSC (Optilink) - 1990

Acquisition

Spin-Off

Digital Telephone
Systems - 1969

CHAT Com. - 1986
SRC Cables - 1986

Advanced Fibre Com. - 1992
Coactive Networks - 1992

ObjectSwitch - 1996
SpectraSwitch - 1996

Hewlett Packard
Co. - 1972

Harris (DTS) - 1980

Intelisys - 1994
Masterwork - 1994
Next Level Com. - 1994

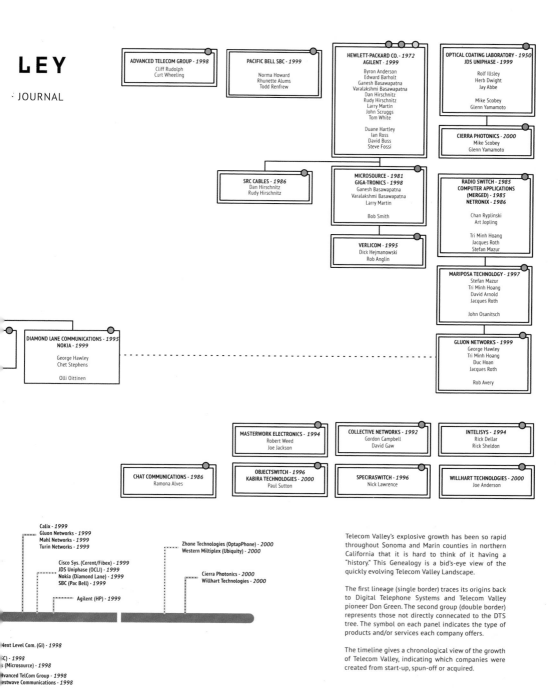

ADVANCED TELECOM GROUP - 1998
Cliff Rudolph
Curt Wheeling

PACIFIC BELL SBC - 1999
Norma Howard
Rhunette Alums
Todd Renfrew

HEWLETT-PACKARD CO. - 1972
AGILENT - 1999
Byron Anderson
Edward Barholt
Ganesh Basawapatna
Varalakshmi Basawapatna
Dan Hirschnitz
Rudy Hirschnitz
Larry Martin
John Scruggs
Tom White

Duane Hartley
Ian Ross
David Buss
Steve Fossi

OPTICAL COATING LABORATORY - 1950
JDS UNIPHASE - 1999
Rolf Illsley
Herb Dwight
Jay Abbe

Mike Scobey
Glenn Yamamoto

CIERRA PHOTONICS - 2000
Mike Scobey
Glenn Yamamoto

SRC CABLES - 1986
Dan Hirschnitz
Rudy Hirschnitz

MICROSOURCE - 1981
GIGA-TRONICS - 1998
Ganesh Basawapatna
Varalakshmi Basawapatna
Larry Martin

Bob Smith

RADIO SWITCH - 1985
COMPUTER APPLICATIONS
(MERGED) - 1985
NETRONIX - 1986
Chan Ryplinski
Art Jopling

Tri Minh Hoang
Jacques Roth
Stefan Mazur

VERLICOM - 1995
Dick Hejmanowski
Rob Anglin

MARIPOSA TECHNOLOGY - 1997
Stefan Mazur
Tri Minh Hoang
David Arnold
Jacques Roth

John Osanitsch

DIAMOND LANE COMMUNICATIONS - 1995
NOKIA - 1999
George Hawley
Chet Stephens

Olli Oittinen

GLUON NETWORKS - 1999
George Hawley
Tri Minh Hoang
Duc Hoan
Jacques Roth

Rob Avery

MASTERWORK ELECTRONICS - 1994
Robert Weed
Joe Jackson

COLLECTIVE NETWORKS - 1992
Gordon Campbell
David Gaw

INTELISYS - 1994
Rick Dellar
Rick Sheldon

CHAT COMMUNICATIONS - 1986
Ramona Alves

OBJECTSWITCH - 1996
KABIRA TECHNOLOGIES - 2000
Paul Sutton

SPECIRASWITCH - 1996
Nick Lawrence

WILLHART TECHNOLOGIES - 2000
Joe Anderson

Calix - 1999
Gluon Networks - 1999
Mahl Networks - 1999
Turin Networks - 1999

Zhone Technologies (OptapPhone) - 2000
Western Miltiplex (Ubiquity) - 2000

Cisco Sys. (Cerent/Fibex) - 1999
JDS Uniphase (OCLI) - 1999
Nokia (Diamond Lane) - 1999
SBC (Pac Bell) - 1999

Cierra Photonics - 2000
Willhart Technologies - 2000

Agilent (HP) - 1999

Next Level Com. (GI) - 1998

SC) - 1998

s (Microsource) - 1998

vanced TelCom Group - 1998
estwave Communications - 1998

Telecom Valley's explosive growth has been so rapid throughout Sonoma and Marin counties in northern California that it is hard to think of it having a "history." This Genealogy is a bid's-eye view of the quickly evolving Telecom Valley Landscape.

The first lineage (single border) traces its origins back to Digital Telephone Systems and Telecom Valley pioneer Don Green. The second group (double border) represents those not directly connecated to the DTS tree. The symbol on each panel indicates the type of products and/or services each company offers.

The timeline gives a chronological view of the growth of Telecom Valley, indicating which companies were created from start-up, spun-off or acquired.